Tomorrow Is
Another Country

THE PRESIDENT AND THE PRISONER

The only picture in existence of Nelson Mandela's secret meeting with President P. W. Botha on July 5, 1989, taken by the president's private secretary, Ters Ehlers. From left to right: Gen. Johan Willemse, the commissioner of prisons; Nelson Mandela; Niël Barnard, chief of the National Intelligence Service; President Botha; and Kobie Coetsee, minister of justice, police, and prisons.

TOMORROW IS ANOTHER COUNTRY

The Inside Story of

South Africa's Road to Change

ALLISTER SPARKS

THE UNIVERSITY OF CHICAGO PRESS

Published by arrangement with Hill and Wang, a division of Farrar,
Straus & Giroux, Inc.

The University of Chicago Press, Chicago 60637
Copyright © 1995 by Allister Sparks
All rights reserved. First published in South Africa in 1994 by Struik
Book Distributors
First published in the United States of America in 1995 by
Hill and Wang
University of Chicago Press Edition 1996
Printed in the United States of America
12 11 10 09 08 07 06 05 04   6 5 4 3

ISBN 0-226-76855-4 (pbk.)

Library of Congress Cataloging-in-Publication Data

Sparks, Allister Haddon.
    Tomorrow is another country : the inside story of South Africa's
road to change / Allister Sparks.
        p.   cm.
    Sequel to: The mind of South Africa.
    Includes bibliographical references and index.
    1. South Africa—Politics and government—1989–1994.   2. South
Africa—Race relations.   I. Title.
    DT1945.S6   1996
    968.06'4—dc20   95-26646
                                                        CIP

⊗ The paper used in this publication meets the minimum requirements
of the American National Standard for Information Sciences—
Permanence of Paper for Printed Library Materials, ANSI Z39.48-1992.

TO MY SONS

Simon, Michael, Andrew and Julian,
who are now founding citizens of this new land

Contents

Acknowledgements

THIS BOOK is a sequel to *The Mind of South Africa*, in which I chronicled the rise and crisis of apartheid and which was published in 1989, months before F.W. de Klerk delivered his epoch-making speech unbanning the black liberation movements and initiating the negotiating process that four years later led to majority rule and the birth of a new South Africa. Here is the story of that extraordinary process, which had in fact begun five years before in clandestine circumstances about which most South Africans will now learn for the first time.

In compiling this record of one of modern history's most remarkable political transformations, I have many people to thank. First of all, the key players in the great drama who opened up to me with unusual frankness. Some were friends in the anti-apartheid movement, others were members of the old regime who knew my views but who were concerned that the history of this amazing time be recorded and who trusted me to give an honest account of it, albeit from my own perspective.

A substantial part of this story was first published in *The New Yorker* on April 13, 1994, and I am grateful to that fine publication for the opportunity it afforded me, and for its rigorous fact-checking procedures. My thanks, too, to a number of colleagues and friends for their help: to Cecil Skotnes for the brilliant woodcut that makes the cover of this book; to Hugh Lewin, my associate at the Institute for the Advancement of Journalism in Johannesburg, who read the manuscript with a professional eye and offered much valuable advice; to Phillip van Niekerk of *The Observer*, who helped fill in some gaps and check facts; to Braam Viljoen who did the same; to Joan Schumann, the Institute's administrator, who printed and shipped the manuscript; to Elisabeth Sifton, my wonderful editor, whose fast work made early publication possible; and to Sue, my wife, for her incisive criticisms and unflagging support through what has been a challenging assignment.

Allister Sparks
Rivonia
September 1994

Tomorrow Is
Another Country

The Tale of the Trout Hook

O N A SUNNY August day in the Southern Hemisphere spring of 1991, a hired helicopter took off from the Waterkloof military air base near Pretoria. On board, with his two young sons, was Roelf Meyer, South Africa's Deputy Minister of Constitutional Development and a key negotiator in the talks then in progress between the government and the African National Congress aimed at ending the country's long-standing system of apartheid. Meyer was flying to the Transvaal Lowveld at the invitation of a Johannesburg stockbroker friend, Sidney Frankel, for a fishing weekend at the Havelock Trout Farm, a luxurious holiday lodge which Frankel shared with a syndicate of well-heeled friends.

Already at the lodge, having driven the one hundred and seventy three miles from Johannesburg, was Frankel with his wife and daughter, and Frankel's other special guest and trout-fishing enthusiast, Cyril Ramaphosa, secretary general and chief negotiator of the African National Congress. "I knew both Roelf and Cyril and I thought this was a good way to let them get to know each other," says Frankel. But he had not forewarned Ramaphosa that Meyer was to join them, and when Frankel mentioned it casually on Friday night Ramaphosa, who was there with his wife, Nomazizi, was put out. He felt he had been trapped into the meeting and was somewhat chagrined as he waited the next morning for the helicopter to land.

Just as it was landing, Frankel's ten-year-old daughter, Susan, doing backflips on the lawn with a friend, fell and broke her arm. It was a nasty compound fracture, and her anxious parents immediately boarded the helicopter to whisk her back to hospital in Johannesburg. That left Meyer and Ramaphosa alone with their families at the trout lodge.

They went indoors and chatted desultorily. After a while Meyer's sons began nagging their dad to take them fishing. Roelf Meyer protested that he knew nothing about fishing, so Ramaphosa, the experienced trout fisherman, offered to teach the boys. The group headed for a dam below the lodge, and there, as Roelf Meyer, too, tried clumsily to cast a line, he got a hook deeply embedded in a finger of his left hand.

They returned to the lodge, where Nomazizi Ramaphosa, a nurse, tried in vain to manoeuvre the hook out. After an hour, with Meyer growing faint with pain, Cyril Ramaphosa intervened. "Roelf," he said, "there's only one way to do this." He poured half a glass of neat whisky for Meyer, fetched a pair of pliers from the tool kit of his car, and took a firm grip on the hook. "If you've never trusted an ANC person before, you'd better get ready to do so now," he told the deputy minister. Ramaphosa pressed the hook down hard to make space for the barb and, with a powerful wrench, pulled it out.

As Nomazizi staunched the flow of blood that spurted from the wound, Meyer muttered: "Well, Cyril, don't say I didn't trust you."

Ten months later Meyer became full minister of constitutional development and took over as head of the government's negotiating team – Ramaphosa's opposite number. The two men became central figures in the process that culminated three years later in the birth of a new nation.

1
On the Banks of the Rubicon

W HEN FREDERIK WILLEM DE KLERK strode to the podium in South Africa's wood-panelled Chamber of Parliament at 11.15 on the morning of February 2, 1990, to open his first parliamentary session as president, everyone expected him to make a reformist statement of some kind. Talk of reforming the apartheid system had been in the air for months. After seven years of racial unrest, there was a clamour for political change: international pressures were on the increase, the country was under economic and diplomatic siege, the black townships were on the boil, living standards for the white minority were declining, and there was a general state of emergency.

The previous president, P.W. Botha, had briefly held out the promise of reform during the early 1980s, but then he had retreated into his irascible shell before suffering a stroke and being removed from office by his National Party. Now the "Old Crocodile", as he was called, was sulking in retirement at a resort called The Wilderness, and this new man had taken over. "FW" had succeeded "PW": the Dutch-descended Afrikaners have a penchant for nicknames. At fifty-three De Klerk was the youngest chief executive in South Africa's history, and he had just won an election victory that gave him a secure five years in office. Surely he would do something substantial.

But expectations were tinged with scepticism. There had been too many letdowns in the past. Everyone still remembered a fiasco five years before when President Botha was supposed to announce a giant step away from apartheid – a "Rubicon speech", according to the advance publicity hype – which turned out to be a damp squib that disillusioned South Africa's few remaining friends in the world and triggered the start of serious international sanctions. When it came to reforming apartheid, the ruling National Party had a long record of being strong on promises and short on delivery. Time and again pledges of reform turned out to be no more than the rhetoric of reformulation. Former opposition leader Frederik van Zyl Slabbert said it was like rearranging the deck-chairs on the *Titanic*. The result was that even when the signs were propitious, as they were now, people tended to ignore all the pre-match puffery and wait to examine the fine print.

Besides, while the problems facing the government were difficult, they were not unmanageable. There was no question of any imminent overthrow of the regime. The army and the police were in firm control; though they could not crush the black resistance, they could repress and contain it. And though international sanctions taken against South Africa because of its racial policies were hurting, they, too, were survivable; nobody imagined there was going to be any foreign military intervention. A determined leader could probably hang on for a number of years, and the Afrikaners, who had provided nearly all of South Africa's leaders since the pioneer days of white settlement in the mid-seventeenth century, were nothing if not determined.

Moreover, reforming apartheid was an extremely difficult thing for South Africa's white minority to contemplate. It was not simply a matter of abolishing racial segregation and admitting an oppressed minority to the mainstream of society, as the United States had done. Here, empowering the black majority meant it would take over control of the country. That was the daunting prospect that had always turned reformism into Potemkinism.

But this time it was to be different. This time the surprise was an announcement that went far beyond anyone's expectations. Not even De Klerk's opening line – "The general election of September 6, 1989, placed our country irrevocably on the road of drastic change" – prepared his audience for what was to come. These masters of double-talk had used such language before. But thirty-five minutes later everything had indeed drastically changed. In that time the new president, short, rotund, balding, polished but without much charisma, head cocked to one side like a sparrow and bobbing on his right foot as he spoke, turned three centuries of his country's history on its head.

He didn't just change the country, he transmuted it. In those thirty-five minutes De Klerk unleashed forces that within four years would sweep away the old South Africa and establish an altogether new and different country in its place. Another country with another constitution and another flag and another national anthem. And above all, another ethos.

He demolished the old Afrikaner vision of a white South Africa, of a *volkstaat* that was theirs by divine right and without which they could not survive as a national entity, and ensured that in its stead a new black-led South Africa would arise, as alien to traditional Afrikaner thinking as Palestinian majority rule is to Israelis.

For the previous fifty years, especially, this "white tribe of Africa", as the 3 million or so Afrikaners are sometimes called, had seemed in the grip of an ethnic paranoia. They had been living at the southern tip of Africa for three and a half centuries and had come to regard themselves as indigenous. During their long sojourn in this remote place their filial ties with Holland, from which most originally came, had withered to almost nothing: their Dutch had mutated into a new language, which they called Afrikaans, and their version of the Dutch Reformed Church had changed on the arid African *veld* into something more earthy and fundamentalist: a fire-and-brimstone faith that addressed the harsh circumstances in which they struggled to survive with a gun in one hand and a Bible in the other.

These factors combined to engender in the Afrikaners a sense of their own uniqueness and vulnerability. Unlike colonial settlers elsewhere in the world, they felt they had no metropolitan home to return to. They were Afrikaners, of Africa, and if they were forced to leave for any other continent – since there could be no further retreat here, no further trek southward, as there had been for the white Kenyans and Rhodesians and Congolese and Mozambicans who had migrated in successive waves to South Africa – they would lose their national identity and suffer cultural death. So alongside their ethnic nationalism grew a sense of themselves as an endangered species, and the more the groundswell of decolonization swept across the world and down Africa, the stronger their paranoia became. South Africa was their God-given homeland, the place which gave them their national identity, and if ever they were forced to share it with the black majority it would cease to be theirs and that would be the end of them, for they could conceive of no nation surviving without a homeland. They therefore equated racial integration with "national suicide".

The Afrikaners are not the only whites in South Africa. There are some 5 million whites in all out of a total population of 41 million, and about 40 per cent of them form a catch-all category known as the "English-speaking South Africans". These include descendants of British settlers who began arriving after Britain annexed the Dutch Cape Colony in 1795, and others who came in greater numbers after diamonds and gold were discovered in the interior in the latter part of the nineteenth century, together with a hodgepodge of immigrants from other parts of Europe. But it is the Afrikaners, because of their numbers and the energy derived from their survivalist imperative, who have always been the driving force in white politics and who have shaped its ethos.

It is they who developed the concept of apartheid. It began in the middle years of this century as a simple policy of racial oppression, but as the cry of black liberation rose after the Second World War it was elevated into an ideology of national salvation. South Africa would have to be ethnically segregated, the blacks parcelled off into tribal ministates, euphemistically called "homelands", so that the Afrikaners could remain in control of their own country and thus of their own destiny. This became Afrikaner nationalism's credo, a civil religion given theological sanction by their church and imposed by their political movement, the National Party. For any Afrikaner to criticize it was apostasy, actively to oppose it was to be regarded as an ethnic traitor.

Among the architects of the policy was one Jan de Klerk, a cabinet minister in the National Party government that came to power in 1948, and later president of the Senate. Because of his role "Oom Jan" (Uncle Jan), as he was called, became a revered figure in the close-knit Afrikaner community. Oom Jan's father, too, had been a prominent nationalist politician and a friend of old Paul Kruger, the patriarchal leader of the Afrikaner people during the thunderous years of the Anglo-Boer War at the turn of the century; Jan's sister had married Hans Strijdom, the "Lion of the North", who was prime minister of South Africa from 1953 until his death in 1958. Verily, they were a family of *volksleiers*, people's leaders.

Now here on February 2, 1990, was Jan's son, Frederik Willem, seemingly destroying everything that father, family, and *volk* had ever stood for. And he himself, too, since throughout his political career FW had given every indication of being on the conservative wing of the National Party. Yet here he was legalizing the whole spectrum of black liberation organizations and their sympathizers, which had been outlawed for the previous thirty years and more – the African National Congress; its guerrilla wing, Umkhonto we Sizwe, (Spear of the Nation); the Pan-Africanist Congress; and the South African Communist Party – and at the same time announcing the impending release of Nelson Mandela and hundreds of other political prisoners, and declaring his readiness to enter into negotiations with all of them to work out a new national constitution in which everyone would enjoy equal rights. In other words, advocating "national suicide".

The impact was enormous. At home, there was a mixture of trauma, exhilaration, and disbelief as different groups struggled to come to terms with a change so profound. Abroad, there was a sense of wonderment and relief. Here, so soon after Mikhail Gorbachev's perestroika revolution, was another miracle of reform: at a stroke South Africa and all it symbolized were transformed. The February 2 speech was to race relations everywhere what the collapse of the Berlin Wall was to communism. It signalled the end of the world's last racial oligarchy.

As the implications sank in, it dawned first on South Africa's neighbours and then on the larger world community that this transformation of Africa's most highly developed industrial country had more than just symbolic importance. Not only was a destructive factor that for decades had destabilized and impoverished the whole southern African region to be removed, bringing the prospect of peace and recovery to millions of people, but a transformed South Africa now had the potential to become an important new influence in African affairs.

South Africa is by far the most significant military and economic power in Africa. Its gross domestic product, at $104 billion, is 60 per cent that of all the other forty-five countries of sub-Saharan Africa combined, and nearly four times the $28 billion of the region's next most developed country, Nigeria. It has a per-capita GDP of $2,600, compared with Nigeria's $230. That makes it a regional superpower in the world's most marginalized continent, the one country that could perhaps provide the engine to pull Africa out of its mire of poverty and desperation. A new South Africa could also play an important part in international affairs. As Archbishop Desmond Tutu, the 1984 Nobel peace laureate, noted on the night the 1993 peace prize was awarded to Mandela and De Klerk, South Africa is a microcosm of the world, embodying all the global issues of white and black, of rich and poor, of developed and underdeveloped peoples. "Once we have got it right," Tutu said, "South Africa will be the paradigm for the rest of the world."

Striking the same theme, Heribert Adam and Kogila Moodley, two veteran analysts of South African affairs, suggest in a recent book, *The Opening of the Apartheid Mind*, that South Africa represents a laboratory test for a new global compromise between the North and the South –

which is urgently needed lest the steeply declining South destabilize the entire globe.*

The North-South divide is potentially the world's most challenging issue after the end of the Cold War. The developed nations appear not to have appreciated this yet. Though it has been years since the end of the self-centred Reagan-Thatcher era and the collapse of communism, they are still too wrapped up in what John Kenneth Galbraith has called "the culture of contentment" to be overly concerned with the deepening plight of the world's poorer countries, most of them in the Southern Hemisphere, tending to view them rather as tiresome beggar nations. Since the Western democracies and the former socialist states of the Soviet empire no longer need to compete with aid projects for the allegiance of the third world, they have all largely forgotten it, dismissed it as irredeemable and irrelevant, and left it to wallow in its own hopelessness. Even the World Bank's structural adjustment programmes seem unable to stop the slide into instability, corruption, and decay, so the countries of the affluent world turn away in exasperation.

But, as Adam and Moodley warn, the powerful North neglects the powerless South at its own peril. In this fast-shrinking world no nation is an island unto itself, immune to the others. The importance of the South lies in its very weakness, in what the authors call *Chaosmacht*, or the capacity to destabilize the entire globe with its instability – through environmental deterioration, the spread of diseases, the stream of economic refugees towards first world affluence, and manifestations of national and religious fundamentalisms.

Most dangerous of all is what I call the politics of desperation. When people feel desperate, and when they feel their desperation is ignored, they tend to do desperate things to attract attention to their plight. They seize hostages, hijack planes, blow up the World Trade Center in New York. Or they develop apocalyptic visions and turn to religious fanaticism, sometimes with homicidal consequences. And

---

* Heribert Adam and Kogila Moodley: *The Opening of the Apartheid Mind: Options for the New South Africa* (1993), p. 12.

desperate nations throw up fanatical leaders who do desperate things at the national level. The sudden, bewildering appearance of such figures – an Ayatollah Khomeini, a Saddam Hussein, an Idi Amin, a Mohammed Aideed – is a feature of our times. In a world of greatly reduced nuclear controls, the politics of desperation in a neglected third world is surely going to be a mounting threat in the twenty-first century.

This disparity of wealth and power between the first and third worlds cannot continue to be ignored – and here lies South Africa's future value in international affairs. A successful new South Africa, embodying as it does all the elements of the global divide and striving now to overcome them, could develop into a model for the gradual solution of the North-South divide. With a leader of Nelson Mandela's international stature, it has the chance to be the interlocutor between the developed and underdeveloped worlds.

None of this, certainly, was in De Klerk's mind when he delivered his February 2 speech. He was motivated by very different concerns and, like Gorbachev, had an entirely different outcome in mind when he embarked on his "Pretoriastroika". Just as Gorbachev could not have known that his restructuring of the Soviet system would lead to the loss of his East European empire, the collapse of communism, and the dismemberment of the Soviet Union itself, so, too, De Klerk did not expect his reforms to lead to black-majority rule and the end of Afrikaner nationalism before the end of the decade.

In speeches he delivered after February 2, De Klerk made it clear that he was as strongly opposed as ever to black-majority rule. There could be no "winner takes all" system, he said, because that would mean black domination. "Don't expect me to negotiate myself out of power," he told Western diplomats. Instead, there had to be a system of "power sharing", a concept which he explained would be government by consensus among the leaders of the various race groups. South Africa was what he called "a nation of minorities": each of its ten black tribes was an ethnic entity, as the whites were, which meant no ethnic group constituted a dominant majority and all should therefore rule jointly by consensus decision-making. In party congresses that followed, these ideas were fleshed out into policy proposals.

The result was an elaborate constitutional plan that provided for a House of Representatives elected by universal franchise and a Senate in which all parties above a certain threshold of support would have equal representation regardless of their strength and which would have to reach decisions by consensus. The executive branch of the government would consist of an all-party "collegiate" cabinet with a presidency that would rotate annually among the leaders of the three or five strongest parties, depending on their electoral percentages. The cabinet would also have to reach decisions by consensus. The effect would be that the black majority in the House of Representatives could draft and pass legislation, but the white minority would have the power to veto it in the Senate and the executive. White-minority rule might end, but black power would be shackled, unable to redress the gross inequalities built up during the apartheid years.

But in freeing the black leaders and legalizing black politics, De Klerk had let the genie out of the bottle. South Africa's huge black constituency could now be mobilized and bring pressure to bear on the government with mass demonstrations and strikes. Suddenly, the white government found it could no longer determine the future on its own. De Klerk's commitment to negotiation meant that he had to begin making compromises.

The black leaders attacked the power-sharing plan as a fraud that would give the illusion of majority rule but in fact freeze apartheid's inequalities. Analysts mocked it as a "loser keeps all" plan. Gradually it was whittled down. First to go was the idea of "group rights" and group representation: political parties would have to serve as the representatives of groups. Next went the ideas of enforced coalition and a rotating presidency. In the end permanent power-sharing itself was discarded.

The final agreement, arrived at in November 1993, was to have a temporary "Government of National Unity": a coalition of all parties that won more than 5 per cent of the vote in the country's first one-person, one-vote election, in April 1994, with each of these parties awarded cabinet seats in proportion to its strength. The leader of the majority party was to become president, with two deputy presidents – one from the party running second and the other from any other party gaining more than 20 per cent of the vote, or, if no party achieved this (which in fact was the case), from the majority party. The cabinet was to rule by majority vote, but with some attempt at consensus.

So it has turned out. The Government of National Unity, installed in May 1994, will rule until the next general election, due in 1999. During those five years De Klerk will be one of the two deputy presidents, but after 1999 the compulsory coalition will fall away and there will be full majority rule. De Klerk will then go down in history as one of the few political leaders who have indeed negotiated themselves out of power.

2

Tennis Court
Diplomacy

S OUTH AFRICA'S NEGOTIATED revolution could be said, like the one in France, to have begun on a tennis court – in this case on the campus of the University of the Orange Free State. For that is where a fortuitous friendship began, in the 1950s, between Hendrik Jacobus Coetsee, later to become minister of justice, police and prisons, and a slightly older student named Piet de Waal.

The tall, lean De Waal played a strong serve-and-volley game; the shorter, speedier Coetsee was one of those tireless retrievers who darted about the court getting everything back and waiting for his opponent to make mistakes. De Waal usually won, and in later years went on to be selected to play for his province. "But I picked up a few sets sometimes," Coetsee says today.

The two were in residence together in the Abraham Fischer Hostel (named after a president of the old Boer Republic of the Orange Free State), which the students irreverently called the Vishuis, or Fish House.* As their friendship grew it was De Waal who persuaded Coetsee to abandon his plans to become a teacher and take a law degree instead. And when Coetsee graduated in 1954, it was again De Waal who got him his first job, in the Jewish law firm of Louis Medallie in the provincial capital of Bloemfontein. "Medallie asked me if I knew where he could find a good Boer lad to take on as an articled clerk, and I introduced him

---

* In one of the many ironies of South African history, President Fischer's grandson of the same name, a distinguished civil-rights lawyer and Queen's Counsel, became leader of the outlawed South African Communist Party. He was sentenced to life imprisonment in 1966 for his underground activities and died of cancer nine years later. He is acclaimed a hero by the new South African government.

to Kobie," De Waal recalls, using the nickname by which Coetsee is generally known.

De Waal, meanwhile, had decided to become a small-town lawyer and moved to the little farming *dorp* of Brandfort out on the wide open Orange Free State plains thirty-six miles from Bloemfontein. Some years later Coetsee bought a farm in the Brandfort district, and when he went to Parliament in 1968 as the National Party MP for Bloemfontein West, he would telephone De Waal from time to time to ask him to arrange for the purchase of fodder and other farming supplies. The old tennis partnership continued.

Fortuitously, it was to Brandfort that, in 1977, James Kruger, the minister of justice, police and prisons, chose to banish the feisty Winnie Mandela, Nelson Mandela's wife, when she became too troublesome for the authorities to handle in the aftermath of the 1976 riots in Soweto. Brandfort was remote but also reasonably accessible to the regional security headquarters in Bloemfontein, so that an intensive round-the-clock watch could be kept on Mrs. Mandela without undue cost or inconvenience. It was fortuitous, too, that when she arrived, bringing the only splash of colour to the drab little town, Winnie struck up a friendship with De Waal's wife, Adèle, and their daughter, Sonja. And it was fortuitous once again when Coetsee, in 1980, replaced Kruger as minister of justice, police and prisons. Thus a tenuous line of communication was established, through the one-horse town of Brandfort and its country lawyer, between the world's most celebrated political prisoner and his jailer.

Winnie Mandela later fell from grace, her impulsive temperament and imperious ways having brought her into conflict with the law, the ANC, and her husband. All that, however, lay in the future. Now, in this place during these turbulent years of the 1980s, she was a hero, a living martyr to the black liberation cause, and despite the discomforts inflicted on her by her persecutors she revelled in the role. Her vivid personality dominated the little town. She shocked the conservative Afrikaner townsfolk, long accustomed to subservient blacks who lowered their eyes and called them *baas*, by striding through the streets dressed like a queen in dazzling African gowns. She kept them waiting while she used "their" public telephone at the post office. She marched into the local liquor store and ordered exotic things like champagne and Cinzano. She pointedly ignored the separate entrances and segregation signs, and tried on clothes in the town's only dress shop.

And she captivated the De Waals. Piet de Waal was reluctant at first to have anything to do with the dangerous newcomer, but then Winnie's Johannesburg lawyer, Ismail Ayob, telephoned him to warn that since he was the only lawyer in Brandfort, and since her restriction order did not allow her to leave the town, he was ethically obliged to handle her legal business; if he refused, Ayob warned, he would report him to the Law Society.

That was a serious threat, so De Waal hot-footed it to the police station down Voortrekker Road to tell the security police officers that his visits to Mrs. Mandela in the little segregated township of Phathakahle (which means Handle with Care), where they had placed her, would be strictly in the line of duty. "I was worried that I would have the security police around my neck," De Waal confesses today. In something of a frenzy, he wrote to both Kruger and his old friend, Kobie Coetsee. The letter to Minister Kruger was a plea, partly on Mrs. Mandela's behalf and partly on behalf of De Waal himself and the other white townsfolk of Brandfort, to review the banning order and move Mrs. Mandela somewhere else. The house she had been allocated in Phathakahle was unsuitable, he wrote. It was too small and had no running water. Moreover, Mrs. Mandela's presence in the little *dorp* was stirring up the local blacks. "Last Friday when she came to my office a huge crowd of blacks gathered outside as though it were Christmas or New Year," De Waal complained. He said he appreciated the delicacy of the matter, but wouldn't the minister please reconsider whether Brandfort was a suitable place for Mrs. Mandela to live. Then, to cover his back, De Waal appended a paragraph pointing out that he was handling Mrs.

Mandela's affairs only because he was the only lawyer in town. "It is an unfortunate position I would rather not be in," he wrote. "I mention this in case you might jump to the wrong conclusion."

The letter to Coetsee was more plaintive and direct. "My good old pal," he wrote in Afrikaans. "I am the only lawyer in town. What must I do?" Coetsee replied warmly, recalling their old tennis-playing days together at the Vishuis, and advising De Waal to go ahead and handle Mrs. Mandela's legal affairs. "Better that than have the overseas press say she couldn't get a lawyer," he wrote. To save his friend from harassment, Coetsee also wrote to Kruger, telling him he had known De Waal "for a lifetime" and that his integrity was "above all suspicion". No need to worry about his associating with Winnie Mandela.

In the event, Mrs. Mandela's restriction order prohibiting her from being in the company of more than one person at a time, and with the police keeping a constant watch on her Phathakahle shack through binoculars from a nearby hillock, the lawyer's house was the only place where she could safely talk with a group. So Mrs. Mandela came to the De Waals' home at 44 Duke Street – for legal consultations and for social meetings. Foreign visitors often met with her there. In January 1985 I took Katharine Graham, then publisher of *The Washington Post*, and a party of the paper's senior staff to the De Waals' home for a long discussion with Mrs. Mandela.

But more and more Winnie came to 44 Duke Street just to visit Adèle. The two became close friends, spending hours together talking about their families and other intimate things and developing what Piet today calls "a remarkable relationship". It was all the more remarkable considering Adèle's family background: she was born Adèle Retief, a descendant of the Voortrekker martyr Piet Retief, who was murdered by the Zulu king Dingaan when he sought to obtain part of Zululand for the Boers in 1838. Their friendship surmounted all differences between them. Winnie called Adèle de Waal "my white sister" and wept when she died in a car crash in 1990. "She became a friend of mine also," says

Piet de Waal. "It began at a professional level, but I also got
to know her as a person. I learned quite a few things from
knowing her, and I came to understand her point of view."

De Waal's attitude to Mrs. Mandela's banishment was
hardened by a personal encounter with Winnie's persecutors
early in 1980. She had been waiting at his home for a
telephone call, and when the call had not come through by
7.20 p.m. – ten minutes before she was required by her
restriction order to be confined to her tiny three-room shack
in Phathakahle – Adèle de Waal decided to drive her to the
township. The De Waals' twelve-year-old son, Werner, accompanied them. The drive took less than ten minutes, and
as they pulled up outside no. 802, Sgt. Gert Prinsloo, Mrs.
Mandela's particular tormenter, stepped out from behind a
wall to arrest her for being late. Adèle de Waal remonstrated
with him, pointing to her watch to show that Mrs. Mandela
was still inside her time limit, but the policeman would have
none of it – and promptly placed Mrs. de Waal under arrest
for entering a black township without a permit. He
threatened to do the same to the boy.

When Sergeant Prinsloo arrived the next day to serve the
summons on Mrs. de Waal, he encountered her furious
husband. "You goddam coward, give me that summons and
I'll phone the minister right away," Piet de Waal fumed.
Scared that he had overstepped the mark, the sergeant
backed off and dropped the matter, but for De Waal it was a
seminal lesson in the kind of gratuitous harassment that
opponents of apartheid were subjected to.

When in October 1980 Coetsee succeeded Kruger as minister of justice, police and prisons, De Waal began to lobby
him cautiously, first to lift the ban on Winnie, then to con-
sider releasing Nelson Mandela himself from prison where
he had been held for seventeen years. This was the first
lobbying of a cabinet minister on the subject by anyone
within the Afrikaner nationalist fold, and Coetsee admits
today that it had a considerable influence on him. "You
could say that's where the whole process started," he says. "I
trusted Piet. What struck me particularly," Coetsee adds, "is

that Piet de Waal and his family could break down the barriers of prejudice and bias in a little place like Brandfort. That told me something indeed."

"Whenever Kobie phoned about matters to do with his farm he would ask, 'How are things going with your client?'" De Waal recalls. "I would give him a report on what she was doing, but then, gradually, I found openings to tell him I thought the government should reconsider its attitude to the Mandelas." Knowing the sensitivity of the subject, De Waal phrased his points carefully. "I would say, 'Look man, this banning order is achieving nothing. If she wants to say inflammatory things they still get reported overseas anyway, so what's the point?'"

Patiently, persistently, he encouraged his friend to make contact with Nelson Mandela.

3

Four Years of Secret Talks

T HE TENNIS PARTNER got his opportunity when Nelson Mandela developed an enlarged prostate gland and, in November, 1985, was admitted to the Volks Hospital in Cape Town for surgery. On the day before the operation Coetsee and Winnie Mandela happened to board the same South African Airways flight for Cape Town. Coetsee stopped by her seat in the economy section of the plane and spoke to her, assuring her of the government's concern for her husband's health. Later, with typical audacity, she strode through to the first-class section of the plane and sat herself down beside the minister. They talked for much of the two-hour flight. By the time the plane landed, Coetsee had decided to visit Mandela in the hospital.

In the five years since he had taken over from Kruger, the new minister had been working quietly on prison reform. The harsh conditions of earlier years had eased. Mandela himself recalls that when in 1963 he first went to Robben Island, South Africa's Alcatraz six miles offshore from Cape Town, the political prisoners were treated as the lowest of the low.* They were classified in D-group on admission– ordinary criminal prisoners started in C-group – which meant they

---

* Mandela went to prison a year before the other ANC leaders. After the ANC was banned in 1960, he went abroad to set up its guerilla wing, Umkhonto we Sizwe, then returned and went underground in South Africa. He was caught in 1963 and sentenced to five years' imprisonment for leaving the country illegally. Mandela was in prison when the other ANC leaders were caught in what is known as the Rivonia Raid, after the small settlement outside Johannesburg where they were hiding, and was brought from Robben Island for the 1964 "Rivonia Trial". He and other members of the ANC high command were sentenced to life imprisonment for "sabotage", a capital offence in South African law at that time.

had the least privileges, with no newspapers, radio, or contact visits (South Africa did not get television until 1976), and
they could not begin advancing to higher categories until
they had completed one-third of their sentences.

D-group prisoners were put to work in chain gangs on the
windswept island, crushing granite and digging lime. The
racist warders abused them routinely. Mandela himself was
never maltreated – his strong personality seemed to restrain
even the worst warders – but he recalls how his colleagues
were often lashed with whips and batons, and how on one
boiling hot day a prisoner was buried up to his neck in sand
and when he cried out for water a warder urinated into his
mouth. Guards would invade the cells late at night, during
the cold, wet Cape winter and force the prisoners to strip
naked and stand on the bare cement floors, spread-eagled
against the walls, often for more than an hour, while the
guards searched through their belongings. James Gregory,
who spent a total of twenty-four years guarding Mandela in
three different prisons, recalls that when he first arrived on
Robben Island in 1966 it was made clear to him that part of
his job was to demoralize the political prisoners in any way
he could.

Some of the "politicals" had been on the island for seventeen years when Coetsee became minister, and he allowed
them newspapers and access to radio and television for the
first time. Until then political prisoners did not qualify for
parole or remission of sentence: life imprisonment, the sentence Mandela and other members of the ANC leadership
had received, literally meant for life. After lobbying his cabinet colleagues, Coetsee eventually secured a minor policy
relaxation that allowed a measure of discretion in granting
remission. "I was convinced that Mandela and his colleagues
would have to be released sometime and that they should be
prepared for that," Coetsee said in an interview.

In March 1982, as foreign pressures for their release mounted, Mandela and four other ANC leaders – Walter Sisulu,
Ahmed Kathrada, Raymond Mhlaba and Andrew Mlangeni
– were suddenly transferred to Pollsmoor maximum securi-

ty prison. At this sprawling red-brick complex, set in a Cape Town suburb, they were placed in a large communal cell on the roof, cut off not only from the other four thousand prisoners jailed there but from the hundreds of other "politicals" still on Robben Island. The move was puzzling, and people speculated that the authorities wanted to end the enormous influence their most famous prisoner had on the stream of young black activists who continually passed through what they dubbed "Mandela University". Coetsee denies this. He says the idea was to enable the government to make discreet contact with the imprisoned leaders, which could not be done on the island without raising a storm of gossip.

Mandela, meanwhile, was putting out his own feelers for a meeting. He had watched black resistance to apartheid ratchet upwards, decade by decade, from when the ANC launched its first campaign of non-violent defiance in the mid-1950s. In 1960 another passive-resistance campaign, this time against the hated pass laws which restricted the movement of black people, culminated in the massacre of sixty-nine passive resisters at a township called Sharpeville, south of Johannesburg. That prompted the government to ban the ANC and the Pan-Africanist Congress, leading to the decision to resort to guerrilla struggle and so to Mandela's own arrest and imprisonment. Sixteen years later a student demonstration against the use of Afrikaans as a medium of instruction in the segregated black schools began in Soweto and triggered a bigger and more sustained uprising which lasted a year and left more than six hundred people dead. Now, in the mid-1980s, the country was in turmoil once again with wave after wave of protest demonstrations that had begun in September 1984 and looked like becoming endemic as defiant young activists squared up to the security forces and as the rising casualty rate brought increasing international pressure on P.W. Botha's embattled regime. Mandela decided the time was right for the ANC to take the initiative in trying to open a dialogue with the government that might lead to negotiations. He wanted to set up a meeting with Botha, and he wrote to Coetsee asking the minister to come and see him in the prison. Coetsee did not respond, but now, in 1985, the opportunity arose for him to see Mandela in the hospital. "Some intuition told me I shouldn't see Mr. Mandela behind bars," he explains – as always, at pains to accord his former prisoner the appellation of "Mr". "I don't know why, I just had this feeling that that was the way I had to do it. Now I have known him only as a free man, not as a prisoner, and I wanted that to remain in his mind as well."

Coetsee remembers the meeting vividly. "If I close my eyes I can see it all now," he says. On the third floor of the big hospital, sealed off by security, Mandela was the sole patient, with two nursing sisters and his surgeon the only other people allowed on the floor. As Coetsee walked into his ward, together with the commissioner of prisons, Gen. Johan Willemse, prisoner no. 466/64, dressed in a blue-checked gown, rose from his chair and greeted his jailers like old friends.

"It was quite incredible," Coetsee recalls. "He acted as though we had known each other for years and this was the umpteenth time we had met. He introduced General Willemse and me to the two nurses, and chided me for not coming to see him sooner. I remember he made a little joke about this being his ward and me being his warder. He took complete command of the situation. He was like the host. He invited us to sit down, and 'General Willemse, are you comfortable and is there anything we can do for you?' I had read a lot about him – all his speeches and all these reports that came across my desk every day – and I was fascinated at what kind of man he must be to have attracted all this international attention and have all these honorary degrees and awards given to him. When I met him I immediately understood why. He came across as a man of Old World values. I have studied Latin and Roman culture, and I remember thinking that this is a man to whom I could apply it, an old Roman citizen with *dignitas, gravitas, honestas, simplicitas*."

Although the two men got on well, it was a wary occasion, with more hints than substance in the conversation.

Mandela sensed a change in the atmosphere from previous meetings he had had with government officials and the overbearing Kruger. He later told me: "Coetsee is a different type of fellow. He was very polite, and although we didn't discuss politics it was clear that he was putting out feelers. But he was very subtle about it. At one point he said to me, 'I am interested in your being put in a situation between prison and freedom.' I asked him whether he meant my whole group of prisoners, and he said no, just me. I was worried about that because it would look as though there was a deal, but I didn't say anything about it to him. All I said was, 'Well, your coming here cuts down our problems by 25 per cent.'"

The ice was broken and a new process had begun, slowly and uncertainly.

When Mandela left the Volks Hospital on December 23, the commanding officer at Pollsmoor, Brig. Fred Munro, met him with the news that he would not be rejoining his colleagues on the roof, but was to be given a cell in the prison hospital on the ground floor. Again Mandela worried that the others would think he had made a deal. He asked Munro why he was being separated from his colleagues, but the prison commander said he didn't know – those were the orders from head office.

Mandela asked for, and was granted, permission to meet with his fellow political prisoners. "Look, chaps," he said, "I don't think we should fight this, because, whether they have it in mind or not, it will open an opportunity for us to make an approach to the government about a meeting between them and the ANC."

That was what Mandela had always had in mind. In 1961, a year after the African National Congress was outlawed, he had written to Hendrik Verwoerd, the chief architect of apartheid and then prime minister (this was before South Africa switched to a presidential system of government), appealing to him to convene a national convention, at which all South Africans would be represented, to draw up "a new non-racial and democratic constitution". Only when

Verwoerd failed to reply to that letter did the ANC decide to abandon non-violent methods and form a military wing. "I started Umkhonto we Sizwe," Mandela says now, "but I never had any illusions that we could win a military victory; its purpose was to focus attention on the resistance movement." So getting to see the government had always been a primary objective.

He knew, too, that popular attitudes on both sides would make this difficult. "I knew it would be opposed by our own people as well as those on the government side," he told me. "I would have to adopt a strategy that would enable me to confront people with a *fait accompli*. I was convinced that was the only way." So confidentiality was essential, for Mandela as well as Coetsee. "I hope you understand now what was going on," says Coetsee. "In a sense this is material for Le Carré."

MORE CLANDESTINE WORK was at hand. Not one to leave anything to chance, Mandela had asked to see his senior legal adviser a few days after his meeting with Coetsee. George Bizos, a barrister of large girth and even larger heart, was a good deal more than just Mandela's lawyer, more than part of the defence team in the 1964 Rivonia trial at which the ANC high command had been sentenced to life imprisonment: he was also his trusted friend and confidant.* Over the years, Bizos, together with attorney Ismail Ayob, had been one of the few people allowed access to Mandela – a fact he took pains to keep quiet about, so as not to jeopardize the precious channel of communication. So Bizos, too, had made a secret visit to the ward on the third floor of the Volks Hospital, staying for nearly three hours – the longest visit Bizos had ever been allowed – while a prison guard waited at the door, discreetly out of earshot. Mandela himself ended

---

* Bizos is now a member of the Judicial Services Commission, a body established under the new South African constitution to recommend appointments to the judiciary. He was appointed to the commission by President Mandela.

the meeting out of concern for the young Afrikaner nurses who were waiting to change his dressings before they could knock off duty. "It was a rare meeting for him, yet he said we should end it so that the nurses could get home to their families," Bizos told me, still astonished at the black prisoner's solicitude towards these members of the racial group that had persecuted him and his people for so long.

"Nelson was worried that news of his meeting with Kobie Coetsee might get out and reach the ANC leadership in exile, and that they might think he was doing deals without their concurrence," Bizos recalls. "He asked me to try to get to Oliver Tambo [the ANC president] in Lusaka and assure him that nothing would happen without their approval."

Happily, Bizos was able to undertake the mission. Because of his friendship with the ANC leaders, for most of his life, he had been denied citizenship rights and a passport, which meant he could not travel outside South Africa, but now his status as a senior barrister was such that the government could not withhold these "privileges", and in middle age he had at last been given a passport. His story is in itself a representative one of persecution and tenacity of spirit.

At the age of twelve, as the German army marched into Greece in May 1941, Bizos and his father, Antonios, boarded a rowboat in the southern Peloponnesian fishing village of Vasilitsi together with seven New Zealand soldiers his father was helping to escape and four other Greeks. With two sets of oars and a sail they set course for Crete, one hundred and fifty miles away. Three days out, as Crete itself fell to the Wehrmacht, the bedraggled refugees were picked up by a British destroyer, *HMS Kimberley*. George remembers being hauled aboard as Stukas dive-bombed the destroyer and the ship's anti-aircraft guns thundered back at them. They were taken to Egypt, where Antonios Bizos was placed in a refugee camp and young George was taken to an orphanage in Alexandria. Two months later they were transported aboard the *Ile de France* to South Africa, where the father got a job in a café in downtown Johannesburg. The café was opposite the offices of the Afrikaans newspaper *Die Vaderland*, from whose balcony members of the pro-Nazi Ossewa-Brandwag movement delivered fiery speeches and, in the 1948 general election campaign, National Party speakers proclaimed the doctrine of apartheid that would carry them to power and keep them there for the next forty-six years. Given his early encounter with its parent philosophy, that was enough to turn the young Bizos into a lifelong opponent of apartheid.

Later, when he went to law school at the University of the Witwatersrand, in Johannesburg, Bizos became an active member of the radical National Union of South African Students, and in 1950 he helped to organize South Africa's first student strike in protest against a quota system for blacks to be admitted to the university's medical school. Thereafter he was labelled an enemy of the state, and his applications for citizenship were repeatedly rejected long after he had lived in the country for the statutory five years required to qualify for nationalization. Once, he recalls, the rejection came from Interior Minister Jan de Klerk – FW's father – with the curtly uninformative response that it was "not in the public interest" to grant him citizenship. So he remained in South Africa on a refugee permit, unable to travel abroad – not even to visit his ageing mother, who had stayed in Greece in the village of Vasilitsi.

Now here he was, aged fifty-seven and silver-haired, preparing to fly to Lusaka on a mission for Mandela. Before leaving he decided to see Kobie Coetsee. "My reasons were twofold," says Bizos. "Firstly, it was a kind of personal insurance policy: I knew the authorities would find out about my trip and I didn't want them to think I was running an errand as part of an ANC conspiracy. But I also wanted to make my own assessment of the situation. Nelson had been very enthusiastic about his meeting with Coetsee and had spoken warmly of the minister, but I was suspicious that they were trying to use him as part of a plan to split the internal and external wings of the ANC and have him lead the internal wing. I still believe that was their plan at the time, but they had underestimated Nelson's intelligence and integrity. I didn't think Nelson would fall for it, but he was unable to speak publicly for himself, and I was worried that they might be able to do things that would compromise him and cause confusion."

Bizos telephoned Coetsee's private secretary to ask for a meeting. More covert arrangements followed, culminating in another encounter aboard an aircraft flying between Cape Town and Johannesburg. This time nature intervened to extend the meeting: Johannesburg airport was fogbound, so the plane was diverted to Durban, where it refuelled and returned to Johannesburg after the fog had lifted. The result was that the two men had a total of four hours' discussion time together. It may have been decisive in determining the course of events.

"Coetsee wanted to know a lot about Mandela, and I spoke about what sort of person he was," Bizos recalls. "I stressed his absolute integrity and loyalty to the ANC, and told him I was quite sure he would never accept his own release before the other political prisoners were freed. At one stage I was behaving so much like an advocate that he told me it wasn't necessary to preach to him. But he showed a very keen interest, and the whole discussion seemed to be an awakening for him."

Bizos flew to Lusaka a few days later and checked into the Pamodzi Hotel. At 10.30 p.m. ANC security guards brought Oliver Tambo to his room. It was an emotional reunion: the two had not seen each other since Tambo had slipped into exile in 1961, two years before his colleagues were arrested in the Rivonia Raid. Tambo, one year older than Mandela, was the prisoner's lifelong soulmate, though wholly unlike him in manner and appearance. Where Mandela was tall and slightly austere, with a *gravitas* derived from his upbringing as a member of the royal household of the Tembu king who had adopted him as a young boy, Tambo was a small man, soft-spoken but shrewd. The two had met as students at Fort Hare University, in Eastern Cape province, in the early 1940s: together they had formed the ANC Youth League; together they had been expelled from the university for taking part in a student strike; and together they had later formed the first black legal partnership in South Africa. Only when the ANC was banned did they part company – Mandela going underground and then to prison; Tambo going into exile to seek aid for the ANC and then taking over as its president when the other leaders were arrested in the Rivonia Raid.

Bizos and Tambo talked animatedly in the Lusaka hotel room until 3.30 a.m., when the exasperated security guards told them it was time to stop. "Tambo was elated at the news I brought him," Bizos recalls. "He told me they had indeed been concerned; they didn't know how ill Mandela was and they were worried that he might be tricked into a deal, but I assured him Nelson was in good health and in full control of the situation. His message to them was that they shouldn't worry, that he wouldn't do anything without their concurrence."

Tambo was anxious to know the extent to which he could discuss such a sensitive issue with other ANC leaders. "I told him Mandela felt he should discuss it with whomever he thought necessary, but not with too wide a circle because of the tentative nature of the talks," Bizos says.

Bizos made a second trip to Lusaka on February 28, 1986, and this time they met in President Kenneth Kaunda's guest house, where Tambo was staying. "By then Tambo had been able to discuss the matter with a small inner circle of other leaders," says Bizos, "and he told me they had full confidence in Mandela's ability to handle the situation. I should tell Mandela to carry on, that he had their full support." It was a vital message for the worried prisoner back in Pollsmoor, and having delivered it, a heartened Bizos decided to seek another meeting with Coetsee – thus establishing the first indirect contact between the government and the ANC in exile. This time Bizos sought the help of a long-time professional colleague, Judge Johann Kriegler, to set up the meeting. "I didn't trust the telephone on such a sensitive matter, so I went to see the minister personally," says Kriegler. A date was set, and the judge accompanied Bizos to the minister's official residence in Pretoria, South Africa's executive capital.*

The staff had been dismissed and Coetsee was alone in the house when the two jurists arrived. Bizos remembers that the minister served them lunch and drinks himself. Kriegler recalls that the meeting was "marked by great circumspection and great carefulness." But the essential messages were communicated. "I reported to him what had gone on between Tambo and myself and between Mandela and myself, and I assured him that there was a serious desire to start talking to the government," Bizos says. "I also told him – and I don't know how pleased he was to hear this – that there were no differences between Mandela and the outsiders, and that, whatever agreements were reached, the ANC in exile would support Mandela."

MANDELA'S CELL in the ground-floor prison hospital at Pollsmoor was eight yards by six, painted pale green, comfortably furnished, with a private bathroom next door and a second cell across a hallway equipped as a gymnasium with an exercise bike for the sixty-five-year-old fitness fanatic. By South African prison standards, this was unheard-of luxury. "It was clear to me they wanted to talk," says Mandela. "I didn't think they were about to release me. I thought they just wanted to have me in a convenient place to talk to me."

That was indeed the reason. Coetsee had reported to President Botha on his visit to Mandela in the hospital, and Botha had instructed him to stay in touch with the prisoner. According to Coetsee the old president wanted to find a way to release Mandela, but he was in a bind: on the one hand, he wanted to show the international community which was putting pressure on him, that he was not inflexible; on the other hand, he did not want to appear weak within his own country. The Old Crocodile was obsessed with always look-

---

* The legislative capital, where Parliament sits, is in Cape Town. Cabinet ministers and other senior government officials have to shuttle between the two capitals, one thousand miles apart.

ing tough and in control. "PW was not a man for concessions," says Coetsee. "He never wanted to show any sign of
weakness. He wanted this thing to be done. He knew it had
to be done. But he didn't want to appear weak."

The result was long and drawn-out. It began slowly.
Coetsee followed up his meeting with Winnie Mandela on
the plane by inviting her to his official Cape Town residence,
a splendid old Cape Dutch mansion called Savernake,
where he told her he wanted to let her go home to
Johannesburg and asked her not let him down by behaving
in too extreme a fashion if he did so. For the pugnacious
Winnie, that was asking too much. She gave no pledge, and
when eventually she did return to Johannesburg nearly a
year later she began the most assertive phase of her life. She
surrounded herself with a group of young toughs who mas-
queraded as a soccer team but who were in fact a private
gang who guarded her and did her bidding. As the gang
became thuggish, Mrs. Mandela's star waned in the black
community. In 1988, the gang kidnapped a group of teenage
boys, beat them, and murdered one, a fourteen-year-old
named Stompie Moeketsi Seipei. The gang leader, Jerry
Richardson, was sentenced to death for this murder, and
Mrs. Mandela was sentenced to six years' imprisonment (reduced to a R50,000, or $14,000, fine on appeal) for being
involved in the kidnapping. This and other wayward behaviour strained her marriage after her husband's release from
prison, and in 1992 the couple announced their separation.
Since then she has made a partial comeback, regaining her
position as chairwoman of the ANC Women's League, winning a seat in the new National Assembly, and forcing her
appointment, through the sheer force of her popular support, as a deputy minister in the new cabinet. But in 1986 all
that lay in the future.

Coetsee had several more meetings with Nelson Mandela
– but again he was at pains not to see him in the prison.
Brigadier Munro drove him in his grey Audi through Cape
Town's oak-lined avenues to Savernake, just eight miles
from Pollsmoor but light-years away in style of accommoda-

tion. There, in the deep-cushioned sitting-room, they talked, and the jailer offered his prisoner canapés and his first drink in twenty-two years, a sherry, medium-cream, a drop of nectar that Mandela says he savours to this day.

They would meet, too, in a "guest house" in Pollsmoor's spacious grounds a mile from the main cell blocks. A car would arrive outside the hospital section to take Mandela there at night, and the discussions would last two to three hours. Sometimes, too, they met in General Willemse's residence close by, a pillared mansion in a faintly American southern antebellum style ironically named *Kommaweer* (Come Again). But as Mandela had anticipated, a year dragged by and the talks seemed to be getting no closer either to a meeting with Botha or to the prisoners' release.

Then came what Mandela regards as a key event. A Commonwealth summit meeting in Nassau, Bahamas, deadlocked over whether this club of former British colonies should join the international sanctions campaign against South Africa, itself a former Commonwealth member expelled in 1961 because of apartheid. The third world member countries were all for it, but the redoubtable Margaret Thatcher was strongly opposed – and without Britain, South Africa's main trading partner, Commonwealth sanctions would not mean much. Eventually a compromise was reached whereby a group of "eminent persons" would visit South Africa to study the prospects for change and report to the next annual Commonwealth summit.

A seven-member Eminent Persons Group arrived in South Africa early in 1986 under the co-chairmanship of Malcolm Fraser, a former Australian prime minister, and Gen. Olusegun Obasanjo, the former military ruler of Nigeria who had distinguished himself by handing over his country to civilian rule in 1979. Shuttling between Pretoria and Lusaka, the group began a round of proximity talks between the white regime and the outlawed black liberation movement. After some hesitation the Botha government granted permission for Obasanjo alone to meet with Mandela on February 21 – just as Bizos was about to meet with Tambo in

Lusaka – and then for the whole group to see him in March and again in May.

The meetings with Mandela took place in Pollsmoor's guest house, a round building with bedroom suites leading off a central sitting-room furnished in lime green. The government went to some lengths to make an impression: the prison tailor was summoned to take Mandela's measurements for a new pinstripe suit – "it fitted like a glove," Mandela says – and also a shirt, a tie, shoes, and underwear. Coetsee was there at the start of the second meeting but he did not stay, even though Mandela invited him to. "I wanted him to feel that he was in charge, that he was the host," Coetsee explains today. "I was so struck by his presence. It was absolutely remarkable – his alertness, his composure, his bearing, the way he met these people as though he had been a pinstriped leader all his life. That was a crucial impression for me. I think that was the day I realized this could be the man."

The Eminent Persons Group reported later that it had found Mandela "reasonable and conciliatory". He had emphasized his commitment to racial reconciliation and "pledged himself anew to work for a multiracial society in which all would have a secure place". Encouraged by what it had found on both sides of the political divide in South Africa, the EPG drew up a "possible negotiating concept" for the release of political prisoners, the lifting of the ban on the ANC and other black organizations, the suspension both of the ANC's armed struggle and of government violence against blacks, and the start of all-party negotiations – almost exactly what De Klerk was to announce four years later.

But that was too much for the hawks in South Africa's military-security establishment. The mission arrived at a time when the country's black liberation movement was making the most concerted organizational drive in its history and the government was responding with a fierce security crackdown. As Chester Crocker, then U.S. assistant secretary of state for Africa, has written, the Botha administration was deeply split: some of its members thought the Commonwealth EPG was an ideal vehicle for forcing the ANC and its allies to make hard choices; others wanted to prevent negotiations until they had first smashed the black resistance movement.* The military-security establishment, always close to Botha, who had been defence minister for twelve years before becoming president, prevailed. According to Crocker, the balance was tipped by Botha's annoyance when the Western powers refused to respond to his government's appeal that they address the issue of violence in the country at an upcoming Group of Seven economic summit meeting in Tokyo. He wanted some recognition of the difficulties he was grappling with and he didn't get it. "Something snapped in the man," wrote Crocker. "Xenophobic anger overtook his common sense."**

On the morning of May 19, the day the EPG was due to meet with a special cabinet constitutional committee, Botha's defence minister, Magnus Malan, ordered a series of predawn commando and air raids on supposed ANC bases in Zambia, Zimbabwe, and Botswana. That same day Botha reversed earlier moves to ease security restrictions and imposed a nationwide state of emergency. Outraged at what it considered deliberate provocation, the EPG aborted its mission and flew out of Johannesburg that night. Their only recommendation: to call for the Commonwealth's imposition of comprehensive and mandatory economic sanctions against South Africa.

There was an international outcry over this wilful destruction of the EPG's negotiating initiative, and reformists in South Africa were cast into a new pit of despair. But not Mandela. He remained optimistic because the Commonwealth group had ascertained that among ordinary South Africans there was a widespread desire for a negotiated settlement and enough potential common ground to get negotiations going. That spurred him to take up the initiative. He

---

* See Chester A. Crocker, *High Noon in Southern Africa* (1993), p. 316.
** Ibid., p. 316.

wrote to the commander of Pollsmoor requesting a meeting with Commissioner Willemse.

"I wrote the letter on a Wednesday and on Sunday Willemse flew from Pretoria to see me," Mandela recalls. "I said, 'Look, I want to see P.W. Botha. I want a meeting between the ANC and the government.' And of course the gate to P.W. Botha was Coetsee. 'Well,' said Willemse, 'it so happens Minister Coetsee is in town. I'll phone him and see if you can go and see him.'"

So another trip to Savernake followed. Coetsee promised to speak to the president. Botha did not respond directly, but his interest was aroused. He instructed Coetsee to probe Mandela more closely and report back to him, but not to breathe a word to other cabinet members, for Botha was still terrified of word leaking out that his government was meeting with the ANC. Coetsee stepped up the frequency of his meetings with Mandela, and in May 1988 he formed a special committee to broaden the discussions, consisting of the head of the National Intelligence Service, Niël Barnard; his deputy, Mike Louw; Commissioner Willemse; the director general of the Prisons Department, Fanus van der Merwe; and Coetsee himself. They had frequent, long (sometimes up to seven hours), detailed talks with Mandela whose diary notes forty-seven meetings in all.

Thus for four years before the rest of the world knew anything of it, the future of South Africa was being explored in secret conversations in hospitals, prisons, and a cabinet minister's home between government officials and their principal political prisoner. At the same time, slowly and carefully, the officials began to take Mandela for secret drives into the countryside to accustom him to the world from which he had been cut off for a quarter of a century.

4

A Prisoner
at Large

ON THE FIRST of these excursions, which began shortly
after his return from the hospital to Pollsmoor,
Mandela had one of the most bizarre experiences of his long
imprisonment. The deputy commanding officer of the
prison, Lt. Col. Gawie Marx, was taking him for a drive
around Cape Town, showing him the sights of the city, and
on their way back Marx pulled up at a shopping centre. He
asked Mandela if he would like a Coke, then jumped out of
the car and disappeared into a café.

"He just left me there, sitting alone in the car with the keys
in the ignition," Mandela recalls. "It was a very disturbing
situation. There I was, I'd been in prison for twenty-two
years, and I didn't know whether I was going to find myself
running away. It was so new, so unexpected. I just didn't
know what I was going to do." He did not, of course, do anything. Whatever else Mandela may be, he is not headstrong.
But the incident reveals not only how respectful the
government officials were towards Mandela but also how
emotionally upsetting it can be for a long-term prisoner to be
tantalized with a glimpse of freedom.

The excursions began modestly with walks into an
agricultural allotment adjoining the prison grounds, where
Mandela was able to stroll on the grass beside a dam and
watch the ducks and other birds. It was a wonderful escape
from the drab surroundings he had lived in for half his adult
life. Later the excursions became more venturesome, as the
prison officials began taking him out almost every weekend,
first around the streets and suburbs of Cape Town, then
further afield on excursions through the scenic peninsula
that extends down to Cape Point, where the Indian and
Atlantic oceans meet at the southwestern tip of Africa.

"What we had in mind was to expose him to the realities of the outside world, to prepare him for release," says Coetsee.

For the warders, too, the excursions were a pleasant diversion from the prison. Several formed warm relations with the fatherly figure they were driving around, and sometimes they became a little daring in what they did with him. Christo Brand, who was just twenty-five at the time, remembers taking Mandela walking on Cape Town's Sea Point beach one evening, and even bringing him to his own apartment to meet his family – after which Mandela sent Christmas cards to Brand's small children. "Life's not the same without the politicals here," says Brand today. "The ordinary criminal prisoners are not nearly so interesting."

All the while the discussions with Coetsee's committee were continuing, and Mandela was pressing for a meeting with President Botha. He had written to Botha, and in early August 1988 he received word that the president might see him before the end of the month. Then Mandela fell ill. On August 12 he was taken to Cape Town's Tygerberg Hospital, where the doctors diagnosed tuberculosis. He would have to have an operation to remove fluid from his lungs, followed by a long convalescence.

"Gee whiz! You know that just destroyed me, because all my concentration now was on these talks," says Mandela. However, the years of prison regimen and work in the quarries had toughened him, and his recovery was quicker than the doctors expected. By the end of September he was able to leave the hospital and was taken to a private clinic in Cape Town, where the talks resumed. Then, in December, he was transferred to the Victor Verster Prison outside the wineland town of Paarl, thirty-six miles from Cape Town, where he was accommodated in the deputy chief warder's comfortable house on the prison grounds.

After that, the excursions into the countryside became even more wideranging. Mandela was taken to the neighbouring towns of Stellenbosch and Wellington, then on a day-long journey up the west coast to Saldanha Bay and the quaint little fishing village of Paternoster; and, on another occasion, one hundred and fifty miles inland to Laingsburg, on the edge of the semi-desert Great Karoo.

He was taken for walks about the streets of Paarl, too, accompanied by prison warders and security officers dressed in civilian clothing. Though he was the world's most famous political prisoner and a living icon to his people, he had been gone from public view for so long that no one knew any longer what he looked like. South Africa's Prisons Act prohibited the publication of pictures of prisoners, and the only photos of Mandela to appear in foreign publications showed a thick-set, middle-aged man quite different from the lean, grey-haired figure who now walked the streets with a small posse of white men. When he and his minders went into shops and fastfood restaurants, no one recognized him.

"Once we stopped at a petrol station to fill up, down near the foreshore in Cape Town, and I got out of the car and spoke to the pump attendants," Mandela recalls. "I made a mistake by greeting them in the African way, and it caused quite a commotion. They seemed to realize this was somebody. I think they may have recognized me."

THE MOVE TO Victor Verster had run into an initial difficulty that casts a small shaft of light on the apartheid government's obsession with concealment. The decision to send Mandela there had been taken by the committee of officials who were meeting with him. "We wanted him to be in a decent place where he could receive people and start playing the political role that we had in mind for him," says Niël Barnard, the National Intelligence Service chief whom Mandela realized was the key figure on the committee. But they had not counted on having to furnish the house where they put him: when the deputy head warder moved out, on transfer to another prison, he had taken all his personal furniture with him, and days before Mandela was due to move, the officials discovered the house was bare. How to furnish it? With their neurotic sensitivity to such matters, the committee members feared that any large expenditure on furniture for their prisoner, if traced through the normal public accounts that had to be tabled in Parliament, would lead to a political outcry. However, the National Intelligence Service had a slush fund for secret projects that did not have to be accounted for to Parliament, so Barnard arranged for it to be used to buy the furniture. In one of the service's more unconventional operations, two agents flew to Cape Town and in two days furnished the house completely. "To this day I have no idea what happened to all that furniture after Mandela was released," Barnard admits.

Life at Victor Verster was infinitely more relaxed than anything Mandela had known before. He virtually had his own household staff in attendance on him. James Gregory, a soft-spoken warder who had been with Mandela for twenty-two years on Robben Island and in Pollsmoor, during which time he had become a friend and admirer (and voted for the ANC in South Africa's first democratic elections in April 1994) headed a team of four assigned to care for him: Maj. Charl Marais; Lt. Jack Swart, head of the prison's kitchen staff; Gregory; and his twenty-year-old son, Brent, then a trainee in the prisons service. Other prison staff were not allowed near the house, which was about two miles from the main prison complex.

"When one went there to see Nelson one usually arrived in the morning and stayed for lunch," recalls Bizos, who made several visits during these closing years of Mandela's imprisonment. "The meal would be cooked by Swart, who was Mandela's personal chef, and Gregory and his son would wait on us at table like a butler and his assistant."

Surveillance was indulgent. "I would end my duty around 4 p.m.," says Gregory. "I knew which rooms Mr. Mandela would use [again the careful use of the apellation "Mr."] and I would go to all the other rooms and close the windows, then lock the front door before leaving by the back door and locking that. But he had a key to the back door, so if he wanted to go out onto the patio and sit beside the swimming pool he could, for as long as he liked."

A prisoner with his own key! Of course there could be no escape from the prison grounds, but even so this was an unprecedented token of status for a prisoner. Compared with the harsh regimen of the earlier years and the heavy responsibilities that lay ahead, the fourteen months Mandela spent at Victor Verster stand out as a relaxed and relatively pleasant interregnum in Mandela's life. He grew fond of his warders, and when five years later he became president he invited all of them all to his inauguration (Gregory's son, by then, had sadly been killed in a car crash). Mandela also became attached to the house. After his release he obtained the plans and had an exact replica built as his holiday home at Qunu, his birthplace in Transkei.

James Gregory was the warder who was closest to Mandela. The two men had established a rare relationship over the years, a Hegelian bond that had broadened into friendship and ultimately, on Gregory's part, almost hero worship. The warder was only twenty-three when he arrived on Robben Island and he remembers that he was filled with hostility when he first saw the imposing figure standing there in his prison overalls, tall and aloof, a powerfully built man who had been a heavyweight boxer. Gregory had grown up on a farm in Zululand and was comfortable in the company of black people, but at his Afrikaans boarding school his head had been filled with the National Party's demonizing propaganda against the ANC and its leaders. "I had been force-fed this line that they wanted to overthrow the government by force and kill all the whites," Gregory recalls, "and as I looked at him I thought, So you are the one. You are this terrible terrorist. You should have been hanged."

Because he spoke African languages, the young warder was placed in the censors' office – a job despised by the prisoners that, ironically, brought him into close contact with them. An inherently decent person, Gregory was shocked that the other censors simply filed away letters containing passages that contravened the prison regulations without telling the prisoners they had been intercepted, leaving the prisoners to wait anxiously and in vain for their letters to be answered. He acted differently: he went to the prisoners and gave them an opportunity to alter the text of their letters. "I think that is where a trust started building up between us," he says.

As the trust grew the prisoners began opening up in their conversations with Gregory – and, as happens to everyone who has ever come into contact with Mandela, the young white warder was influenced by the black leader's strong but empathetic personality. "I was amazed at how positive and cheerful they were," he says. "I mean, if I had a life sentence I would just curl up in a corner and die, but here they were with high morale, joking and carrying on as though it was everyday life. I couldn't understand this, I was curious." He began questioning Mandela about the ANC, then spent hours in reference libraries checking what he had been told. "I started realizing that what he was telling me was the truth. That changed my attitude towards him tremendously."

As the relationship warmed, the prison authories assigned Gregory more directly to the ANC leadership group. In effect, he became Mandela's personal warder. "I think [the authorities] realized I was doing a proper job, and because I got along with the prisoners it took a lot of stress out of the situation, so it was useful for them," he says. When Mandela was transferred to Pollsmoor, Gregory was transferred with him, and he accompanied him again to Victor Verster. He found the relationship enriching; it transformed his whole outlook on life; and Gregory speaks today in almost reverential tones of his former charge, recalling with pride how Mandela telephoned his daughter, Natasha, to congratulate her when she graduated from Stellenbosch University. But it was not always easy or pleasant. His fellow warders looked at him askance, and often made derogatory remarks behind his back. Socially, Gregory found himself shunned. "I ended up living like a hermit," he says. "I couldn't go to friends, I couldn't go to parties, because the moment I got there I was bombarded with questions about Mandela, and I couldn't answer because I knew they would twist things around, so I just kept quiet and kept to myself so that I didn't have to explain myself all the time."

Nor was the relationship itself always easy. Mandela, with his iron will, could sometimes be difficult. Gregory recalls how, while they were at Pollsmoor, Mandela asked for a supply of blue Pantene hairdressing lotion, which he had heard was good for the scalp. Gregory tried to buy some but could not find any. Soon afterwards Mrs. Helen Suzman, the noted civil-rights parliamentarian who took a special interest in prison conditions, visited Pollsmoor and after chatting with Mandela asked him, in the presence of the commanding officer and other senior warders, whether he needed anything. "Yes," Mandela replied, "I have asked for some blue Pantene but they haven't given me any." Commanding Officer Fred Munro glared at Gregory. "See to it that he gets this stuff," he ordered. "Yessir," the warder replied.

An ordeal worthy of Monty Python followed. As Gregory recounts it, he ordered young Christo Brand to scour the city's pharmacies for blue Pantene. Brand reported back that the manufacturer had discontinued the line, but Mandela would have none of it. "The commanding officer can't promise me this while Mrs. Suzman is here, and now that Mrs. Suzman has gone you tell me I can't have it," he admonished. "You must understand how serious this was," says Gregory, seeming agitated even today as he recalls the confrontation. "I mean, us cheating him like that. It could have caused an outcry." The anxious warder got on the telephone and called pharmacies throughout the Cape Peninsula. "I would ask each pharmacy for the name of ten others, then call them, but the answer was always the same: 'It's discontinued.' I would go back to Mr. Mandela and say, 'I can't get any, they don't make it anymore,' but he would reply, 'I was promised this in front of Mrs. Suzman, and now she's gone you tell me I can't get it.' I would say to him, 'I can get you the yellow kind, bottles and bottles of it' – but, no, it had to be the blue one." Eventually, to Gregory's enduring relief, the indefatigable Brand found a pharmacy that had a forgotten carton of blue Pantene in its storeroom. He bought the lot.

The warders performed other little favours, too. Mandela eats sparingly and tried while in prison to obtain health foods. He was particularly fond of a wholewheat bread produced by a small bakery near Pollsmoor, and Christo Brand would buy loaves there and store them in his deep freeze at home to keep Mandela regularly supplied.

Gregory was his main chaperon on excursions outside the prison. It was he who took Mandela on the long drives to Paternoster, Saldanha Bay, and Laingsburg. He recalls that the two of them went for a stroll along the beach at Paternoster and stumbled on a group of German tourists taking photographs of the little fishing boats being pulled up on the sand. If any of the tourists had realized who the tall black man was walking so casually among them, he could have made a fortune by taking the scoop picture of the year, but none did, and Mandela and Gregory returned to their car to chuckle over their anonymity.

On another outing, Gregory recalls, they were returning to Victor Verster and were held up for two hours as roadworkers carried out a blasting operation in the Bain's Kloof pass between Ceres and Wellington. Gregory bought some fish and chips at a nearby roadhouse, and as they sat there having an impromptu picnic about fifty other cars pulled up and scores of people milled around them as they waited for the road to reopen. Again no one recognized the world's most famous political prisoner in their midst.

"Whenever he asked to go anywhere, I would take him," says Gregory. "Those were my instructions. He would read something that interested him – about the salt pans at Saldanha Bay, or the floods that had devastated Laingsburg a few years before – and he would ask if I could take him there. Once he heard that there was snow on the Matroosberg mountains beyond Worcester and he wanted to see it. He wanted to walk in the snow and play in it, but when we got there the snow was too high up the mountain, so all he could do was look at it."

Security was Gregory's nightmare on these ventures. "The arrangements were left to me, but my instructions were that we had to keep this man safe, we had to make sure nothing happened to him – even if it was to cost our lives." They travelled armed – Gregory carried a 9 mm. parabellum pistol – and in a convoy of two or three cars. "This was not to stop him escaping," Gregory emphasizes. "We knew he wouldn't attempt that. But we had to protect him at all costs, and that was a nerve-racking business, knowing how sensitive the whole issue was."

Gregory would notify the other members of the convoy only moments before leaving, and even then would not give them the destination. The cars would not travel in line but would take turns at being in front so as to appear part of the general traffic stream, remaining in contact all the while via a radio intercom system. Only once did they have a security scare. On their way back to Victor Verster from General Willemse's home at Pollsmoor, where Mandela had been in a meeting with the committee of officials, the rear car in the convoy radioed Gregory to report that a grey Chrysler was trying to wedge in between them. "'What must I do?' this guy at the back asked. I said, 'Take him out.' You know, bang him off the road. That was all I could do. My orders were to do anything to protect Mr. Mandela." As it turned out, the Chrysler was a police car that picked up the exchange on its own intercom and hastily reassured the convoy drivers. Through it all, says Gregory, Mandela remained completely unruffled.

For the most part, Mandela's life at Pollsmoor was extremely busy. He received visitors, up to a dozen at a time, he read avidly, and he worked hard preparing himself for his talks with the committee of officials and his hoped-for meeting with Botha. "He turned the place into an office," Bizos recalls. It was also a negotiating centre. He met not only with the committee of officials, but, on special request, with the ANC leaders still in prison at Pollsmoor and other political prisoners on Robben Island, some of whom were young men and women he had never met before who had been jailed for their involvement in the great black uprising of the 1980s. Meeting this younger group was especially important, for they represented a new and internally based element in the liberation struggle whom Mandela had hitherto known of only by name and reputation. They, too, would have to be co-ordinated into his strategy, together with the ANC in exile, yet once again he would have to be cautious about how much he revealed. He could not tell them of his secret talks until he had his *fait accompli* in place.

For the young revolutionaries, it was almost a sacramental experience to be brought into the presence of the messianic figure of their liberation songs and dreams. I recall seeing the Reverend Allan Boesak, a co-founder and one of the patrons of the umbrella opposition organization called the United Democratic Front, as he emerged, face glowing, from his first encounter with Mandela. "I have just had one of the great experiences of my life," he breathed to a cluster of reporters at the gates of Victor Verster.

Popo Molefe, the UDF general secretary, who had just been sentenced to twelve years' imprisonment for his part in the uprising, was one of those whom Mandela asked to see. The authorities included his name in a list of ten to be brought from Robben Island, but someone blundered and another Molefe, not Popo, was told he was to be taken to see the great man. This other Molefe, who was serving a sentence for a criminal offence, realized there must have been a mistake, but the opportunity to meet Mandela was too good to miss, so he kept his mouth shut and joined the group. At Victor Verster the visitors formed a line in the house, and Mandela began greeting each in turn, asking after their families by name. When he reached Molefe he shook his hand warmly. "And how is Pinda?" he asked, referring to Molefe's wife. As the man stared back blankly, Mandela's face hardened. "You're not Popo," he snapped, and moved on to the next in line.

The embarrassed authorities straightened things out quickly, and the real Popo Molefe was brought to Victor Verster the following week, but the incident revealed a personality trait that has astonished many who have met Mandela since his release, and that is his close attention to personal detail, his almost card-index memory for people, which enables him to recognize men and women he may not have seen for years or may have met only briefly in a crowd. It reveals itself in the cards he sent Christo Brand's small children, and his phone call to Natasha Gregory when she graduated. He has called my home and greeted my young son Julian by name when he answered the phone. I was the first journalist to interview Mandela after his release, and as we began talking in his sitting-room in Soweto, we were interrupted by a family member who announced that some tribal elders from his home village in Transkei had arrived to pay their respects. The old men were shown into the room, and Mandela proceeded to ask them for news of their extended families, who had married whom and what children and grandchildren had been born in the twenty-seven years he had been away, and one could see him mentally card-indexing all the names. "This is no trick of political showmanship," Nadine Gordimer, the Nobel literature laureate, has written of the man she knows well. "Seemingly trivial, it is a sign of something profound: a remove from self-centredness; the capacity to live for others that is central to his character."*

In this spirit of selflessness Mandela prepared himself for what he knew was the mission ahead of him. As the talks with the committee of officials went on through 1988, the ground was slowly prepared once again for a meeting with Botha. And again the word came through that the president might be prepared to see Mandela soon. Then in January 1989 Botha suffered a stroke.

---

* *Sunday Times*, Johannesburg, 12 December 1993.

5

Tying the
Shoelaces

A S THE PALL of another delay settled over Mandela and the committee of officials, they kept up their meetings. The talks had been going on through all the dark years of the most prolonged and intensive black uprising in South Africa's history, which had begun in September 1984 and was still shaking the country to its foundations despite Botha's attempts to clamp down on it with two states of emergency and a savage use of force. By 1989 more than four thousand people had been killed and fifty thousand detained without trial; international sanctions were being applied; and the rand currency had crashed. Mandela wanted to negotiate, but he could not get beyond these secret talks.

What was discussed over all those years was a narrow band of issues that, had the political will been there, could have been resolved in a fraction of the time. But Botha was hesitant and heavily under the influence of his military-security establishment. So the meetings tracked over the same old ground, session after session, waiting for some decisiveness at the top. Coetsee was seeking the elusive formula for an "honourable release" – for freeing Mandela in a way that would make Botha look flexible to the Western world but not weak to the folks at home. Niël Barnard had a brief to sound the ANC leader out on three issues: Was he prepared to accept that violence was not the way to solve South Africa's political problems? What was his attitude to communism, given the ANC's long-standing alliance with the South African Communist Party? And did he still insist on majority rule, or was he prepared to settle for something less?

Mandela, for his part, was single-minded in wanting a meeting with President Botha to discuss with him the possibility of a negotiated settlement. In addition, he wanted to press the government to release his colleagues in the ANC leadership group who were also serving life sentences – especially Walter Sisulu, who was now in his mid-seventies. Not once did he raise the question of his own release.

Botha's obsession with not appearing weak was the main stumbling block. He kept searching for some formula for Mandela's conditional release, but Mandela, too, had an iron will and remained resolute. Back in January 1985, Botha had made an offer that only complicated the issue. The president had just returned from a rare trip to Europe where, according to Coetsee, he had been encouraged in the idea by some conservative politicians, one of them Franz-Josef Strauss, the Bavarian Christian Socialist politician whom Pretoria regarded as one of its few friends in the world. Says Coetsee: "PW called a special meeting of key people and told us, 'I've got the answer now.'" The plan was to offer to release Mandela if he would "unconditionally reject violence as a political instrument" – in other words, renounce his 1961 decision to go over to an armed struggle after the ANC was outlawed. "PW told us he thought this was a brilliant solution," says Coetsee, "because if Mandela refused, then the whole world would understand why the South African government could not release him."

But Coetsee argued against it. "I had studied the man and I knew he would never accept this," he says. "There was no way Mandela was going to renounce the ANC's armed struggle, for which he had spent all those years in prison. We had to put it in a positive way, asking him to commit himself to a future peaceful process rather than asking him to renounce the past." Also, the deal was one-sided. There was nothing in it for the ANC. After years in exile, during which the organization had built up a high international profile, its leaders would be unlikely to sacrifice their strongest bargaining chip for nothing more than Mandela's personal freedom. "I warned that the ANC would decline the offer and that we would be painting ourselves into a corner," says Coetsee. He got support from Louis le Grange, the minister of law and order, who, though a hawk, had also met

Mandela and taken the measure of the man. But the rest of the cabinet opposed them, backing Botha.

"We argued right up to the last minute," Coetsee recalls. "He was going to make the announcement in Parliament and he had his speech already prepared, but Le Grange and I worked on an alternative draft of the last few pages. We followed the president right into the parliamentary chamber and stood with him for a moment behind the speaker's chair. He had his speech in one hand and our text in the other. He hesitated, then, slapping his text, said, 'No, this one carries the support of the cabinet.'"

As Botha walked to his bench Le Grange cursed under his breath. "Go ahead and fuck it up then," he muttered. Coetsee followed the president to his bench to make a final plea, but Botha glared at him and snapped: "I have already decided."

Botha gave the speech as he wanted to, and the response was as Coetsee feared. Winnie Mandela flew to Cape Town with Ismail Ayob to get Mandela's reply. The following Sunday, February 10, 1985, a huge rally was held in Soweto's Jabulani Stadium to pay tribute to Archbishop Tutu on winning the Nobel peace prize for his outspoken opposition to apartheid over many years. Mandela's daughter Zinzi, aged twenty-four, who was then the only family member not silenced by a banning order, mounted the platform to read her father's statement flatly refusing to give any undertakings until his people were free of apartheid.

> I cherish my own freedom dearly but I care even more for your freedom. I am no less life-loving than you are. But I cannot sell my birthright, nor am I prepared to sell the birthright of my people to be free. I am in prison as the representative of the people and of your organization, the African National Congress, which was banned. What freedom am I being offered while the organization of the people remains banned? . . . Only free men can negotiate. Prisoners cannot enter into contracts.

As Mandela's daughter's voice rang out, the big crowd erupted in a wild display of cheering and chanting. They were the first words anyone had heard from Mandela since his final address to the court that imprisoned him twenty-one years before, and if ever the South African government had doubted the durability of his stature in the black community, it could do so no longer.

The trouble was that Botha was now stuck with his demand that Mandela had to renounce violence before he could be released. Any withdrawal of that would make Botha look weak. So the talks in the prison dragged on inconclusively. Botha made several half-hearted attempts to extricate himself. He tried to lure Mandela with an offer of release if he would agree to go to the nominally independent tribal homeland of Transkei, where he was born, and where his nephew, Paramount Chief Kaiser Matanzima, was now president under the apartheid system. But Mandela wrote back warning that if he were taken to the tribal territory he would defy all restrictions placed on him and walk to Johannesburg. More bizarrely, on another occasion Botha sought Western applause by offering to release Mandela if the Soviet Union would free Andrei Sakharov and Anatoly Scharansky, and if Angola would return a South African soldier captured there trying to sabotage the country's oil industry. That, too, was a lead balloon.

The only benefit to flow from Botha's bungled release offer was that it increased Coetsee's credibility as an adviser. Botha was never one to admit a mistake, but it became clear from then on that he and other members of his cabinet were more inclined to heed what the justice minister had to say. Gradually, Coetsee was able to bring them around to accepting a new formula that would get over the difficulty of requiring Mandela to renounce violence. He would be asked to commit himself only to "positive development and reconciliation", without having to renounce anything. Coetsee knew from his discussions with the prisoner that he would agree to this.

Meanwhile, in the house at Victor Verster, Mandela was carefully putting his own thoughts together and trying as best he could to consult with his ANC colleagues. He was unhappy about acting on his own, but the circumstances left him little choice and he was growing more and more concerned at the increasing conflict in the country and the deepening racial polarization that could result. He was worried, too, that the authorities might establish a second line of communication with the ANC and that the two lines might then be at cross purposes.

Mandela managed to persuade the prison authorities to let him send an occasional fax, and once even make a telephone call, to Alfred Nzo, the ANC secretary general in Lusaka. This, together with Bizos's trips to Lusaka and the visits to Victor Verster by political activists from outside and political prisoners from Pollsmoor and Robben Island, meant that a rudimentary system of consultation was established. Mandela hoped this would be enough to ensure that he did not come into conflict with any other element of the liberation movement – but, as we shall see, he was mistaken and some serious misunderstandings did in fact arise. At the time, however, he felt reassured enough to write an eleven-page memorandum setting out his position on the issues that Coetsee and the committee of officials were raising, and urging a meeting between the government and the ANC as a first step towards reaching a negotiated settlement on the country's future.

He was characteristically forthright. The ANC had a long history of campaigning peacefully for political rights, he wrote, but when the government made that illegal the black organization had the right to take up arms against an oppressive and morally repugnant system of government. Oppressed people through the ages had done the same. "Africans as well as Afrikaners were, at one time or another, compelled to take up arms against British imperialism," he added, in a telling passage that went to the heart of Afrikaner nationalist pride. There was no way, therefore, that the ANC was going to abandon its armed struggle until the government showed a willingness to give up its monopoly of political power and negotiate directly with the country's real black leaders.

Mandela was equally blunt about communism. The ANC was not communist, he declared, but the South African Communist Party had supported its struggle against racialism since the early 1920s, through long lean years when it had no other allies, and the ANC was not the kind of organization to dump its friends. "Which man of honour will ever desert a lifelong friend at the instance of a common opponent and still maintain a measure of credibility among his people?" he asked.

As for majority rule, Mandela said, it was a pillar of democracy worldwide. It was the right thing for whites, he noted, but when black South Africans demanded it they were told it would be a disaster – that if they wanted political rights they would have to find some other formula. "White South Africa simply has to accept that there will never be peace and stability in this country until the principle is fully accepted," he wrote.

Yet Mandela was also conciliatory. In any negotiating process, he said, two fundamental issues would have to be reconciled: the black demand for majority rule, and white concerns stemming from this demand. Attention would have to be given to structural guarantees ensuring that majority rule did not mean black domination of the white minority. "Such reconciliation will be achieved only if both parties are willing to compromise," he added. Mandela concluded the memorandum by suggesting a two-stage process. First the government and the ANC should meet to work out what could be done to create a proper climate for negotiations, and then the negotiations themselves could take place.

Mandela sent the memorandum to Botha in March 1989, after the president had recovered from the stroke. Here, for the first time since Verwoerd spurned Mandela's letter asking for a national convention twenty-eight years before, was a concrete ANC offer to negotiate a peaceful settlement of South Africa's bitter conflict, reversing the organization's commitment to the revolutionary overthrow of white minority rule. A week later, Mandela received word that Botha was ready to see him.

It was Coetsee and Barnard who had prevailed on the Old Crocodile to agree to the meeting. "I spent an hour with him telling him there was no way he could lose out if he saw Mandela," Barnard recalls. "'If the meeting goes wrong and jumps the tracks and all that,' I said, 'you will still be remembered as the one who tried to keep things moving forward to a solution. But if it goes well it will be the beginning of South Africa's settlement politics, and history will acknowledge you for that.'" In the end Botha consented, leading to one of the most unusual encounters in modern politics.

NiËL BARNARD WAS the key organizer of the secret meeting between the white president and the apartheid state's prime black prisoner, which was scheduled to take place on the evening of July 5, 1989. Botha was, as usual, fearful of political repercussions if his own constituency learned of the meeting. "I had to smuggle him into *Tuynhuys* past the security police," says Barnard, referring to the early Cape Dutch home alongside the Houses of Parliament where the president has his Cape Town office.* This in itself was risky. "They came to ask me my blood group in case there was a shootout and I got injured and had to have a transfusion," Mandela recalls. And again, as when he met the EPG four years before, there was a flurry of concern that he should look smart. So again the prison tailor was sent for, Mandela's measurements were taken, and a new suit was purchased. And a new shirt and tie and shoes.

"They told me to be ready by six o'clock in the evening," Mandela recalls. "I was. But when they saw me they said, 'Your shirt is creased.' I said, 'But, heh, it's new, it's just out of the shop.' There were these folds that you get in a new

---

* Despite the elaborate precautions, news of the meeting leaked out anyway. President Botha flew to an Eastern Transvaal resort the next day in the company of Foreign Minister Pik Botha and the administrator of the Transvaal, Daniel Hough. There he mentioned the meeting, someone tipped off the newspapers, and to Botha's intense anger the story was across the front pages within a week.

shirt, and they said, 'That's not good enough.' I had to take it off and let them iron it. Then, when I put it on again, one of the senior prison officers said my tie was badly tied, so he tied it again."

They drove in a protective convoy of cars – two ahead and two behind – to *Tuynhuys*, bluffing the security police at the gates that this was a politician from an African state making a clandestine nighttime visit, and parked in an underground garage. An elevator took them directly to the ground floor of *Tuynhuys*. They stepped out and walked to the door of the president's office. As they were about to enter, Barnard glanced down and noticed that Mandela's shoelaces were undone. During all his years in prison Mandela had worn laceless loafers and he had forgotten how to tie shoelaces properly. So the chief of the National Intelligence Service got down on his knees before the prisoner to tie his shoelaces outside the president's door.

"It shows how scared they were of President Botha," Mandela says today. "Everything had to be just right."

As it turned out, the meeting between these two iron-willed men was surprisingly serene. Barnard and Coetsee were worried that Botha's famous temper, worsened by his recent illness, would erupt in the face of Mandela's forth-rightness. They had urged both men to avoid controversial issues and keep the meeting at the bland level of an ice-breaking courtesy visit. But, Mandela says, "I was very tense. I thought I was going to meet this finger-wagging man I had seen on television, and I didn't know how I might react. But when I entered the room he came in from the opposite side and walked towards me with his hand outstretched. That was the way the whole thing went. He was charming and the whole conversation was very warm."

Towards the end of the meeting Mandela raised the subject of Walter Sisulu, seizing the opportunity to urge the president directly to release his old friend and colleague on compassionate grounds. Ducking the issue, Botha told Barnard to look into the matter. On the drive back to the prison, Barnard recalls, he and Mandela had a blazing row when he told Mandela there was no chance Sisulu would be released at that stage, that the political climate wasn't right for such a step. Mandela remonstrated with the National Intelligence chief, telling him he was a civil servant whose duty it was to carry out the president's instructions, not to question them.

(Later, Barnard had a row with Botha as well, after the president's retirement. The Old Crocodile had ordered that his conversation with Mandela be recorded clandestinely. Barnard, troubled by the ethics of this, had nonetheless complied, but after Botha ceased to be president he destroyed the tape, keeping only his own written notes of the meeting. Botha, fuming over a claim made by De Klerk that he was merely carrying on with a policy Botha had initiated, demanded a release of the tape to demonstrate, he said, that he had warned Mandela about communism. He refused to accept that the tape had been destroyed, but Barnard insists that it was. "I destroyed it myself," he says. "It should never have been made.")

So the meeting with Botha for which Mandela had striven for so long turned out to be inconclusive – a courtesy meeting with no substantive discussions and no subsequent decisions. Mandela went back to prison and the waiting game resumed. Yet in some subtle way a line had been crossed. As Coetsee says, after that there was no way of stopping the process. It was just a matter of time – and the man.

6

An Underground
Rescue

THROUGHOUT THE GREAT uprising of the 1980s, the
resistance to the South African government was led by
the umbrella organization called the United Democratic
Front, a loose alliance of hundreds of community, church,
professional, sports, workers', students', women's, and
youth groups. This was an effective spearhead, but it had
only tenuous contact with both the imprisoned ANC leaders
and the exiled ANC's headquarters in Lusaka. When word
began to leak out from Victor Verster Prison of Mandela's
contacts with the government, particularly of his memorandum to P.W. Botha, a ripple of concern ran through the
UDF. Was the old man doing a deal behind their backs? Was
he selling out? Had the government at last managed to turn
him, having isolated him from his colleagues and taken
advantage of his advancing years and perhaps failing health
(after all he had been hospitalized twice)?

Going right back to when they were all together on
Robben Island, there had always been tensions within the
ANC's imprisoned leadership group (which went under the
rather pompous sobriquet of the Higher Organ in those early
days) between those unequivocally committed to the revolutionary overthrow of the apartheid government and
those who believed that, while the guerrilla campaign was
an effective way to dramatize the anti-apartheid campaign
and increase pressure on the government, the solution
would eventually have to be found at the negotiating table.
Mandela was firmly in the negotiation camp. Although he
had started Umkhonto we Sizwe, he never had any illusions
that it could win a military victory and he did not hesitate to
say so in the discussions they had on the island. The radical
group had its roots partly in the Communist Party, with its

commitment to revolutionary strategy, and partly in a tradition of non-collaboration that ran back to the 1930s when
an organization called the Non-European Unity Movement,
especially strong among the mixed-race "coloured" community of the Western Cape Province, tried to deny legitimacy to segregationist political institutions by boycotting
them. This tradition had gained strength and spread all over
the black communities of South Africa when the regime
began co-opting black leaders to head the tribal homelands
and other apartheid institutions in the 1960s and 1970s; to its
more extreme adherents, the very notion of nego-tiating with
the government had became tainted with the collabor-
ationist brush. The issue had led to lively clashes within the
Higher Organ between Mandela and Govan Mbeki, the old-
est of the leaders arrested at Rivonia, a lifelong member of
the Communist Party, and the leading figure in the radical
group. Fellow prisoners on Robben Island recall a particularly sharp exchange in 1968 when Mandela initiated a
debate in the Higher Organ on whether the ANC should
start thinking about how to open lines of communication
with the government. Mbeki was outraged and, say some,
retained a lingering suspicion of Mandela's "moderation"
after that.

In mid-1987 an event occurred that revived this tension
between them. Mandela, now separated from his colleagues
in the hospital section of Pollsmoor Prison and talking to
Kobie Coetsee and the committee of officials, was negotiating for the release of his fellow prisoners – particularly the
seventy-eight-year-old Mbeki and Walter Sisulu, two years
younger. Eventually the authorities agreed to release Mbeki
alone, and with typical crassness precipitated an incident
that severely embarrassed Mandela and, indirectly, nearly
derailed the negotiating process two years later.

Without explaining anything to either Mbeki or his
lawyer, the prison commander on Robben Island isolated
Mbeki as a preliminary step to releasing him. When the
lawyer heard of this, she asked permission to see Mbeki, but
permission was refused, again without explanation. She then

lodged an application for a court order to gain access to her client. This was one week before Mbeki was to be released, and the authorities erupted with anger. "The commissioner of prisons called me in and said they were cancelling the whole deal," Mandela recalls. He pointed out that the embarrassment was their fault, not his, and managed to placate the angry commissioner, who agreed that the release could go ahead if Mandela would persuade Mbeki and his lawyer to drop the court action. That meant bringing Mbeki from Robben Island so Mandela could talk to him.

Mbeki himself takes up the story: "The commander of Robben Island prison came to my cell about five o'clock one morning. I was cleaning my *balie* [prison slang for a slop pail], but he said, 'Leave your *balie*, get dressed and come with me.' He took me out into the corridor, where all the warders were lined up against the walls. I walked between them down to the prison entrance, where there was an ambulance backed right up against the door. They made me get in. The ambulance pulled away. At first I thought it was headed for the docks, but it turned off in another direction. I didn't know where they were going or what they were going to do with me."

When the ambulance stopped, Mbeki found they were alongside a speedboat ramp. A speedboat was tied up and he was told to board it. They roared away towards the mainland, from which the ageing prisoner had been cut off for twenty-three years. They pulled in to a Prisons Department jetty, where Mbeki was hustled into a small room and left alone.

"A man in a dark suit came in and greeted me," he says. Without explanation he was ordered into a car which again had backed right up against the building. Two hefty men slipped into the back seat on either side of him and the car drove off. "The man in the dark suit introduced himself as the minister of justice's private secretary, but he still didn't say what this was all about. Through the window I saw a sign that said Tokai." This meant they were headed for Pollsmoor.

They drew up outside the prison, and Fred Munro, Pollsmoor's commander, slipped into a front seat; Mbeki knew him from Robben Island. Suddenly Mbeki spotted Walter Sisulu coming down a flight of steps. He hadn't seen his old comrade for five years, and frantically he tried to open the car door, then the window, to call out to him, but there were no handles on the inside. "I banged on the window and shouted to Walter, but he didn't hear. I turned to Munro and said, 'What's the matter with Walter?' He replied, 'Oh, Walter can hardly see these days.'" It was a gratuitous lie: Sisulu's sight was fine.

From there the bewildered Mbeki was taken to the prison guest house, and after a while Mandela came in. It was a long and difficult meeting. In order to persuade Mbeki to drop his court action, Mandela had to tell him he was negotiating with the government for his release, yet he did not want to disclose the substance of the negotiations, both because he had agreed with Coetsee and the committee of officials that he would not do so and because of his own concern that his colleagues, Mbeki particularly, would object. As he has said, he had decided that the only way to pull off the tricky exercise was to confront them with a *fait accompli*.

So Mandela was less than open with Mbeki. "He indicated to me that he was having talks with the government, but he wouldn't go into detail because he said he had given an undertaking that he wouldn't talk about it," Mbeki recalls. "He said Walter and the others didn't know either. When I asked why he was being kept apart from the others, he replied that he didn't regret it – it was probably a good thing."

Later, after his release in November 1987, Mbeki was allowed to meet again with Mandela in Victor Verster Prison. Again they had several hours together, and again Mbeki asked him about his talks with the government; again Mandela refused to give details. Mbeki is cautious today about how he expresses himself on an issue that aroused such strong emotions at the time, but clearly, given his earlier misgivings about Mandela's interest in negotiations, these elliptical responses sounded suspect to him. "I was not very happy about the fact that he seemed either not to have sufficient confidence in me to tell me the full story, or, alternatively, that the other side might have come to some arrangement with him which he felt he couldn't break," Mbeki says. "But beyond that, my concern was not of a nature to doubt his integrity as a leader."

By the winter of 1989, Mbeki was living in relative freedom in his home town of Port Elizabeth, where, despite severe security-law restrictions, he managed to hold court as a sage of the liberation movement and meet many of the key figures in the UDF who would visit him for advice. When a truncated report of Mandela's eleven-page memorandum to President Botha reached Mbeki, it revived his old suspicions – and his doubts were quickly transmitted to the UDF. Word moved through the grapevine that Mandela's behaviour was suspect and that UDF members should not respond to invitations to visit him in Victor Verster Prison.

Mbeki says today he knows nothing about any orders telling UDF members not to see Mandela; but Allan Boesak remembers them. "There was a huge debate about it," he says. "People were worried, because they didn't know what Mandela was talking to the government about."

Indeed, a major crisis loomed. By acting on his own, to present his movement with a *fait accompli*, Mandela had unwittingly violated a cardinal principle of the UDF, which was that you did not act without a mandate from the people. That had become an obsessive requirement within the internal resistance movement. As Boesak puts it: "He had not consulted, and there was no greater sin in the UDF." The reaction might easily have derailed the whole settlement process, but for the fortuitous intervention of a shadowy figure who had slipped into the country clandestinely a few months before – paradoxically to intensify the revolutionary struggle, but who in fact rescued the negotiations.

SHORTLY AFTER THE ANC held a "national consultative conference" in Kabwe, Zambia, in June 1985, the newly elected national executive committee had begun to talk about infiltrating a leadership group into South Africa to link up with the activists and give direction to the uprising. It took two years for this idea to come to actuality: finally it was launched in great secrecy by Oliver Tambo under the code-name Operation Vulindlela – a Zulu word meaning "open the road", which was later shortened to Vula, simply "open". The man Tambo chose to head Operation Vula was Mac Maharaj, an Indian member of the ANC who had served a sentence of twelve years on Robben Island, where he had been close to Mandela, and then gone into exile a year after his release in 1976. Maharaj was a member of the ANC's national executive committee and one of the sharpest minds in the liberation movement: that Tambo was prepared to risk him on such a mission shows how badly he felt the need for not only an effective activist but also intelligent appraisals of the situation within the country. In the months that followed, Maharaj became Tambo's eyes and ears inside South Africa.

When Maharaj left Lusaka in early 1988 he told colleagues and journalists, myself included, that he was going to Moscow for a kidney transplant operation, the outcome of which was uncertain. His gaunt appearance made this an entirely believable story, but in fact he was a wiry man in robust health. He did indeed go to Moscow, but not for surgery: the Soviets, always helpful to the ANC, fitted him out with false passports, including an Indian passport in the name of Robin Das, and some sophisticated disguise equip-ment. From there Maharaj flew to Amsterdam, where he linked up with a colleague, Siphiwe Nyanda, a senior Umkhonto we Sizwe guerrilla who went under the *nom de guerre* Gebhuza. The pair were joined in South Africa two years later by Ronnie Kasrils, a former chief of intelligence of Umkhonto we Sizwe.

Gebhuza, who came via Brussels, met Maharaj in the transit section of Amsterdam's Schiphol Airport. There they changed names, appearances, and flights. "It was a simple matter of going into a toilet, taking out the false passport, putting away the old one, changing your appearance slight-ly, making a small alteration to the air ticket, then boarding the new flight as though you were a continuing transit passenger," says Maharaj.

The disguises were sophisticated and effective – but unexpectedly troublesome. Maharaj had shaved off his moustache and distinctive goatee and affixed a set of special dentures over his teeth to change the shape of his face: one plate over the back molars pushed out his cheeks slightly, another over his front teeth made his mouth protrude a little. "The essence of disguise is that you must do it incrementally, not try to make a big, spectacular change," says Maharaj.

The problem arose after take-off. "We found we couldn't eat," Maharaj says. "The crumbs fell down between these plates and your gums and your tongue couldn't get down there to scoop them out. It was like having metal filings at the bottom of your mouth. Terribly uncomfortable." So they went without food. Maharaj spent a hungry night in the transit lounge of Nairobi airport, then flew on the next day to Swaziland. Gebhuza arrived on a separate flight, and from there the two prepared to make their risky entry into South Africa.

More serious problems arose. First, the underground team that was to meet them on the South African side of the border misread a coded message and thought they were arriving from Zimbabwe. This meant Maharaj had to make hasty rearrangements, which involved persuading a local man whom they did not know to come across the border, meet them at the pick-up point, then drive them to Johannesburg. This risky business was made more so when Maharaj realized that the delay meant they would now be making the night crossing at full moon. Then Maharaj's blazer, with all their money and a diary containing the coded names and addresses of all his key contacts in South Africa, was stolen.

Feeling the pressure build up, Maharaj decided to make a dash for it, to cross the border at a busy point used by African peasants rather than at some secluded place where they might be spotted accidentally, and to do so in broad daylight. He and Gebhuza disguised themselves as peasants. "I didn't have to darken my face much," Maharaj says. "I was wearing tattered blue overalls, a rolled-up balaclava on my head, and I carried a stick the way African peasants do." They also had pistols and AK-47 assault rifles concealed under their overalls. "That was so we could defend ourselves if intercepted," Maharaj says. "I had arranged for a group of our men to take up positions on the Swazi side of the border, so that they could provide cover fire for us if anything went wrong. We would then have had a chance to fight our way back into Swaziland."

But nothing went wrong. Maharaj and Gebhuza walked across the border unchallenged in the midst of a group of peasants. Their Swazi contact picked them up and they made a rendezvous with a woman from the ANC underground who took them to a spot where they could change their clothes and appearances once again. She took their weapons to return them to Swaziland, and the two men and their hired driver headed for Johannesburg. They asked the driver to drop them at The Carlton, Johannesburg's premier hotel – "to cut the link in case he had begun to realize who we were, which I think he had," Maharaj explains. From there they caught a taxi to a more modest hotel in Hillbrow, and Maharaj began the difficult business of trying to link up with the UDF leaders whose contact numbers he had lost.

He moved to Durban and established that as his main base for what soon became an expanding underground network. Over the next year Maharaj set up a remarkable system of communication with Lusaka. Using a small laptop computer equipped with a modem, he transmitted coded messages from public telephone booths to contacts in London and Amsterdam, who retransmitted them to Lusaka. The coding system was sophisticated but easy to use – a computerized version of a self-erasing "one-time pad", which meant that each message was encoded in a particular way that changed automatically once the message was sent, so that the next message was encoded differently. The receiver had a set of decoding systems set up in the same order. This meant that if messages were intercepted, the interceptor could not break the code by tracing consistencies from message to message: they were all different.

"We would put our message on a tape recorder, go out at night to find a phone booth, put an acoustic coupler on the mouthpiece, and play the tape," Maharaj explains. "We would collect our messages in the same way, then run them from the tape into the computer through the decoding process and get the message in a printout. It could handle four to six pages in three minutes."

So for the first time ANC exile headquarters in Lusaka were in direct and regular contact with an underground agent inside South Africa. Later, Maharaj established a way of communicating with Mandela in prison, and it became a unique three-way contact that was to prove invaluable in the events that followed. "When I sent Tambo his first report from Mandela he got so excited that he immediately bombarded me with a ten-page reply," Maharaj recalls.

"I had told him that Mandela needed a thorough briefing, and he asked, 'How long?' I said, 'I can send him ten or twelve pages, no problem.' So he prepared this personal briefing in which he told Mandela to go ahead with what he was doing. He said to him, 'Look, there is only one problem: don't manoeuvre yourself into a situation where we have to abandon sanctions. That's the key problem. We are very concerned that we should not get stripped of our weapons of struggle, and the most important of these is sanctions. That is the trump card with which we can mobilize international opinion and pull governments over to our side.'"

Communicating with Mandela was in fact a lot simpler than the computer talk with Tambo. Since Mandela, in Victor Verster Prison, was being allowed to receive visitors, it was a simple matter for Maharaj to arrange for couriers to carry messages. "I would print out a message in a small typeface on a thin strip of paper that could be folded in such a way that you could pass it to him while you were shaking hands," he explains. "It was a trick we had learned on Robben Island." The courier would carry a small tape recorder in his pocket with a concealed microphone, so that

Mandela could dictate his reply as though conversing with the courier. By nightfall the reply would be in Tambo's hands in Lusaka.

"I offered Mandela other techniques, such as invisible pens," Maharaj says. "I even told him that if he could describe some article, a wallet or item in the house, I could have an exact replica made, and then just swap them and exchange the messages in that way. That would give him more time to prepare his replies. But he rejected these as too complicated. I think he was also nervous that there might be hidden video cameras in the house."

It was in the course of Mandela's dictating one of these "letters" to Tambo that the trouble arose. To those gathered in the room, it sounded like a briefing, but the courier had his tape recorder on and Mandela was in fact giving the exiled president a full report on the memorandum he had just sent to President Botha. The trouble was, some of those present misunderstood parts of what he was saying; they did not have the full context, and to them it sounded suspiciously as though he was offering to do a deal with Botha. When they reported what they had heard to Mbeki, he was alarmed; the UDF grapevine was alerted, and further meetings with Mandela were put on hold.

When Maharaj heard of this, he moved swiftly. He called for the tape, transcribed the full text, and verified immediately that the Mbeki-UDF suspicions were unfounded. He transmitted the text, together with an explanatory note, to Tambo in Lusaka. That done he dashed to Johannesburg to see the UDF leaders, then to Port Elizabeth where Mbeki lived. "When they saw the full text of the letter they realized they had misread Mandela's intentions," Maharaj says. "Within days we were able to sort the matter out. I sent a message to Mandela explaining how the trouble had arisen. He promptly sent invitations to Govan Mbeki and the others involved to come and see him."

But the concern had reverberated as far as Lusaka, and that took longer to quell. Although Maharaj's messages had kept Tambo informed, the ANC president had not briefed his national executive committee fully for fear of leaks that would endanger the Operation Vula agents and jeopardize his precious communication links with Maharaj and Mandela. Then in August, 1989, Tambo suffered an incapacitating stroke and was hospitalized in London. Only when Maharaj managed to slip out of South Africa for a brief visit to Lusaka several months later was he able to allay the remaining doubts about Mandela's motives.

The trickiest crisis to threaten the negotiating process from the ANC side was over at last – saved by an operation originally intended to step up the revolution. As things turned out, Operation Vula was later to trigger a crisis of its own. But for the moment things were set fair for a major change in the prospects for peace.

7

The Old Era Ends

A S SOUTH AFRICA'S worst winter of discontent drew to a close in August 1989, it became clear to everyone that there would be no meaningful political change until there was a change of national leadership. P. W. Botha, always a difficult man with an explosive temper, had grown more irascible and authoritarian with the years, and he became worse after his stroke. He was also becoming more reluctant to press ahead with his earlier reformism. He had started a process but was failing to follow through. In fact, he seemed to have gone into reverse.

Botha's twelve-year presidency was characterized by contradictions. During the first phase, from 1977 until the mid-1980s, he introduced a number of significant reforms. Raising the slogan "Adapt or Die", he had done the unthinkable in 1983 when he rammed through a racial reform at the cost of splitting the National Party. That reform had breached the political colour bar for the first time by giving the Asian and mixed-race "coloured" people the vote in their own separate parliamentary chambers. Botha also abolished the hated pass laws that restricted the movement of black people into the cities, he increased the black education budget and scrapped laws that prohibited interracial sex and marriage. And he pledged to move on restoring South African citizenship to blacks living in the tribal homelands (they had been declared statutory foreigners under the policy of territorial and political segmentation).

All this required courage, yet the reforms were piecemeal and Botha appeared to have no clear vision of where he was leading South Africa. He perceived the need for reform but could not bring himself to contemplate ending Afrikaner hegemony. He had been a party apparatchik since the age of twenty and he was now in his seventies: that was too much of a personal investment to renounce. So his programme became an exercise in limited reform, changes that would give blacks the vote without giving them power – a token vote in some new restrictive constitutional structure. The result was that, while the social and economic circumstances of black people improved, Botha's political changes amounted to little more than a reformulation of the old system of racial domination. Apartheid was dead – long live neo-apartheid!

Instead of mollifying the black population, this inflamed them. Botha had fallen into a trap that has caught ruling elites through the ages, that of imagining he could placate the clamour of the oppressed masses with a few token concessions and material benefits. He had failed to heed Alexis de Tocqueville's warning that "the most perilous moment for a bad government is when it seeks to mend its ways"; that revolutionary movements tend to arise, not out of circumstances of absolute deprivation and oppression, but when things begin to improve and loosen up and when the aspirations of the oppressed rise and they feel they have a chance to liberate themselves at last. Whites regarded the reforms as major concessions, but blacks saw them as an insult to their aspirations. As they watched Botha's tortuous attempts to conjure up the illusion of political rights without the reality of power, they denounced him as a confidence trickster. The result, to the surprise and dismay of the whites, was that Botha's reform policy unleashed the most furious and sustained black uprising in South Africa's history.

When the rebellion intensified after 1984, Botha became increasingly confused and angry. As Archbishop Tutu quipped, he "lost the convictions of his courage". He still wanted reform, but his obsession with not appearing weak meant he could not make concessions in the face of the uprising. He would have to crush it first. And so Botha declared a draconian state of emergency, moved troops into the black townships, clamped restrictions on the press, and cracked down on the political activists. International outrage at the harshness led to sanctions and disinvestment, to which Botha responded with what U.S. Assistant Secretary of State Crocker saw as "xenophobic outrage". He became obsessed with the idea that he had to resist Western attempts to meddle in South Africa's affairs, and so he scuttled the Commonwealth group's initiative and in effect told the world to go to hell. "Don't underestimate us," he thundered at a special congress of the National Party in August 1986. "We are not a nation of jellyfish."

That special congress marked the turning point in Botha's presidency. The congress had been announced six months earlier with the declared intention of endorsing a new reformist constitution that would give blacks some form of representation in the central government, but by the time it arrived Botha had gone into reverse and the special congress was yet another damp squib. From then on, as South Africa became increasingly isolated and em-battled, Botha grew ever more defiant and angry. The ANC stepped up its guerrilla activities and several bombings and land mine explosions resulted in whites being killed. This led to security-force action against ANC targets in neigh-bouring countries and against radical groups inside South Africa. Assassinations and hit-squad operations became commonplace.

The rising spiral of violence sharpened the divide in the government between those who wanted to negotiate and those who were determined to crush the rebellion before there could be any thought of negotiating (and then not with the ANC but with more malleable black leaders). The rift ran not only through the political branch of Botha's administration but through the security and intelligence services as well. Niël Barnard and Mike Louw, who of course were secretly talking with Mandela, were becoming con-vinced that negotiations with the ANC were not only pos-sible but necessary; Military Intelligence, which spearheaded counter-insurgency operations and provided the hit squads, was strongly opposed. The hawkish "securocrats" of MI, always close to Botha, were obsessed with what they saw as a communist threat to South Africa, with Moscow using the ANC as a stalking horse, and they reinforced the president's reluctance to show weakness. Increasingly, Botha swung around to their view that the uprising had to be crushed to make space for a new deal negotiated with the "moderates", meaning those blacks who were already collaborating in the apartheid structures plus any others who might be co-optable once the uprising was crushed.

Botha had given a glimpse of the new deal he had in mind at the ill-fated 1986 congress. The National Party, anticipating the reformist step that never came, accepted the principle of extending the vote to blacks "in a single South Africa" – ostensibly abandoning apartheid's old objective of dividing the country into separate ethnic states. Botha spoke of giving blacks political representation "up to the highest level". But it was the old double-talk again. What Botha had in mind was not a conventional vote for direct representation in the central legislature, but an indirect system of balloting through the homelands and township councils to give blacks their own segregated place in Parliament. More particularly, he did not have ANC participation in mind. His idea was to isolate the militant black leaders and groups, and negotiate a new deal with "moderates".

Despite the denials one hears today from those who were involved, it is difficult to escape the conclusion that the purpose of the government's talks with Mandela was to explore the possibility of co-opting him as leader of such moderates – perhaps along with members of the exiled ANC whom the government's analysts regarded as nationalists and moderates, as compared with the communists and other militants. Whatever the initial intention, it soon became clear that Mandela's fixity of purpose and loyalty to his organization ruled out any such possibility – and by then, in the hard years between 1986 and 1989, those who were meeting with Mandela were coming to view both him and his organization in a different light.

As the unrest continued, South Africa's isolation deepened, and Botha's attitude toughened, frustration levels began to rise among many leading Afrikaner political thinkers who had become convinced of the necessity of reform. These extended beyond the politicians in the *verligte*, or reformist, wing of the National Party into the very heart of the Afrikaner establishment, into the Afrikaners' secret brotherhood, the Broederbond – a powerful inner body of the white tribe's political intelligentsia who had played a pivotal role in directing the Afrikaner nationalist movement from its earliest years.

It was the Broederbond which had first devised the apartheid ideology and functioned as the primary think tank for shaping government strategy thereafter. But after the late 1970s its role began to change as more Afrikaner intellectuals perceived the need for reform. It became the main agency for trying to find a way out of the Afrikaners' historic dilemma: how to abandon apartheid and come to terms with the black majority without losing control of the country and ultimately the national identity of the Afrikaner *volk*.

Pieter de Lange, who took over as chairman of the Broederbond in 1983 after a bitter power struggle with con- servatives, had his first contact with members of the ANC at a Ford Foundation conference on Long Island, New York, in 1986. There he met Thabo Mbeki, the ANC's director of information and adviser to Oliver Tambo (today Mbeki is first deputy president of South Africa). Then forty-four and with a master's degree in economics from Sussex University, Mbeki was already the ANC's most polished diplomat, urbane and witty with a geniality that quickly undercut all the stereotyped images of Pretoria's propaganda factory. The two men talked for about three hours after the conference session one evening, and De Lange invited Mbeki to lunch with him and his wife the next day.

Both men remember the occasion well. De Lange em- phasized his belief that South Africa had to undergo political change, but Mbeki was sceptical. White South Africans tended to say such things when they were abroad but showed little inclination to act when they were at home. "I remember him telling me that if South Africa was not on the way to resolving its racial conflict by 1990, then the country would be in serious trouble," Mbeki recalls. "I said he would find it very difficult to convince us that we were going to see the kind of changes he was talking about with a man like P. W. Botha in power.

"His reply was interesting. He said, 'Look, we Afrikaners thought we needed many things to secure our future: segregated living areas, no mixed marriages, and all that. We thought if we didn't have them, this black continent would swallow us up and the Afrikaners would cease to exist as a people. But the reality is that we can remove the Group Areas Act [enforcing segregated living areas] tomorrow and it's not going to make any difference, because your people don't have the money to move into the expensive white suburbs. So from your point of view it will be a meaningless change, but for us Afrikaners it will mean we will wake up one day and realize that nothing has changed, that we are still all right, we've not perished as a people because the Group Areas Act is not there. That will open the way to asking the question: Why do we need a white government anyway?'

"So he made the point that these changes which we regarded as cosmetic were significant in changing the thinking of the Afrikaner people. That would open the way – despite P. W. Botha."

When the two men lunched the following day, De Lange told Mbeki that on his return to South Africa he intended devoting himself to national reconciliation. Again the ANC man was sceptical. But a few months later Mbeki saw a newspaper report that De Lange had resigned as principal of the Rand Afrikaans University in Johannesburg to devote himself to promoting interracial understanding. "Then I understood why he had insisted that I should come to lunch with his wife, because he made that commitment in her presence," says Mbeki. "What it meant was that he was going to go on the road as chairman of the Broederbond to convince his people that there had to be movement."

De Lange recalls that at the end of the meal on Long Island, Mbeki asked what message he should take back to his leader, Oliver Tambo. "I told him that South Africa was getting ready for the changes that were necessary, and that the Afrikaner would insist on retaining his cultural identity and the necessary instruments to do so – language, education, religious freedom. I think he was quite surprised and pleased."

De Lange did indeed lobby for reform, but it was a cautious, tentative exercise conducted far from public view in the secret inner cells of the brotherhood and with its main concern being how to manage reform without jeopardizing the security and identity of the Afrikaner *volk*. But cautious though it was, given the Broederbond's history and status within the Afrikaner nationalist establishment, it was important in getting the chemistry of change under way. I remember interviewing De Lange at the time of his resignation from the university, when he spoke of his vision of the way change might come to South Africa. He drew the analogy of tensions building up at the core of the earth to the point where they produced a shift in geological structures that created whole new oceans and continents, leaving living creatures to adapt to an altogether new environment. His worry, he said, was whether there was sufficient mutual trust to enable South Africans to make that adaptation. "The lack of mutual trust is due to the lack of meaningful contact," he said. "There is a tremendous need for more contact to build up mutual understanding."

De Lange spoke regularly to Botha, conveying the message that the ANC was more moderate than Afrikaners realized, that "the stereotyped images on both sides were starting to break down with the contacts". Botha and his senior ministers also met periodically with the Broederbond executive at a secret mountain retreat called Hawekwa, near the Western Cape town of Wellington, to discuss ideas on political transformation.

De Lange claims that the Broederbond was well ahead of the National Party in its reformist thinking. According to him, the Broederbond had accepted by 1984 – a full year before Coetsee's first meeting with Mandela – that black South Africans would have to be given the vote and that

Afrikaners would have to be prepared for this seismic change. Working documents setting out ideas on constitutional reform were circulated, and De Lange says that by early 1986 a majority of the brotherhood's twenty thousand members voted to accept the principle of full citizenship rights for blacks – although there is no evidence to suggest that any of them were yet thinking in terms of unbanning the ANC and negotiating with it. Most had in mind a deal with the Inkatha movement's Mangosuthu Buthelezi and other traditionalist black leaders.

But however limited the brothers' thinking may have been at that stage, De Lange reckons it was at least another year before a majority in the cabinet came round to the same conclusion. And by then Botha had stalled. Though he had a great opportunity to make a historic breakthrough, an unassailable political power base, encouraging reports from the committee meeting with Mandela and from his most trusted think-tank, and a personal impression of his own of Mandela's stature and reasonableness, President Botha had gone into a freeze.

As the frustrations built up among reformists, De Lange recalls, a National Party parliamentarian called on him to suggest that the Broederbond and a group of *verligte* National Party MPs mount a revolt against the president. De Lange refused, but soon afterwards told a regional meeting of the brotherhood that he didn't believe political change could come about "until the personalities at the top are changed".

THE FRUSTRATIONS WERE intensified by the fact that business leaders and white opposition parliamentarians had broken new ground by flying to Lusaka for meetings with the ANC. These discussions attracted a lot of publicity, but Botha made it clear he disapproved and that for Afrikaner nationalists in particular it would be tantamount to ethnic treason to meet with such enemies of the state. When a group of Afrikaans students at Stellenbosch University planned a trip to meet with the ANC, the government seized their passports.

But the ANC leaders were putting out feelers. After Bizos's visit with the news of Mandela's secret meetings in the prison, they wanted to learn more about what was going on in South Africa's ruling establishment. Mbeki recalls Oliver Tambo saying around that time, "I have a nightmare that we are going to get a message from P.W. Botha one of these days saying he is ready to negotiate, and we won't understand it because we don't know how they think." And I remember that when I interviewed Tambo in Lusaka in February 1986, he asked me whether I would talk to a group of his colleagues about my perceptions of what was happening within Afrikaner nationalism. Next day I addressed twelve members of the ANC leadership group on the conflicts I could see developing in the ruling establishment and the growth of a·reformist movement at its core.

Clandestine invitations began to filter through. Sampie Terreblanche, a professor of economic history at Stellenbosch, and a fellow academic, Willie Esterhuyse, received a message that the ANC would like them to visit Lusaka. Both were influential Afrikaners, members of the Broederbond and advisers to the government. Both were also reformists and keen to accept the invitation. But before they could leave, Botha summoned them to an office he was then using on the eighteenth floor of the Hendrik Verwoerd Building in Cape Town. "He told us how important the two of us were to him," Terreblanche recalls. "Then he said that he didn't want us to talk to murderers and that we should not go." Meekly, the two men abandoned the trip. Terreblanche, a little shamefacedly, says he wonders today what would have happened if they had defied the Old Crocodile and told him they were going anyway. "You know, I think he may have hurled us through that eighteenth-floor window," the silver-haired professor muses with a small chuckle.

But within a year both Esterhuyse and Terreblanche became involved in yet another extraordinary series of clandestine meetings with the ANC in Britain – this time with Botha's indirect knowledge and approval. The concept of these meetings arose, paradoxically, after a fruitless meeting in London between Oliver Tambo, Thabo Mbeki, and a group of British businessmen with interests in South Africa. The ANC leaders were anxious to get their message across to the British business community, but the meeting was poorly attended and unresponsive: British companies were mostly unsympathetic to the ANC at that time, viewing it as a radical revolutionary movement in the mould of the Irish Republican Army and the Palestine Liberation Organization.

But one man at that meeting took a different view. Michael Young, head of communications and corporate affairs at Consolidated Goldfields, a major British mining house, had been a political adviser to Prime Ministers Alec Douglas-Home and Edward Heath after Ian Smith's unilateral declaration of Rhodesia's independence from Britain in 1965.* The protracted conflict over UDI had instilled in him a lifelong interest in the stormy racial politics of southern Africa. When Margaret Thatcher replaced Heath as prime minister, Young, who regarded himself as a left-wing Tory, left the Conservative Party to join the Liberals. Now, at the age of forty-one, he felt that British business – and especially his company, which had a major subsidiary in Johannesburg – should be doing more to help bring about political change in South Africa. So after the London meeting, Young had a private word with Tambo to ask what British business could do that would address more than just the symptoms of the apartheid problem.

"He thought for a moment, then said, 'I would like to see if we couldn't have a dialogue with the Afrikaners,'" Young recalls. It was not an easy thing for a British multinational corporation to organize, but Young took it up with Consgold's

---

* Ian D. Smith, leader of the white minority in what was then the self-governing British colony of Rhodesia, proclaimed a unilateral declaration of independence in 1965. His rebel government defied world condemnation, international sanctions, and a ruinous civil war for fifteen years before succumbing. The country gained recognized independence under black majority rule in 1980 and was renamed Zimbabwe. The term UDI found its way into the political vocabulary of the region as a result.

chairman, Rudolph Agnew. To his surprise Agnew, a flamboyant right-wing Conservative, agreed and put up the funding for Young to organize a series of secret meetings between the ANC and top Afrikaner establishment figures. "It was a remarkable and pretty courageous thing for Agnew to do," says Young, who today runs his own private consultancy business in London. As it turned out, this highly significant decision led to the first direct contact between the South African government and the exiled ANC leadership.

Young flew to South Africa to seek out possible collaborators. "I wanted members of the political elite who were close to P. W. Botha," he says. Before leaving he spoke to Fleur de Villiers, a former South African political journalist then doing consultancy work for Consgold in Britain. De Villiers steered him to Esterhuyse and Terreblanche, but after that played no further role, according to Young. Esterhuyse was enthusiastic, and he and Young set about making preliminary arrangements. Then something even stranger happened.

Someone tipped off South Africa's National Intelligence Service: a tapped telephone, perhaps, or an agent in the know. A report reached Niël Barnard, who went to see Esterhuyse. "I didn't ask him how he found out," says Esterhuyse – and Barnard himself still won't say. Barnard had been as fiercely opposed as Botha to private groups meeting with the ANC, on the grounds that they might get at cross-purposes with the government's intentions. But not this time. "He told me the government wanted an informal contact with the ANC," Esterhuyse recalls, "and he asked whether I would be willing to report to him on the discussions we were going to have."

Esterhuyse was hesitant about acting as an intelligence agent – literally acting like a spy – but at the same time could see the value of making a link between the ANC and someone so close to the president. He told Barnard he would do so provided he could tell Thabo Mbeki and Jacob Zuma, the key ANC figures, about it. Mbeki confirms that the Stellenbosch political philosopher kept to his pledge. "He squared with me right at the beginning," says Mbeki. "I knew all along that he was talking to Barnard – and that Barnard was reporting to P. W. Botha."

Other participants did not know, however. "I could see there was a kind of meeting within a meeting, with Esterhuyse going into huddles with Mbeki," says Terreblanche. "I suspected he was reporting back to someone, but I didn't know for certain."

In fact he was being very precisely a go-between. Mbeki says, "He would come to me and say, 'Look, these matters – this, that and the other – are of concern to the government. Can you get a sense from your people what their views are on these matters?'" Esterhuyse would then convey the ANC responses to Barnard, together with questions from Mbeki about the government's attitudes on specific issues. Thus a form of proximity talks began between the government and the exiled ANC. Barnard, of course, was also seeing Mandela as a member of the committee of officials, and Mandela, in turn, was being kept in touch with external ANC thinking by Bizos. It was a round-robin of indirect talks.

Nor were these the only points of contact. Willem de Klerk, the future president's brother, usually known by his nickname, "Wimpie", was among the Afrikaners Esterhuyse invited to participate in the secret meetings, and he, too, reported back surreptitiously to the man who was ultimately to make the decision to release Mandela and unban the ANC.

Wimpie de Klerk was an interesting man, a theologian turned journalist who became a major *verligte* influence as an executive member of the Broederbond. He was plucked out of a professorship at Potchefstroom University to take over the editorship of the National Party's official mouthpiece, *Die Transvaler*, when it was challenged by a new *verligte* competitor. At the time I was editing the country's most vigorously anti-apartheid newspaper, the *Rand Daily Mail*, yet I established a warm relationship with De Klerk. We lunched together periodically and tried to keep our differences on a reasonable basis. Wimpie was considered well to the left of his brother, who at that time was leader of the

National Party in Transvaal province and still deep in his conservative mode of thinking, yet he retained close fraternal contacts with him. In line with his family loyalty, Wimpie told his brother he was going to have a series of meetings with the ANC in exile. FW replied tersely that such meetings were against party policy and he therefore wanted to know nothing about them. "Too bad," replied Wimpie, "I'm going to report back to you anyway, whether you like it or not."

"I'm not going to respond to your letters," came the brother's reply, "but thanks very much. I'm most grateful."

Wimpie de Klerk duly wrote to FW after each of the three meetings he attended, giving his own frank assessment of the ANC. He also gave verbal reports to the Broederbond on his return. "The essence of my message was, 'Look, boys, everything is OK. We can do business with the ANC. They are not that radical. They are willing to negotiate. They are willing to compromise. They see the Afrikaners as an indigenous part of the South African population. They are not that dangerous. There's a flexibility even in their economic outlook." True to his word, FW did not reply to these reassuring observations, but Wimpie thinks they had an effect nonetheless.

"They were a kind of mock negotiation," says Wimpie de Klerk of the secret talks. "We were told that the ANC wanted to meet Afrikaners who had constituencies back home and that they wanted us to convey messages from them to those constituencies. They, in turn, would report to Lusaka. That is why I reported to FW."

Yet the meetings were considered top secret. President Botha had denounced any talks with the ANC, and so members of his government could not be seen enagaging in them. That is why Barnard had to set up an indirect line of contact. And as far as the participants were concerned, the Old Crocodile knew nothing of them. "If P. W. Botha were to hear about what we are doing he would smash us into oblivion," Wimpie de Klerk wrote in his personal diary. Yet PW did know, because Barnard was keeping him informed.

It was an elaborate exercise to have contact without running the political risk. If the meetings were found out, they could all be blamed on renegade individuals.

"The first few meetings were full of tensions and suspicion," Young recalls. "There was fear among the Afrikaners, who didn't know what would happen if word of the meetings leaked out. It was my understanding that if that happened the government would withdraw their passports to dissociate itself from the talks." But then the tensions eased and "barriers between the two sides broke down quite dramatically." Indeed, the meetings remoulded long-held perceptions on both sides. On the Afrikaner side they dissolved the demonized image of the ANC that had been built up by years of propaganda, while on the ANC side they sensitized the black liberators to white anxieties, particularly Afrikaner fears about their survival prospects under black rule.

The effect on individuals was profound. "For me personally it was one of the most liberating experiences of my life," says Esterhuyse. He was a *verligte*, but there was a difference between his intellectual understanding of what needed to be done and his existential experience of face-to-face interaction with these black liberationists he had been conditioned to hate. He recalls the chill that ran down his spine on his first encounter with the ANC men. Harold Wolpe was there, a white member of the Communist Party who had been arrested in the Rivonia raid and then made a daring escape with three others from police headquarters in central Johannesburg. "It was quite a shock," says Esterhuyse. "I hadn't realized we were going to meet him, and when I recognized his face all the resentment we Afrikaners had felt for these people flooded back and I thought, Jeez, these are the guys that gave us so much trouble. I mean, they were the devil incarnate."

But the ice was quickly broken. The first meeting, an exploratory one to test the feasibility of a wider dialogue, was held in a small hotel at Henley-on-Thames. "We had our discussions in a cellar, and I remember as I walked down the stairs thinking how appropriate that we should be meeting underground," Terreblanche recalls. Aziz Pahad, an Indian member of the ANC who led its delegation at this first meeting, greeted Esterhuyse's group in Afrikaans. Pahad and Esterhuyse soon discovered they had mutual acquaintances in South Africa. As with all the clandestine meetings between white and black South Africans taking place around this time, the bond of the fishing story – of mutual attachment to the same country despite racial and political differences – asserted itself. The men shared jokes and anecdotes and reminiscences and a kind of unspoken fellowship arose among them.

There were twelve meetings in all between November 1987 and May 1990. After the first one, all the others were held at Mells Park House on a Consgold estate in the village of Mells, near Bath in Somersetshire. The mansion, a fine example of the work of the *fin-de-siècle* architect Edward Lutyens, is set in acres of parkland, ideally secluded for this clandestine purpose.

Esterhuyse took more than twenty prominent Afrikaners to Mells Park House at various times, including church and business leaders. Most, though not all, were Broederbonders. They included Attie du Plessis, a brother of the minister of finance, Barend du Plessis; Sampie Terreblanche's brother, Mof Terreblanche, one of F. W. de Klerk's closest friends; and Ebbe Domisse, editor of *Die Burger*, the most important of the pro-government Afrikaans-language newspapers. The final meeting, which took place after De Klerk's February 2, 1990, speech, was also attended by a member of the cabinet, Dawie de Villiers, a former ambassador to Britain who was then minister of mineral and energy affairs. Thabo Mbeki led the ANC delegations to all the Mells meetings, and as always his smooth reasonableness impressed the Afrikaners he encountered, demolishing their stereotyped image of the ANC as an organization of crude ideologues and revenge-seeking terrorists.

There was a set routine. Everyone foregathered at the manor house on a Friday evening and dined together. On

Saturday and Sunday there were formal sessions with a set agenda in a conference room. Michael Young would chair them, and they would range over political developments in South Africa, the rise of international pressures, sanctions, the state of the economy, the possibility and implications of releasing Nelson Mandela, and what both sides believed could be done about the deepening racial conflict.

Important though the formal discussions were, the informal relationships and friendships were even more significant. The conference sessions would end in mid-afternoon and small groups would go walking in the woods together, then gather for dinner and, afterwards, for a chat around a log fire in the library. At that point Michael Young would slip away and leave the South Africans to themselves. Sometimes the conversations around the fire would continue until the small hours of the morning, and that is when the real business of mutual discovery took place. One of Wimpie de Klerk's diary entries reads:

> For me personally they meant a great deal: the luxury trips and accommodation; the experience of sitting close to the fire and engaging in political breakthrough work to bring the National Party and the ANC to dialogue; the bonds of friendship that developed between Thabo, Aziz, Jacob Zuma and myself; the access to direct confidential information; the position of intermediary, because from the beginning until now I have conveyed "secret messages" from the ANC to FW and even the other way around, but FW was and is very cautious.
>
> Our agendas are very concrete and direct: on Mandela's release and ANC undertakings in that connection; on the armed struggle and a possible suspension of it by the ANC; on the various steps that must be taken before pre-negotiation talks with the government can take place; on constitutional issues such as a transitional government, minority safeguards, an economic system, etc; on concrete stumbling-blocks and the exploration of compromises to get out of deadlocks; on sanc-

tions; on ANC thinking on all kinds of South African political issues and on government thinking on those self same issues.

I am convinced that the discussions have greatly improved mutual understanding; created a positive climate of expectations; brought a mutual moderation and realism to our politics; channelled important messages to Lusaka and Pretoria; and even included the germs of certain transactions. In general, therefore, a bridge-building exercise between NP Afrikaners and the ANC. . .

Our little group's unique contribution has been that we engaged in extremely authentic private discussions that were taken seriously by both sides and that it exposed Thabo, Aziz and Jacob to Afrikaners for the first time, and that they found an affinity with us and so with the group we represent.

As Esterhuyse saw it, the Afrikaners underwent a fundamental shift of position over the course of the meetings. At first they tried to explain and rationalize the situation in South Africa from their perspective as mandarins within the system, arguing that things were changing and that blacks should be patient. "Give us time and eventually we'll sort things out," was the *verligte* line. But then came the tough ANC questions: How could any group of people claim the right to govern others without their consent? How could the continued denial of basic human rights be countenanced, even in the short term? How could the banning of authentic black organizations such as the ANC be justified? How could black people accept that the future of South Africa could be decided without their democratic participation? How could blacks be expected to tolerate a second-class status that Afrikaners themselves had experienced and taken up arms against at an earlier stage in their history? How did white South Africans, especially Afrikaners, imagine they could continue defying the world indefinitely? And above all, how could these *verligte* Afrikaners argue that an evil system such as apartheid could be amended or reformed? It could only be abolished.

Then came a change. At a meeting in late 1988, says Esterhuyse, the Afrikaners began to shift ground under this barrage of unanswerable questions. "We moved from trying to explain to posing the questions: Where do we go from here? What needs to be done?" The critical moment occurred during a discussion about Mandela. "Thabo Mbeki made the point that one could get nowhere just having talks with Mandela, in or out of prison, without enabling the exiled movement to take part in the whole process to give it legitimacy. He made the point very firmly – and he convinced all of us because it was so bloody logical." From then on, says Esterhuyse, the group discussed "not just procedures but mechanisms – the idea of a government of national unity, and so on."

There were other moments of revelation. Mbeki recalls a discussion in which one of the Afrikaner participants, "who was still very much stuck in the apartheid mould," kept returning to the issue of group rights, arguing that this was fundamental to any future settlement. "I remember Jacob Zuma saying to him, 'Look, I'm a Zulu and so is Chief Buthelezi, and if we got together we could speak Zulu to one another, we could do the traditional dances, we could do all sorts of things, but there's no way you are going to find Chief Buthelezi and me in the same party. The fact of our Zuluness doesn't result in our sharing common political perspectives and aspirations, so you can't say that negotiations must be between Zulus and Afrikaners and so on.' And this Afrikaner chap says to him, 'I've never thought about it like that. Of course, you're right. I can eat *boerewors* with Andries Treurnicht [the Conservative Party leader at that time] but you won't find us in the same party. I see your point: you're not saying you won't negotiate, you want to negotiate, but as political groups not as race groups . . . '"

There were even moments of concrete achievement. After the formal conference session one afternoon in January 1990, as the participants gathered in the bar for a sundowner, the conversation turned to the international sports boycott against South Africa and specifically to a series of demonstrations then disrupting a boycott-breaking tour of South Africa by an English cricket team led by the England Test captain, Mike Gatting. One of the Afrikaners asked Mbeki, 'Why don't your chaps stop all this nonsense? All we want to do is watch cricket.' This triggered a discussion of the boycott, during which it was suggested, half jokingly at first and then more seriously, that they should negotiate an agreement – to stop the demonstrations in exchange for abandoning the second leg of the Gatting tour, following which the ANC undertook that if a political solution to the South African conflict were reached it would give its full support to South Africa's re-entry into international cricket. Once the participants at Mells had agreed on this formula, one of the Afrikaners telephoned the South African Cricket Union while the ANC called the anti-tour South African Cricket Board. "By eleven o'clock that night we had a deal," says Esterhuyse, who adds that he now uses this as a case study in his political science lectures to illustrate that "negotiations don't always have to be formal, you can also use Glenfiddich to resolve a problem."

THE MELLS MEETINGS were not the only encounters the ANC had with white South Africans at this time. Contacts were widening all the time: in August 1987, a former leader of the parliamentary opposition, Frederik van Zyl Slabbert, took a group of some fifty Afrikaner dissidents for a week-long meeting with ANC leaders in Dakar, Senegal; in July 1989, fifty ANC leaders hosted a delegation of one hundred and fifteen whites, representing thirty-five opposition organizations, in Lusaka; and later that month an ANC delegation met in Zimbabwe with a group of Afrikaans writers.

But the importance of the Mells meetings was that they were with people deep inside the Afrikaner nationalist establishment, members of the Broederbond and others whose contacts ran right to the top of South Africa's ruling oligarchy. That is why they were conducted in such elaborate secrecy, and why they were of seminal importance: while they gave these members of the Afrikaner establishment a more reassuring impression of the ANC as a rational and pragmatic organization that was ready to negotiate if all restrictions were lifted, they also gave the ANC a better insight into the Afrikaner nationalist mind and some understanding of, if not actual sympathy for, the fears and concerns that lay behind much of the government's political behaviour.

On the strength of this improved knowledge, the ANC prepared a document setting out for the first time its formal proposals on how to move towards a negotiated settlement. The document, adopted at a meeting of the Organization of African Unity in Harare, Zimbabwe, on August 21, 1989, committed the ANC to intensify both the liberation struggle and the drive to mobilize international pressures against apartheid, but at the same time it declared the ANC's belief that "a conjuncture of circumstances exists which, if there is a demonstrable readiness on the part of the Pretoria regime to engage in negotiations genuinely and seriously, could create the possibility to end apartheid through negotiations." It set out five preconditions for negotiations – lifting the state of emergency, ending restrictions on political activity, legalizing all political organizations, releasing all political prisoners, and stopping all political executions. If these things were done, the document said, all armed violence could be suspended while the two sides agreed on constitutional principles and then on a mechanism for drafting a new, nonracial constitution.

This Harare Declaration, as it was called, amounted to the ANC's opening bid in the negotiating process to come. Looking back, the course it outlined was remarkably close to the events that actually followed. But at the time of its drafting and of Willie Esterhuyse's continuing discussions in Mells Park House, there was still one massive obstacle in the way of real progress. The Old Crocodile was still in office.

THE COUP, WHEN it came, was partly of Botha's own making. In February 1989, after recovering from his stroke, Botha unexpectedly announced his resignation as leader of the National Party, though he retained his government position as president. This created an unprecedented constitutional situation: the South African system, inherited from Britain, provides for the leader of the strongest political party to be head of government. For the two roles to be separated meant detaching the chief executive from his political power base.

There were four candidates to replace Botha as party leader: Roelof "Pik" Botha, the foreign minister; Barend du Plessis, the finance minister; Chris Heunis, the constitutional affairs minister; and F. W. de Klerk, minister of national education. Of these the first three were regarded as reformists and De Klerk as the conservative candidate. Du Plessis had Botha's backing. The choice lay with the National Party's one-hundred-and-thirty-member parliamentary caucus, and there De Klerk edged out Du Plessis by eight votes.

Though Botha never fully explained his reasons for resigning the party leadership, he apparently wanted to elevate himself "above politics" in order to head a "national forum" of selected ethnic leaders who would discuss how he might give blacks their own segregated place in the central government. The plan was, as we have seen, a non-starter: merely a further refinement of the apartheid system that spurned all the bridge-building taking place with the ANC. But by his unorthodox constitutional move the president had exposed his flank to the growing forces of frustration in his administration. A whites-only general election was due in September, and the National Party faced the embarrassment of going into it under a leader who had no power. That, and Botha's health, gave De Klerk the pretext to make his move.

At 8.30 a.m. on a wet wintry Monday, August 14, De Klerk led fifteen of South Africa's most senior politicians to *Tuynhuys* to confront President Botha. It was the first time in the country's history that cabinet members had met with their chief to tell him to go, and it was not a pretty scene, as a copy of the cabinet minutes leaked to a South African newspaper reveals.

It was Botha who had summoned them. He was furious because Zambia's president, Kenneth Kaunda, had announced that he was going to meet with De Klerk on August 28 – a meeting Botha said he had not been told about. He felt slighted and his famous temper was on the boil. But the cabinet members had decided that now was the time to confront him.

The meeting began with a prayer by Dawie de Villiers, the minister of mineral and energy affairs, who is also an ordained minister of the Dutch Reformed Church. It ended three stormy hours later with Botha telling De Klerk to make sure his relationship with the Lord was in order. But at first Botha listened quietly as the cabinet members paid their tributes, told him what a great leader he had been, how much they admired what he had done for *volk* and fatherland, but how out of concern for his health and for the welfare of the country and the party they felt it would be best if he would take a little break and appoint an acting president – at least until after the election.

One by one the ministers asked him to go, among them the minister of defence, Gen. Magnus Malan, who had been Botha's protégé and friend for twenty-three years. He was the Brutus of the piece. "I wish I could bypass this day," Malan lamented, but in the circumstances he had to support the others.

Botha erupted, lashing out with all the fury of his violent temper. "So," he sneered, "you regard me as a superman, do you? If I'm so wonderful, such a superman as you describe, why are you treating me like this?"

"Your health, Mr President —" De Klerk began.

Botha turned on him. "Yes," he snarled, "that is the coward's way. What you are implying is that I can't think for myself. Why don't you come out and say so?"

"That's not what I said," De Klerk protested.

"Why not?" Botha demanded. "Why do you insinuate it with a smile on your face and a dagger in your hand?"

"Mr. President, that's not what I'm insinuating," De Klerk protested again.

There was no calming the angry chief. "Look, you'll go too far," he thundered. "I am fit. Is any one of you in possession of a medical certificate that proclaims you to be healthy? Let me hear, how many of you are sitting here with pills in your pockets while you drag my health into this matter? Oh, so that's going to be your new tack, your new propaganda: he's not *compos mentis*!"

Botha railed on, telling his ministers he still had the right to fire them all, calling them hypocrites, telling them that they were weak and useless, that they were no good on television, that they came across too apologetically, not as fighters, that they were letting the party down. He also accused them of "playing with the ANC".

He refused to appoint an acting president, insisting that he was not ill, but said he would resign that night after going on national television to tell his people why. Then he stood up, glared around the room, and said: "Thank you, gentlemen. Good-bye."

Botha did go on television that night to announce his resignation and state his case, but the broadcast turned out to be a long, rambling bluster that left viewers confused. They didn't know what it was all about, except that the Old Crocodile was angry. In these squalid circumstances De Klerk was appointed acting president the next day – and a new era began.

8

The Calling of De Klerk

D E KLERK, the party conservative, had had little to do with the Mandela issue when he became president. Indeed, as he confessed in an interview, it was not until late 1988 that he became aware of the secret negotiations with Mandela. They had been taking place for nearly four years without his knowledge. The reason, he explains, is that the issue did not fall within his ministerial authority, and Botha was keeping knowledge of the secret meetings restricted to those directly involved. "I was not part of the inner circle dealing with security – in fact, I was never part of any inner circle of Mr. P. W. Botha's," De Klerk says, with just a hint of rancour in his voice. It was in his capacity as leader of the National Party in Transvaal province that he eventually learned of the prison meetings. "When I found out about them I was fully supportive," he says, insisting a little disingenuously that he was not so conservative as he appeared. "I was often troubled in my own mind, and it became more and more difficult for me as a loyal party spokesman in a leading position to defend a policy which increasingly I believed had to go."

De Klerk strongly denies that he underwent a sudden Damascus Road conversion. It was not a question of morality, he says, but of practical politics. Nor was his conversion merely a personal matter; it was part of a gradual realization within the National Party that apartheid was unworkable and had to be changed. In line with this, De Klerk still will not apologize for apartheid, which he dismisses as simply a political mistake that had to be rectified. It began, he insists, as "an honourable vision of justice" – one that would allow separate development for white South Africans and the various black tribal groups. Only when it proved to be unworkable did it become unjust, he says, "and when we realized that, we changed it." This is a disingenuous argument by any reckoning. From the early 1960s, when Hendrik Verwoerd first enunciated the policy in its full form, a whole range of political analysts, myself included, pointed out that the racial arithmetic of South Africa was loaded against it; that white South Africa was inextricably dependent on the black labour force; and that even if the policy could somehow be implemented beyond the highest expectations of even its most optimistic planners, population growth patterns were such that there would still be a five-to-one black majority in so-called white South Africa by the end of the century. The whole elaborate exercise would be for nothing.

If the lesson of the trout hook – of black and white South Africa's mutual dependency – was obvious as long ago as that, it is hard to believe that an intelligent man like De Klerk could not see it for himself fifteen or twenty years later. His self-exculpatory statements have angered many of apartheid's longtime opponents, who believe they cast doubt on the genuineness of De Klerk's conversion. "Apartheid was not a political mistake, it was a fundamentally evil thing," fumed an aged and angry Archbishop Trevor Huddleston, head of the international Anti-Apartheid Movement, at a special service in Soweto's Regina Mundi Cathedral to honour him on his return to South Africa after a thirty-six-year absence in July 1991.*

Leon Wessels, the first National Party cabinet minister to apologize publicly for apartheid (in June 1990), says he suspects the reason De Klerk won't do the same is because it would amount to a repudiation of his father. De Klerk may also be sensitive to the deeply conservative views of his wife, Marike. Pieter Potgieter, an early Afrikaner reformist and

---

* Trevor Huddleston, an Anglican priest and member of the celibate order the Community of the Resurrection, became a legend in the black community when he lived from 1944 to 1956 in Sophiatown, a racially mixed quarter of Johannesburg which was demolished under the apartheid policy soon after he left. Huddleston's book *Naught for Your Comfort* (1956) was one of the most widely-read indictments of apartheid ever published.

professor of politics at Potchefstroom University, De Klerk's alma mater, recalls how Marike de Klerk berated him after he addressed a National Party Women's Federation meeting in Pretoria in 1983, soon after a white referendum had endorsed President Botha's constitutional reform giving Asians and coloureds their segregated role in Parliament. She had been campaigning with her husband in the Waterberg region of northern Transvaal province, where white racism is at its worst. Potgieter says he spoke of the need for further constitutional changes that would extend political rights to the black majority. Mrs. de Klerk interjected from the audience to say, "If you had been in the Waterberg and witnessed the trauma of our people there, you wouldn't talk such nonsense."

Whenever the change occurred in De Klerk, he certainly concealed it from those closest to him. His image in the cabinet was that of a conservative. In 1982, when the hardliner Andries Treurnicht broke away from the National Party in reaction against Botha's proposed reforms, De Klerk was the natural choice to take over as Transvaal leader to counter Treurnicht's new Conservative Party in its stronghold there. Leon Wessels, one of the government's key constitutional negotiators, has a framed newspaper cartoon hanging in his office showing De Klerk resisting Botha's abolition in 1985 of the most notorious of all the apartheid laws, the Immorality Act, which made sex across the colour line a crime. It is a reminder that a mere four years before he took over the leadership of the country, this acclaimed reformer was still supporting not only apartheid's grand vision of territorial separation but also its meanest aspects of social segregation.

As late as March 1989, a month after De Klerk had succeeded Botha as National Party leader, his brother, Wimpie, warned in a magazine article that he was unlikely to turn sharply to the left. "He is too strongly convinced that racial grouping is the only truth, way and life," Wimpie de Klerk wrote. "He is too dismissive of a more radical style." The course his younger brother would follow, he predicted, was a careful, centrist one, hoping to "hold the middle ground by means of clever footwork, small compromises, drawn-out

studies and planned processes, effective diplomacy and grow-
ing authority through balanced leadership and control."
That "is his style, his nature, his talent and his conviction."
There would be no leap of faith in a liberal direction.*

Wimpie de Klerk, whose frustrations had grown while the
meetings in Britain with the ANC were going on, was so
convinced that FW's appointment did not bode well for
reform that he went ahead with plans to help form a new
liberal opposition party, the Democratic Party – although he
withdrew from it in an act of familial loyalty when FW was
inaugurated as president in September, 1989.

These cautionary predictions seemed to be borne out
when De Klerk, having been sworn in as acting president,
waged a reactionary election campaign. He gave no indication during that campaign of any intention to begin negotiating with the ANC, let alone of unbanning it or any of
the other black liberation movements. On the contrary, the
National Party denounced the new Democratic Party as
traitorous because some of its leaders had met with the ANC.
It made widespread use of a smear poster showing one of the
Democratic leaders, Wynand Malan, talking to Joe Slovo,
then general secretary of the South African Communist
Party, in Lusaka. Yet within a month of the September 6
election De Klerk released Walter Sisulu and seven other top
black political prisoners in what was obviously a trial run for
bigger events to follow.

When, and why, did De Klerk change his colours? The
evidence suggests that his claim that he changed along with
the party is at least partly true. He was above all a party-
liner, and the explanation he offers today for his earlier
position is that as Transvaal leader he had to consolidate the
party's conservative support in that province against Treurnicht's challenge. "It was my job," he said in the interview.
"My speeches were focussed on my main opposition."

When, in 1986, the National Party had accepted the principle of "a single South Africa", De Klerk had accepted that,

* *Leadership*, March 1989, pp. 61-66.

too. But Leon Wessels believes the full implications of the decision – that it meant abandoning apartheid's core concept of territorial division – made more of an impact on De Klerk than on most other members of the party. De Klerk himself says of that event, "Once we had gone through the process of reassessment I took a leap in my own mind, more decisively than many other National Party politicians, that power-sharing with blacks was the right course for a new political dispensation."

From that point on, there occurred what Wimpie calls "an evolutionary conversion". Others agree. No one among his closest colleagues and friends was aware of any blinding moment of change, yet imperceptibly, incrementally, De Klerk shifted one hundred and eighty degrees. "He's still the same person I've always known," his closest friend and old law-firm partner, Ignatius Vorster, says, yet Vorster confesses to being puzzled about exactly when and how the trans-formation occurred. "My guess is that at some stage – I don't know when – he realized that if you go on like this you are going to lose the game, the cup, the league, everything," Vorster, who is now dean of the law faculty at Potchefstroom University, says. "He is a pragmatist who carries very little ideological baggage with him, and once he had reached that decision, he acted. Then his strategic sense took over. As a lawyer FW always had a great sense of timing. If he had been a rugby player he would have been an excellent flyhalf."

Wimpie de Klerk, who has talked about this at length with his brother, believes there were several other important phases to the evolutionary conversion. The first was when De Klerk had to campaign against Treurnicht's hardliners in the conservative heartland, the Deep North of South Africa. "Listening to their arguments, their ideologies, their stubbornness, he realized it was a matter of racism rather than identity," says Wimpie. "He reacted against that, and I believe it was the beginning of an estrangement between FW and the conservative part of the National Party." As provincial leader, De Klerk also became involved in a policy

think tank headed by Chris Heunis, then minister of constitutional development. For the first time, De Klerk was
confronted with the problem of how to accommodate the
black majority in the political system. Until then he had held
portfolios such as posts and telecommunications, mines and
energy affairs, that had little to do with race policy, and he
had met few black people of any political standing. Now he
was brought face-to-face with the realities of a failing
ideology.

Heunis's think tankers, many of them young Afrikaner
academics, were grappling with the fact that the policy of
parcelling off South Africa's black population into ten tribal
ministates had been stymied by the refusal of six homelands
to accept nominal independence. In addition, the lesson of
mutual dependency was asserting itself more forcefully than
ever: the stream of black people to the industrial cities was
continuing despite stringent influx control laws, and thus the
black population in what was officially classified as "white"
South Africa was swelling ineluctably. The dream of total
racial separation was clearly unattainable, and, with township unrest on the rise and international pressures intensifying, a way had to be found to include these urban blacks
in the political system. How could this be done without
endangering white control?

Botha's 1983 constitution had created a complicated tricameral Parliament, with separate chambers for white,
coloured, and Asian legislators. Each of these chambers had
autonomy over its race group's "own affairs", while "general
affairs" affecting all South Africans had to be agreed to by all
three chambers. There was a catch, however. Not only was
the white chamber by far the largest of the three, the majority
party there provided the president who in turn selected his
cabinet from the ruling white National Party. Moreover, if
either the coloured or Asian chambers refused to pass a
"general affairs" bill – a rare event, given the malleability of
the "moderate" non-whites who collaborated with the system – it could be referred to a National Party-dominated
President's Council for an automatic veto override.

Now the policy planners were thinking of adding to this tokenist structure a separate black parliament, indirectly elected from township councils established under the apartheid system. This could join the homelands and the tricameral Parliament in an overarching Council of States, in which each race group would still have autonomy over its "own affairs", and the whites would still have the last word in "general affairs".

De Klerk was caught up in this tortuous model-building and, according to his brother, it exposed him to reformist thinking in the National Party. "At that stage he still believed you could find a solution within the apartheid concept, but it would have to be a more enlightened kind of apartheid," says Wimpie.

Then, on February 2, 1989, came De Klerk's election as National Party leader. Suddenly he was no longer the party-liner, the conformist follower. Now he had to put his own stamp on party policy. He began by withdrawing for a few weeks to contemplate this new responsibility. His brother sees this as the most important phase in FW's evolutionary conversion, for it was then that he came to the conclusion that Heunis's models couldn't work. "Instead, he began developing the concept of a policy based on the protection of minority rights," says Wimpie. "The blacks would have to become part of the new parliament. They would be in the majority, but minority rights could be protected through a bill of rights, a system of enforced coalitions – that sort of thing."

There were other influences, too. As party leader De Klerk made several trips abroad – a rare experience for a governing politician from this pariah country. He met Britain's Margaret Thatcher, Germany's Helmut Kohl, and the leaders of Portugal, Italy, Ivory Coast, Mozambique, Zambia and Zaïre. All emphasized the need for South Africa to change, the dire consequences of continued isolation if it did not, and their readiness to welcome South Africa back into the community of nations if it would abandon apartheid.

Herman Cohen, U.S. Assistant Secretary of State for Africa in the Bush Administration, says he became aware of a schizophrenia in South Africa's attitude to foreign pressure. It liked to put on a face of defiance, but behind that lay a yearning for the understanding and approval of outsiders. "In public they didn't want to be seen calling in outsiders, but privately they wanted our advice and approval," says Cohen. "This opened the way for what I called invisible mediation, as we were able to tell them what would and would not be acceptable to the international community."

But of all the international influences, none was greater than the Gorbachev reforms that began unravelling the communist empire, for they eased Pretoria's phobia that the black struggle against apartheid was a conspiracy directed from Moscow. It took the monkey off De Klerk's back and enabled him to justify to his people what would otherwise have appeared to them a suicidal course of action.

The negotiations which brought independence to neighbouring Namibia in October 1989 underscored this point. South Africa had administered the former German colony under the terms of an old League of Nations mandate for nearly three-quarters of a century. Now, as Gorbachev's Soviet Union began settling regional conflicts and removing points of friction with the United States, a deal was struck to have Cuban troops pull out of Angola in return for South Africa's withdrawal from Namibia. The South West African People's Organization, an ANC clone, won the Namibian independence elections that followed, and South Africa handed over the territory smoothly and peacefully to an enemy it had been fighting for thirty years. "Namibia showed the South Africans that this kind of change would not necessarily have catastrophic results," says Sir Robin Renwick, British ambassador in South Africa at the time.

Economic sanctions and campaigns to withdraw investment in South Africa added significantly to the pressures on De Klerk to act. These, together with the racial unrest, had plunged South Africa into the deepest financial crisis of its history. Business confidence was at an all-time low, and increasingly the cry was raised, "We can't go on like this!" The interplay of different policies towards South Africa, with Thatcher's Britain standing out as a solitary opponent of sanctions while more and more of South Africa's other major trading partners applied them, made for some creative diplomatic strategies. As Renwick admits, this enabled him to emulate the time-honoured "good guy, bad guy" technique popular with interrogation teams: he urged De Klerk to make concessions that would enable Thatcher to resist the mounting pressure on her to join the international campaign, particularly in the weeks leading up to a Commonwealth summit meeting in Kuala Lumpur, Malaysia, in October 1989. "Yes, certainly, we did that," says Sir Robin, "although it wasn't just a case of, You must give us something, but, In your own interests you must move."

But the climactic event in De Klerk's evolutionary conversion was undoubtedly his inauguration as president on September 20, 1989. Despite his denial of any Damascus Road experience, friends and relatives say De Klerk talked of being seized by a powerful sense of religious "calling" on that day, which his favourite pastor, the Reverend Pieter Bingle, reinforced in a sermon at the inauguration service in Pretoria.

De Klerk is a religious man, a member of the *Gereformeerde Kerk*, the smallest and most strictly Calvinist of the three branches of the Dutch Reformed Church in South Africa. In line with its interpretation of Calvinist theology, the *Doppers*, as the church members are called, believe they may receive a *roeping*, or call, from God to perform a specific task at a particular time in particular circumstances. It was on this theme that Bingle preached at the inauguration service. Taking Jeremiah 23, verses 16 and 22, as his text, he told the new president that he was standing "in the council chamber of God" to learn the will of the Lord, and that he should act upon it rather than heed the words of the false prophets. As God's instrument, Bingle went on, De Klerk should heed the traditions of his people but have the courage to break new ground. "He who stands in God's council chamber will be aggressive enough to tackle problems and challenges fearlessly," he sermonized. "New ways will have to be found where roads enter *culs de sac*, or are worn out or cannot carry the heavy traffic. Excess baggage will be cast aside. Certain things will stay and others will have to be discarded. Those stuck in the grooves of the past will find that besides the spelling, depth is the only difference between a groove and a grave."

De Klerk was deeply affected. "He was literally in tears after the service," says his brother, who was at a post-inaugural gathering of close friends and family members. "In tears he told us we should pray for him – that God was calling him to save all the people of South Africa, that he knew he was going to be rejected by his own people but that he had to walk this road and that we must all help him. He got very emotional, confessing his belief that God had called upon him and that he couldn't ignore the call. I remember, too, that he said, 'I am not a fundamentalist, I don't think I am important in God's eyes, but I believe in God and I believe I am being called upon to perform a specific task at this time in this new situation.'"

De Klerk admits that the inauguration ceremony was an emotional experience for him and that he wept afterwards. "I am more emotional than I appear on the surface," he says. "And, yes, I did feel a strong sense of calling. Not in an arrogant way, as though I felt I was being looked upon as somebody special who had been singled out by God Almighty to do this job. I was very conscious, and I remain very conscious, of my shortcomings, and I constantly try to overcome them. But, yes, I also believe that God directs things here on earth, and as a result I had to accept that my election as president was something He wanted to happen, and therefore in my relationship – my vertical relationship – I have a direct responsibility and I must try to live according to that."

The first clue the public had that the new president was different from the Old Crocodile had come a week before the inauguration, after the police had opened fire and killed a number of demonstrators in a coloured township outside Cape Town. The angry black community planned a protest march into the city, to be led by Archbishop Tutu, the Reverend Allan Boesak, and other church dignitaries. During the Botha years, the march would have been banned, it would have gone ahead in defiance of the ban, and there would have been a bloody clash with the police. That cycle had been repeated many times. Now De Klerk acted differently. After getting assurances from the church leaders that their own marshalls would control the demonstration, he allowed it – and thirty thousand people marched peacefully to the steps of City Hall. Permission for other public demonstrations followed. It was the first step towards normalizing political life in South Africa.

September of 1989 seems to have marked the culmination of De Klerk's evolutionary conversion – the moment when he made the decision in his own mind to release Mandela and begin negotiating with the ANC. Thereafter, it was only a matter of bringing his party along with him, and of deciding when and how to do it. How to manage the release was especially problematical. There were fears of an uncontrollable emotional surge in the black community when this messianic figure emerged from his long entombment; the government was haunted by visions of the mass demonstrations that had followed the Ayatollah Khomeini's return to Teheran in 1979 and overwhelmed the regime of Shah Reza Pahlavi. Another problem was how to lessen the impact on the Afrikaner constituency. Botha's strategy had been to introduce changes incrementally, but the ANC had thwarted that by discrediting each step as it was taken. De Klerk decided that boldness was the only way to overcome both problems. He would take a series of quantum leaps to break free of the paralysis and throw his opponents off balance.

The first of the leaps came in the predawn hours of Sunday, October 15 – a few days, it should be noted, before Thatcher had to face her Commonwealth critics in Kuala Lumpur. Police cars pulled up outside the family homes of Walter Sisulu and five other ANC life prisoners, and released them back to their families. Also released were Jafta Masemola, founder of the military wing of the Pan-Africanist

Congress, and Oscar Mpetha, an ANC member who had been jailed for terrorism at the age of seventy-six. This was a hugely emotional moment. Albertina Sisulu, a rock of stability for a family that had seen a husband imprisoned for twenty-five years, one son banned and detained, another jailed for resistance activities, and yet another son and a daughter exiled, permitted herself to shed her first tear in a quarter of a century. "I don't know how I'm going to cope with having him around the house all the time," she murmured as she hugged her silver-haired husband of seventy-seven.

That night Soweto was in ecstasy. Word had gone around a few days before that the men were to be freed, and on Saturday tens of thousands of people marched through towns and cities across the country, waving still-banned ANC flags and banners. Now, on Sunday evening, as Soweto revelled with songs and booze and bonfires, the released prisoners reassembled in the packed Holy Cross Church for a boisterous press conference. Through the hubbub Sisulu managed to give a hint of the conciliatory days that lay ahead. To an excited questioner who asked whether a black government would soon take power, he replied: "We believe that in our lifetime there will be a government that includes black people. We are not seeking a black government as such. We are seeking a democratic system in which a black man can be president and a white man can be president. There is no question of judging people on the basis of colour."

Cautious though Sisulu was, the fact that he and the other released prisoners could speak openly in the name of the ANC and that the crowds could carry ANC flags and banners without being arrested meant the ban on the organization had effectively ceased. It was clear, too, that this was a test for Mandela's release.

All this Mandela himself had negotiated in his continuing meetings with Kobie Coetsee and the committee of officials. "He insisted all the time that the others should be released first," Coetsee recalls. "He was like the captain of a ship. He wanted to see them safely outside before he himself left."

De Klerk, meanwhile, was planning his next quantum leap.

ON ANOTHER SUNDAY, seven weeks later, De Klerk and his entire cabinet, with fifty officials and advisers, boarded two Hercules transport planes at Waterkloof military air base and flew to a game reserve called D'Nyala near the small town of Ellisras, in northwestern Transvaal. There, deep in the wild bushveld near the Botswana border, the inner core of the government huddled together for two days, December 4 and 5, of brainstorming and strategizing. A *bosberaad*, or bush conference, it was called, and it set a pattern of collective policy formulation and negotiation that broke with the authoritarian culture of the past. Over the next four years, D'Nyala became De Klerk's Camp David: he headed there seven times with his party colleagues or members of other political organizations to resolve crises in the drawn-out negotiations.

D'Nyala is an exotic setting for such delicate political polemicizing: a cluster of thatched buildings and quaint log cabins set among browsing giraffes and antelopes, all enclosed behind a high electrified fence, a secluded island in the heart of the most reactionary community of white racists in the whole of South Africa. "Man, this is lion country," is how the chief game ranger, Jan van Breda, describes the area, referring to the local populace rather than the animals in his little reserve.

The decor is equally exotic. At the heart of the complex is an ornate conference centre; beside it is a VIP accommodation unit with two huge crystal chandeliers hanging from a simple thatch roof and flanked by two tall tree stumps protruding from the floor. Upstairs are two elaborate suites with pink marble bathrooms and, in the presidential suite where De Klerk stayed, a pink jacuzzi with gold taps. As he descended from his room down a broad wooden staircase De Klerk would have seen, stretched out on the floor below, the stuffed body of a ten-foot crocodile staring at him with the admonishing eyes of his predecessor.

At the head of this establishment is Jan van Breda, a chubby, cheerful Afrikaner with a bushy moustache and the first signs of a beer belly beginning to protrude above the khaki shorts of his game-ranger's uniform. In his forties, Van Breda had spent his life developing the earthy skills of bushcraft; now suddenly he found himself privy, the way a butler at a royal banquet is, to high matters of state and personal interactions leading to one of the most remarkable political transforations of modern times. He served his guests meals and early-morning coffee, got on first-name terms with them, and in the evenings after the formal discussions sat with them around a campfire in a reed-enclosed *lapa* under the wide African night sky.

Van Breda remembers that first *bosberaad* with De Klerk, his cabinet, and advisers particularly well, because it was his trial by ordeal, as it were. He received his instructions from the provincial Department of Nature Conservation: prepare to accommodate seventy of the country's most important politicians, including the president, for the weekend. Security and confidentiality were primary concerns, so Van Breda and his wife did the catering themselves. "I was very nervous because we had never done anything like this before," he recalls. "I felt the reputation of our whole administration was at stake, so we worked very hard and got everything in order.

"Man, it was beautiful. Everything was shining, spick and span. We had candles, champagne, flowers, everything laid out here in the *lapa*. They arrived at seven on the evening of December 3 and we had arranged dinner for nine o'clock. They had just unpacked their things and were beginning a pre-dinner drink when an almighty thunderstorm hit us. God, man, I have never seen such a storm in my life. The rain came down in buckets, thunder and lightning, the whole works. It flooded everything out, swamped the flowers, drenched the tables – and put out the lights."

Poor Jan van Breda had not made provision for such an emergency. There was no reserve power plant in the game reserve, and he had no oil or gas lamps. He couldn't cook the dinner and his guests were plunged into pitch darkness. He got on the phone to the regional headquarters of the Electricity Supply Commission in Brits, two hundred miles away, but they were not sympathetic. "They said, 'Look, we've got a problem right through the region and you're at the end of the line. We won't be able to do anything until the morning.'"

Desperately Van Breda tried to persuade the electricity suppliers to give him priority attention. "I said, 'Look here, man, you've got to do something quick, I've got the whole cabinet here, the state president and all,' but the guy at the other end just laughs and says, 'Yeah, tell me that one again.' I phoned the power station in Ellisras and said, 'Please, man, help me,' but they told me to phone the regional headquarters in Brits. It was catch-22. I was frantic, phoning everyone, yelling at them all to help me, but no one would believe my story. I was trying at the same time to get some light going. All I had were the few candles we had had on the tables for dinner. I tried to light a few of them, but they were wet and broken.

"The provincial administrator, Danie Hough, went to President de Klerk to apologize and say dinner was going to be a bit late. The president was very nice about it. He said not to worry, they understood that crises like this happened sometimes. But I was in a flap, I tell you, running around in such a panic that I got a nappy rash between my legs from all the sweat."

In the end the minister of energy affairs came to Van Breda's rescue with a call to the Electricity Supply Commission that the technicians at last took seriously. Power was restored in time to serve dinner at midnight – and the big bush conference began on schedule the next morning.

THE OUTLINES OF the government's new strategy were established at that first *bosberaad*. "The purpose of the meeting was to come up with a new constitutional vision, and to decide what to do about the political prisoners and banned parties," Leon Wessels recalls. "We reached agreement fairly quickly on the release of prisoners, but there was some heated debate about unbanning the political organizations, especially the South African Communist Party." Roelf Meyer, then still a deputy minister, recalls that Magnus Malan, the hawkish defence minister who had served P. W. Botha loyally and, with him, had evolved the "total onslaught" philosophy in the 1980s that turned South Africa into a militaristic state, spoke out against unbanning the SACP. But others argued that if any party remained outlawed its allies would mount such a massive campaign in its support that the government's moral advantage would be obscured and it would have to give way in the end.

No comprehensive plan was adopted at the conference, says Wessels, but it was clear where the party was headed. "I think the *bosberaad* fine-tuned the president's mind. Everything was there. He just had to put it together." A week later, De Klerk had the first of three meetings with Mandela in *Tuynhuys*, an amicable encounter that left Mandela with the impression of De Klerk as "a man of integrity"– although later the relationship soured and Mandela was to accuse him of duplicity.

After the meetings, De Klerk went on vacation. December is high summer in South Africa and, like August in the Northern Hemisphere, a time when the country packs up and leaves town. Friends who visited the president's official holiday home, Botha House, on the Natal south coast, noted that De Klerk seemed distracted and spent hours staring at the ocean. He seemed, they said, to be wrestling inwardly with himself. De Klerk admits it was what he calls "a very pensive holiday", and that he spent hours contemplating the speech he would have to make on February 2. "I like to sit alone and think when something is being born, when I have to translate a vision into words, into statements, into decisions which must be formulated," he says. He was grappling, no doubt, with those issues deep in the Afrikaner psyche that had turned Botha back from the banks of the Rubicon – the reluctance to go down in history as the one who ended Afrikaner hegemony, and perhaps the Afrikaner *volk* itself, one who would be denounced by his people as a *volksverraaier*, an ethnic traitor. Possibly, too, he dreaded the pain of breaking with his family heritage, even repudiating his own father.

The wrestling continued after his return. Leon Wessels accompanied him on flights to Mozambique and Transkei in mid-January, and says it was evident De Klerk was still struggling with his speech. In the end he wrote the text himself, by hand, over several days – the first part while sitting at the kitchen table in his holiday cottage at Hermanus, near Cape Town, and the final draft in his official Cape Town residence. "I wrote the second part sitting at the dining-room table," he recalls, "because we had the television set in my study and Marike wanted to watch her favourite show. I eventually finished the speech just before midnight on February 1"– less than twelve hours before it had to be delivered. He kept the text secret to avoid leaks, informing only a few close advisers of the main points. "I didn't tell the National Party caucus. I didn't even tell my wife what I was going to announce," he says.

Niël Barnard was part of the inner circle that was consulted. "There was a hell of a row in the last hours before the speech was delivered over the unbanning of the Communist Party," he recalls. Again Magnus Malan objected, but again the argument prevailed that it would be counter-productive to leave a cause for continued campaigning.

And so De Klerk went to the podium to deliver his blockbuster.

The effect of that speech was simply enormous. I was one of about two hundred reporters assembled in a briefing room adjoining Parliament half an hour before De Klerk delivered it. The doors were locked, and we were handed copies of the text and told we could not leave until De Klerk had finished speaking. A hush settled over the room, then a rising buzz as we read the text before watching De Klerk on closed-circuit television. I recall my own astonishment as I flipped through the pages. "My God, he's done it all," I murmured to my *Washington Post* colleague, David Ottaway. My first thought was – and still is – that De Klerk didn't appreciate the full implications of what he was doing.

Despite his insistence that he would not agree to majority rule but only what he called "power sharing" in a system of enforced coalition, I was convinced that the process De Klerk was unleashing would generate its own momentum and lead to majority rule before the end of the decade. With the Gorbachev analogy in mind, I rewrote the last chapter of my book, *The Mind of South Africa*, for its paperback edition predicting this.

But in at least one respect De Klerk was critically different from Gorbachev. He stayed with the changes, he did not try to freeze the process. He came to recognize that you cannot reform an oppressive system, that if you start to relax it you have to go the whole hog. There cannot be perestroika, only abolition. He accepted that as it became evident. His own process of change kept pace with events, which is what has saved him – and South Africa. And so he remains on the scene, although in a lesser role. This second acceptance, even more than the first, is the real measure of the man's reflective intelligence.

9

The Spooks
Move In

BUT I MOVE ahead too fast. Before any of this happened, while South Africa was still on the cusp of a new presidency, another phase of even more secretive and extraordinary meetings began. After two and a half years of indirect contact through the talks at Mells, the small group of men meeting with Nelson Mandela decided that the time had come for the government to make direct contact with the ANC in exile.

They had a problem, though. While Barnard had been able to talk President Botha into agreeing to allow members of the National Intelligence Service to have a face-to-face meeting – that way it could still be explained away as an intelligence-gathering exercise if there were a leak – Mandela was adamant in refusing to sanction any form of direct contact between the government and the ANC in exile. He remained suspicious of the government's motives, believing they would try to drive a wedge between himself and his colleagues outside the country; indeed, dividing the ANC and separating Mandela from the rest of the liberation movement were fundamental goals in the Botha regime's strategy. But Barnard had become convinced that direct meetings were essential to establish more formally where the exiled ANC leaders stood on the issues he and his fellow committee members had been discussing with Mandela – and in the end he decided to go ahead without Mandela's approval. He claims it was his only act of deception in their long relationship. It is also certain that Mandela soon became aware of it, although he never broached the subject with Barnard.

Without informing Mandela of his intentions, Barnard asked Esterhuyse to get in touch with Mbeki and set up a secret meeting with the NIS. What followed was one of the more theatrical episodes in what Kobie Coetsee had called a tale worthy of Le Carré. In June 1989, Esterhuyse flew to Britain and met Mbeki in a London pub. The ANC man was hesitant at first, but by now a bond of trust existed between them and Esterhuyse persuaded him to agree to a NIS-ANC meeting. "I gave Thabo a personal assurance that if I picked up anything that indicated to me that it was a trap, or that something could go wrong, I would alert him," Esterhuyse says. The agreement obtained, Esterhuyse told Mbeki to expect a telephone call from an NIS agent named Maritz Spaarwater – who would announce himself as John Campbell. The purpose of the call would be to set up a meeting somewhere in Switzerland.

Spaarwater, a tall, lean man with a greying beard and debonair manner, was an old hand in the espionage business. He had travelled Africa clandestinely for years, got to know Zambia's President Kaunda well, and once met with Namibia's Sam Nujoma at State House in Lusaka at a time when the leader of the South West African People's Organization was as much of a demon to white South Africans as any member of the ANC. Now, at the time this new assignment landed on his desk, he was the NIS chief director of operations, which meant he was in charge of all intelligence gathering.

Specifically, his job was now to make all the security arrangements for this first-ever meeting between the apartheid regime and its outlawed enemy. As he puts it, "To make sure that we got there and back without being recognized and without the thing being blown in public, which would have caused a bit of a problem."

Operation Flair, they called it, with the international intelligence community's enthusiasm for militaristic code names. Over the next three months covert phone calls were made back and forth between Pretoria and Lusaka and Dar es Salaam, as "John Campbell" set up the details with Mbeki and Jacob Zuma, who had given themselves the code names John and Jack Simelane.

Formal authorization for the mission came late, as various hitches delayed the meeting, and in the end it coincided fortuitously and somewhat confusingly with the dramatic change of occupancy at *Tuynhuys*. On August 16, the day after De Klerk was sworn in as acting president, a carefully worded proposal was placed before South Africa's State Security Council. In his first act as head of state, De Klerk presided over the meeting of this powerful inner body of the administration and approved the proposal. Yet, perhaps because he was distracted by the other dramatic events of the moment, or by the elliptical wording of the proposal itself, he seems not to have registered its import. When Mike Louw and Spaarwater reported back to him a month later, De Klerk was nonplussed by what they had done.

The cunning craftsmanship of the proposal, drafted by members of the committee of officials seeing Mandela, reflects the delicacy of the issue in government circles at that time.

It is necessary that more information should be obtained and processed concerning the ANC, and the aims, alliances and potential approachability of its different leaders and groupings. To enable this to be done, special additional direct action will be necessary, particularly with the help of National Intelligence Service functionaries.*

This could mean everything or nothing: the authorization of the first direct meeting with the ANC itself, or simply more spying on it. If news of the meeting leaked out, the State Security Council resolution could be used to explain it away: after all, it was the NIS's job to undertake investigative work. On the other hand, the wording also lends strength to those who believe it was the government's intention all along to try to split the ANC and do a deal with what they perceived to be its more malleable elements.

---

* Resolution of State Security Council meeting no. 13 of 1989.

The government was still taking no chances. The general election was due on September 6, so the NIS was instructed not to act on the resolution before then. More calls followed between John Campbell and John Simelane, and it was agreed that they should meet at the Palace Hotel, Lucerne, on the evening of September 12.

The NIS's special-equipment department got to work and prepared false passports for Louw and Spaarwater in the names of Michael James and Jacobus Maritz, as well as for three field agents who were to accompany them. The five men flew to Lucerne via Zurich. They were filled with anxiety. They had chosen Switzerland for the rendezvous because it and Britain were the only European countries that did not require South Africans to have entry visas, and they felt they would be less conspicuous in Switzerland. Still, they were mindful that they had antagonized the Swiss authorities eight years before when a South African undercover agent, Craig Williamson, was found to have infiltrated an anti-apartheid aid agency in Geneva. There would be little sympathy for them if they were caught violating Swiss law again. In addition to which they had to take care not to be spotted by agents of the U.S. Central Intelligence Agency, or the British, French or German intelligence services, which would have delighted in exposing a secret South African meeting with the ANC.

Early on the evening of September 12, Louw and Spaarwater checked into rooms 338 and 339 of the Palace Hotel, rooms that formed a suite with a small sitting-room between. Since Mbeki and Jacob Zuma were flying in to Geneva and would travel by road to Lucerne, the three field agents waited at Geneva airport to monitor the ANC men's arrival, then tailed them all the way to Lucerne. It was a measure of the mutual suspicions surrounding the meeting. "We wanted to see whether they had any support staff and whatever else they might be bringing along," says Louw. In fact they had only a driver, an ANC supporter living in Geneva.

The ANC party arrived shortly before 8 p.m., they asked

at the reception desk for the rooms of Messrs. James and
Maritz and were shown upstairs. It was a tense moment. "I
remember we said, 'How can we expect these guys to trust
us?'" Louw recalls. "I mean, we might have been sitting
there with guns and the moment they opened the door just
blown them away. So we opened the door so that they could
see in, and we stood there in full view.

"We could hear them coming, talking, and then they came
around the corner and they could see us standing there.
Thabo walked in and said, 'Well here we are, bloody terrorists and for all you know fucking communists as well.' That
broke the ice, and we all laughed, and I must say that from
that moment on there was no tension."

They talked until three in the morning, a long, exhausting
session covering all the tough issues of Mandela's continued
imprisonment, the government's continued banning of the
liberation movements, the ANC's alliance with the Communist Party and its commitment to guerrilla violence. It
was agreed that the meeting was "an investigation, not a
negotiation", which meant the two sides set out their positions and there was little bargaining. But when Louw and
Spaarwater flew home the next morning, they had a clear
message to deliver to their new acting president: the ANC
was willing to negotiate.

They were in for a shock when they did so, however. As
Louw began presenting his report at *Tuynhuys* on September 17, De Klerk stopped him in mid-sentence. "Who gave
you permission to go and negotiate with the ANC?" he demanded angrily.

"Luckily, I had a copy of the State Security Council resolution with me," says Louw, "and I was able to show it to
him and explain that we had gone on an investigative mission, not a negotiating one. I think he was upset not because
he was opposed to the idea, but because he felt he wasn't
involved. He didn't know what was going on and he hadn't
been properly briefed. But the moment he saw the State
Security Council resolution he relaxed and said, 'Tell me all
about it.'"

And so De Klerk, the conservative, was put in the picture
for the first time. "From that moment on," says Louw, "he
took the ball and ran with it."

NATIONAL INTELLIGENCE headquarters is a grey, featureless
building on Pretoria's Skinner Street. There is nothing to
indicate the nature of the business conducted there except
for a strip of heavy bars covering the frontage and a row of
security cubicles and X-ray machines across the foyer. Inside,
the decor is a startling cream and bright orange, and one
soon becomes aware of a number of erect young men with
close-cropped hair striding about – the stereotype of intelligence agents worldwide.

The upstairs hallways are decorated with portrait sketches
of South Africa's past security chiefs and heads of the secret
service's various departments. An unmarked door leads into
a small waiting-room with the NIS flag in one corner – a blue-
and-white drape with a spray of three peacock feathers, a
luminous secret eye at the point of each, all clasped together
at the base by a wolf's hook, a sinister device derived from
feudal Germany that is shaped like two facing S's with sharpened points, one of which is hammered into a tree trunk and
the other baited with meat to catch the wolf as it leaps for the
lure. "This symbolizes our work," a helpful agent explains.
"It is a warning that you are being watched by secret eyes,
and in counter-intelligence you lay traps to entice and hook
your adversary."

Beyond the waiting-room is Louw's office, the inner sanc-
tum of what was once apartheid's KGB. Here is where "Lang
Hendrik" van den Berg presided decades ago – Tall Henry,
with his wispy white hair, thin lips, and steel spectacles, who
was Prime Minister John Vorster's hatchet man during the
hard years of apartheid.

Van den Berg and Vorster, interned together for their pro-
Nazi sympathies during the Second World War, formed a
formidable duo when Vorster became minister of police in
1960 and then prime minister in 1966. Vorster consolidated

the security services under an umbrella body called the Bureau of State Security, or BOSS, and placed his old comrade, who had been chief of the security police, in charge. Vorster drafted South Africa's draconian security laws, providing for bannings and detention without trial, and Van den Berg implemented them with ruthless efficiency. Anti-apartheid activists disappeared in the night, to be locked away in solitary confinement, tortured, and interrogated. More than a hundred died in the detention cells. Many more were broken. Thousands were forced into confessions and sent away to join Nelson Mandela on Robben Island. Tall Henry, more than anyone else, was responsible for crushing black resistance to apartheid during the 1960s and 1970s.

Mike Louw was there in those days, a minor cog in the machinery of oppression. Now he is head of the organization, and, in one of the many breathtaking ironies that characterize South Africa's political transformation, he has helped to unban the ANC and bring it back to rule the country.

A shift in the nature of the organization came soon after P. W. Botha replaced Vorster as prime minister in 1979. In a move to break up his predecessor's power base and boost his own *maquis* in Military Intelligence, Botha dismantled BOSS and restructured it under new leadership as the National Intelligence Service. He appointed Niël Barnard, an academic from the University of the Orange Free State then only thirty-one years old, to head it. As we have seen, Barnard was drawn into the secret discussions with Mandela, leading in 1992 to his appointment as director general of the Department of Constitutional Affairs – at which point Louw replaced him as head of the NIS. But in 1990 Louw was busy with his plans in Switzerland.

LOUW AND SPAARWATER were back in Lucerne five months after their first visit – on February 6, just four days after De Klerk's epochal speech. They were meeting Mbeki in the Palace Hotel once more, accompanied now by Aziz Pahad in place of Jacob Zuma. Again the NIS men were travelling under false names with false passports, still anxious to avoid detection and political embarassment back home. But this time the nature of the meeting was different.

"Everyone was in high spirits," Louw recalls. "Aziz kept asking, 'What now? How do we proceed?'" That, in fact, was the essence of what had to be discussed. Unbanning the ANC, PAC, and the Communist Party was one thing; getting them safely back into South Africa, past security forces trained to shoot them on sight and with a white population indoctrinated against them for generations, was quite another. Most of the exiles had broken apartheid and security laws still on the statute books, so indemnity had to be arranged. And how could the notorious apartheid tricksters be trusted? Wasn't this just a massive plot to lure everyone back home and then pounce on them, lock them up, and laugh at how easy it had been to eliminate the naïve black liberation movement?

If political prisoners had to be released, the knotty question of exactly who was a political prisoner had to be resolved. Then there was the matter of starting the negotiating process. There would have to be an initial phase of talks about talks, of deciding who would represent whom and what form the process should take.

That is what now began in the Palace Hotel in Lucerne. "This was a different kind of meeting," says Louw. "We were not feeling each other out any more. Now we were starting to set up structures and make practical arrangements." The government representatives also wanted a positive response from the ANC to De Klerk's statement. As Louw explains: "We told them the state president had taken an enormous risk, and if they did not respond positively the whole mood in the country would swing decisively to the right. An eventual destructive war between themselves and the right wing would then be the only result." They wanted a positive response from the ANC's executive committee, "greater discipline" in controlling the protest campaign inside South Africa, and an agreed formula for ending the guerrilla struggle.

It was hard work, with tough haggling over some points, but the atmosphere was more relaxed, and again there was a further thaw in personal relationships as the men got to know each other better. There were lighter moments, too. As the meeting ran deep into the night, Pahad kept nodding off, whereupon Mbeki would nudge him with his foot and say, "Aziz, wake up, don't leave me alone with these Boers."

They set up working committees to deal with the most urgent problems, again succumbing to the spook trade's love of militaristic code names: Group Alpha (Mandela's release), Bravo (the release of detainees), Charlie (setting up discussions at the political level), and Delta (maintaining contact between the NIS and the ANC's intelligence service).

The meeting ended with a security scare for the NIS men. "We became aware that we were under surveillance," says Spaarwater. "I'm pretty sure it was the Swiss. And we were there on false documentation, false passports and cover names, which of course constitutes a criminal offence. So we decided to get out in a hurry."

Louw flew out directly, while Spaarwater left by road, driving through the night across the border into France, where he caught a plane back to South Africa the next day. "I kept wondering what I would do if I was arrested," says Spaarwater. "I decided I would simply tell them what we had been doing and say, If you want to destroy this initiative at the beginning, then go ahead, be it on your own heads. I think it would have worked."

The scare notwithstanding, the two men were back in Switzerland a fortnight later, although they took the precaution of shifting venue to the Bellevue-Palace Hotel in Berne, the Swiss capital, an ornate old building overlooking the Aar River. Barnard and Fanie van der Merwe, who had been part of the committee of officials that had met with Mandela in prison, accompanied them; Mbeki and Pahad were there for the ANC, with for the first time one of the guerrilla commanders, Joseph Nhlanhla. Once again the cautious South African government representatives travelled under cover names and with false documentation.

Louw, as Mike Hicks, checked into room 321, where the group held its meeting.

Barnard recalls his own nervousness on what was his first venture to meet the ANC in exile. As head of the NIS he was especially vulnerable, and he felt the tension acutely. "We can laugh about it today, but for us to go and see the ANC in Europe then was a hell of a thing," he says. "We had to prevent the KGB and CIA and other intelligence services from finding out. It was a very sensitive operation."

He remembers that soon after they went to the dining-room of the Bellevue-Palace for dinner, Mbeki and the other ANC men came in and sat at a separate table. The two groups pretended not to know each other, but with whispers and sideways glances Louw pointed out to Barnard who was who at the ANC table. Only Nhlanhla had them stymied: the NIS men had no idea who he was. After the meal, Pahad phoned up to room 321, contact was made, and the third meeting began.

It was a longer meeting than the others, continuing throughout the following day as the two sides laid the ground for the return of the exiles and prepared for the first meeting that would take place inside South Africa between the government and the ANC's national executive comittee. A hitch arose immediately: Joe Slovo, general secretary of the South African Communist Party, was a member of the ANC executive, and Barnard made it clear that this *bête rouge* of the Pretoria regime, its most demonized adversary, would be unacceptable as a member of the delegation to such a politically high-risk event. But Mbeki was equally adamant: no Slovo, no meeting; the ANC could not permit the government to determine who would represent it at the negotiations.

Barnard got on the phone to De Klerk. The president was appalled. "He gave me an absolute no," Barnard recalls. "He said, 'How can you expect me as head of state to welcome the leader of the Communist Party into the country?' I said to him, 'Sir, I must warn you that there is no other way. If they choose their team and they include Slovo, then they include him. How can it be otherwise?'

"I went back to Mbeki, and we consulted further. He said he could go back to his president and put our case to him, but he could tell me now that it wouldn't succeed. So I phoned President de Klerk again, and there, from the hotel in Berne, we eventually reached agreement that each side could choose whomever it pleased in its delegation: if the ANC wanted to include Slovo, that was its business; if we wanted to include Eugene Terre'Blanche or some other crazy right-winger, they couldn't object. It may not seem much today, but it was a big step then."

A fourth and final secret meeting followed two weeks later at the Noga-Hilton Hotel in Geneva, at which a joint steering committee was set up to make detailed arrangements for the return of the exiles and for the first formal meeting between the government and the ANC on South African soil. Everything was now set for the first phase of the negotiations to begin. But first the ANC members of the steering committee, who still faced possible arrest under South African security laws that had not yet been rescinded, had to be smuggled into the country.

10

The Negotiations Begin

NINE DAYS AFTER De Klerk's speech, on February 11, 1990, Nelson Mandela was released. As billions around the world watched on television, he walked with the stiff gait of an elderly man through the gates of Victor Verster Prison to freedom, with his wife, Winnie, beside him. "Gee, you know, I never expected there would be so many people there," he told me later, as though still astonished that he should have become such a celebrity.

Late that afternoon Mandela addressed a feverishly excited crowd of thousands on Cape Town's Grand Parade, peering uncertainly in fading light at the script of a speech through spectacles that kept slipping from his nose. It was a carefully composed address, not a grand Martin Luther King oration, aimed at countering any lingering suspicions about his talks with the government and any possible attempts by the regime to use his release to sow further dissension or try to split the liberation movement. Methodically he paid tribute to all elements of the movement – "I salute Joe Slovo, one of our greatest patriots" – and pledged his own obedience to its collective decisions. "I am a loyal and disciplined member of the African National Congress. I am therefore in full agreement with all its objectives, strategies, and tactics." In words aimed more at the doubters among the leaders than at the mass audience before him, who knew nothing of what he had been doing in prison, Mandela declared he had "at no time entered into negotiations about the future of our country, except to insist on a meeting between the ANC and the government." Negotiations could not begin immediately. There would first have to be extensive consultations with the people.

These reassurances were necessary. The speed with which De Klerk had acted had thrown the ANC and its supporters off balance and revived earlier doubts in the minds of those who were reluctant to abandon the revolutionary struggle for an uncertain negotiation that might compromise their cherished ideals. In addition, Oliver Tambo's stroke had crippled him just as De Klerk was taking over, and there was no one to pull the amorphous organization's various factions together and provide a coherent response to the rapid changes. When Walter Sisulu and the other prisoners who had been released in October visited Lusaka in January 1990 for their first reunion with the leadership in exile, there were signs of serious discord. I was there at the time and almost every member of the national executive committee that one spoke to had a different response to what was happening – from doves such as Thabo Mbeki to hawks like Chris Hani, chief of staff of the guerrilla force, who seemed thoroughly disconcerted and made a bellicose speech calling for intensified armed struggle.

When I returned to Lusaka with Mandela in March, the mood had stabilized. Doubts about what he had done in prison had dissipated, and there was a coherence in the ranks again. After he addressed the national executive committee, everyone fell into line behind his view of how to deal with Pretoria and spoke glowingly of his political acumen and sense of strategy. Although Tambo was still nominally president, it was clear that the power vacuum caused by his illness had been filled. Even Hani had shifted ground, and in an interview spoke enthusiastically not only of the need for the political leadership to negotiate, but for his military wing to start discussions with the South African Defence Force as well.

It still took nearly two more years for the constitutional negotiations to get under way. First there was a series of preliminary meetings, beginning with a grand première from May 2-4 at Groote Schuur, the gabled mansion at the foot of Table Mountain which Cecil John Rhodes bequeathed in 1902 as the official residence of South Africa's prime ministers. Arrangements for this historic first meeting between the leaders of the ANC and the South African government, begun in Berne and Geneva, were completed in equally clandestine circumstances inside South Africa by a joint steering committee set up at Berne. In order to do its work, the ANC members – Penuell Maduna, head of the ANC's legal department, Jacob Zuma, its intelligence chief, and a man named Gibson Mkanda – had to be smuggled into South Africa. By this time, the ANC itself had been legalized but individual members had not yet been indemnified against prosecution for their violations of the security laws: indeed negotiating an Indemnity Bill was the steering committee's first task. Maduna, Zuma, and Mkanda were therefore still wanted men when the NIS flew them to South Africa on March 21. Louw and Spaarwater met them on the airport apron, whipped them past Customs and Immigration, and took them to an NIS safe house in Pretoria's eastern suburbs. Later they were transferred to a small country inn, the Hertford Hotel, twenty miles north of Johannesburg, where they were joined by two internal members of the liberation movement, Mathews Phosa and Curnick Ndlovu. Government members of the steering committee, including Roelf Meyer, later to become minister of constitutional affairs, met quietly with them there.

The work was fraught with suspicion on both sides. The ANC members feared they were being led into a trap, that once they were all in the country they would be seized and imprisoned; the government feared that the ANC would take advantage of the amnesty arrangements and the suspension of counter-insurgency operations to infiltrate guerrillas into the country for a major revolutionary thrust.

The suspicions were both cause and effect. Three times government members of the working comittee had to report that resistance within the National Party had delayed presenting the Indemnity Bill to Parliament. "The ANC men got very jumpy," one of the government members recalls. As a result the ANC kept a contingency plan in place. Operation Vula, with Mac Maharaj at its head, had expanded into a major underground network that had succeeded even in filching some of the NIS's counter-insurgency files. Now Maharaj called for a review of the operation. Should Vula continue, and if so, how?

After intensive debate the ANC decided to keep Vula in place but change its function. In part this was "an insurance policy", as Ronnie Kasrils called it, in case negotiations failed or a government trap appeared. The decision also reflected Tambo's old concern that the ANC should not allow its venture into negotiations to result in the movement being "stripped of our weapons of struggle." Sanctions, the guerrilla force, and Operation Vula would all remain in place until it was clear that the process was irreversible. As Maharaj puts it, Vula should "defend the gains we had achieved" by maintaining mass mobilization. There should be no easing up, just because the leaders were talking.

So Maharaj, Nyanda, and Kasrils remained underground. When the security police finally uncovered Vula and arrested Maharaj and Nyanda in July 1990, it seemed to confirm the government's worst fears: the police claimed Vula was a communist plot to overthrow the government by force under cover of the negotiations; and Maharaj, Nyanda and seven others were charged with "attempting to overthrow the government by force." The charges were eventually dropped and the prisoners freed.*

Organizing the Groote Schuur meeting in such an atmosphere of tension and mutual suspicion was a nightmare. Rumours and reports reached the government daily either of right-wing plans to disrupt the event or of massive left-wing demonstrations to welcome the revolutionaries home. Either one made for anxiety, and the government planners arranged for two alternative venues in case things went wrong – one at the Ysterplaat Air Force Base near Cape Town, and another aboard a ship in the Simonstown Naval Base.

Temporary indemnities were eventually issued to all the ANC members who would be attending – Joe Slovo included – and they were flown to the Cape, where they were

---

* Mac Maharaj is today minister of transport in Mandela's Government of National Unity, and Ronnie Kasrils is deputy minister of defence. Siphiwe Nyanda (Gebhuza) is general secretary of the National Union of Mineworkers.

accommodated in the Lord Charles Hotel at Somerset West, across False Bay from Cape Town itself. Security arrangements had to be tight, but the ANC members were still profoundly mistrustful of their erstwhile hunters, now supposedly protecting them, so they refused to tell the security guards where they were going when they slipped away to meet members of the internal political organizations. "That meant our people got jumpy," a government organizer recalls, "because here were these guerrillas running around the countryside refusing to reveal where they were going."

In the end the three-day meeting passed off without a hitch. The first substantive agreements were reached in a pact called the Groote Schuur Minute, facilitating the release of political prisoners, the return of exiles, and the amending of security legislation. Pictures were taken of the two delegations, showing a smiling Slovo standing among the men who had hated and hunted him for so long.

Three months later, on August 7, the two sides met again in Pretoria, and after a day-long session Mandela announced the unilateral suspension of the ANC's armed struggle. It was a major concession for which he got little in return, and it stirred the first ripples of concern among ANC radicals who thought he was giving away too much and allowing De Klerk to get into too commanding a position.

FOR MEMBERS OF the newly legalized resistance movements, their return to South Africa was more difficult than any of them had imagined. They had dreamed of it for so long, but now that the moment had arrived it was fraught with complications. Both the ANC and the Pan-Africanist Congress had to transfer their exile headquarters back home and acclimatize themselves to a country they had not seen for decades. Returning exiles, released prisoners, and local activists, many meeting each other for the first time, had to integrate themselves into cohesive political movements and get ready to engage with the government. More difficult still was changing from the culture and habits of mind of an underground revolutionary movement to those of a political organization getting ready to engage in conventional politics.

As the black parties struggled with all this and ended a series of preliminary agreements with the government, De Klerk refined his strategy for a "power sharing" constitution instead of majority rule. He wanted to build an anti-ANC alliance around Chief Mangosuthu Buthelezi's Inkatha movement and other black political organizations that had been established under the apartheid system, and with the coloured and Asian minorities which he assumed would share the whites' fear of black majoritarianism. Of these organizations, Inkatha was the most significant – and, as events were to show, the most problematic. Buthelezi, a Zulu prince who had formed close ties with Tambo and Mandela during his student years, had accepted the position of chief minister of the Zulu tribal homeland, called KwaZulu. He did so with the approval of the ANC leaders who, despite their dislike of the homeland system, hoped Buthelezi would be able to use his position to establish what would in effect be an internal political platform for their outlawed movement. But the relationship soured and Buthelezi turned Inkatha into a Zulu ethno-nationalist party opposed to the ANC. De Klerk now hoped to harness this strong anti-ANC sentiment to his cause. He also wanted to take advantage of the confusion in ANC ranks and allow time for Mandela to be demythologized, to go from being a messianic figure to being just another fallible politician unable to bring instant deliverance to his people. And he wanted international, particularly Western, sympathy to shift from the ANC to his own administration as the world responded to his boldness and shrank from the ANC's commitment to socialism. That would mean sanctions would be lifted, and the ANC, which had based so much of its strategy on winning international support, would be seriously demoralized and weakened.

Gerrit Viljoen, a former Broederbond chairman who was then De Klerk's constitutional affairs minister, spelled out the government's constitutional thinking at a round of four provincial congresses of the National Party during 1990.

There should be a bicameral Parliament, consisting of a House of Representatives of three hundred members elected by universal franchise, and a Senate of one hundred and thirty members – ten from each of ten federal regions or states, plus ten from each of three "background groups" in the population, English, Afrikaners, and Asians (in a major racial concession, the Afrikaans-speaking coloured people were now to be regarded as Afrikaners). What this would mean in practice is that the ten black tribal groups, the English, the Afrikaners and the Asians, would each be represented by ten senators in a racially structured upper house. Bills would have to be passed by both houses, but would require a two-thirds majority in the Senate, meaning that the whites and their allies in the old apartheid parties would easily be able to block any attempt to change South Africa's socio-economic structure.

The executive branch would consist of twenty-six cabinet ministers, half drawn from the regions and "background groups" and half appointed by the president. The president, in turn, would not be a single individual but a rotating chairmanship of what Viljoen called a "collegiate cabinet" that would have to reach decisions by consensus. So the executive, too, would have a veto power over any attempt at socio-economic restructuring. Both Viljoen and De Klerk claimed this concept was drawn from the Swiss constitution, but they failed to note that Switzerland's practice of forming a coalition government of its three main political parties, whose leaders then rotate annually as chairman of the cabinet, is not rooted in that country's constitution but is a voluntary arrangement that the parties agreed to in 1959 and can withdraw from at any time. Voluntary coalitions are one thing, compulsory coalitions quite another.

As if this were not enough, Viljoen also advocated a twenty-six-member Advisory Council, drawn half from the ten regions and three "background groups" in the Senate and half from the popularly elected House of Representatives. This hybrid council would have to decide – by a two-thirds majority – which of the conflicting versions of a bill emerging from the two houses of Parliament should become law.

Again it meant a veto power over the popular will in the House of Representatives.

What this all amounted to was a formula for giving the illusion of popular democracy but denying the substance. South Africa would trumpet that it had a system of one-person, one-vote, but the parliamentary chamber elected under that system would be unable to change anything. The power of "No" would remain in the hands of the old oligarchy.

The apartheid thinkers had come a long way, but they were still not quite free of their ideological mindset. Initially, they had tried to prevent black political participation at the centre. When this proved impossible, they tried to grant it in ways which ensured that the white political representatives still had the final say. Now that they were having to go the whole hog and grant universal franchise, they were still trying to ensure that whites could protect the status quo by vetoing black decisions.

The administration made no bones about its aims. It was not enough to entrench group values, such as language, culture, and religion, said Viloen; group political rights also had to be protected by special structures and procedures. The party had made the important concession that race groups should no longer be defined by law: membership of any race group should be a matter of personal choice, and anyone who did not want to be assigned to one could be regarded for political purposes as part of an amorphous non-group. But those who took their group membership seriously and wanted to stick to their own kind should be free to do so. As Viljoen explained in an interview after one of the congresses: "Those who want to live, worship, work, or play in specifically defined communities should have the right to do so in the new South Africa, but without laws making it compulsory." They should be able to have their own racially exclusive schools, with equal state subsidies, all of which fell under what Viljoen called *volksregte*, or people's rights, people in this sense meaning an ethnic group.

De Klerk himself was even more explicit in rejecting the

principle of majority rule and endorsing group rights. At the
Transvaal congress of the National Party on October 18, 1990,
he spoke of building a new South Africa that would recognize "the reality of the need for people and communities to
remain themselves and be able to preserve the values that
are precious to them – so that the Zulus, the Xhosas, the
Sothos, and the whites can each feel secure in their own
distinctiveness."

The notion that the government was negotiating for black
majority rule was "one of the great untruths" being spread by
the right-wing Conservative Party, De Klerk said. "It is a lie.
The National Party has said repeatedly that we reject it, that it
will lead to the domination of minorities. We stand for power
sharing and not for simple, typical majority rule. We are not
sellouts of anyone. We are going to make it safer for our descendants and for the descendants of all South Africans."

The critical question was, Who would negotiate the new
constitution? De Klerk wanted it to be done by a convention
of all existing political organizations, rather than an elected
constituent assembly as had been done in Namibia. He knew
that his National Party and its allies would be reduced to
minority status in a one-person, one-vote election for a constituent assembly, while the ANC would be likely to win a
big majority, enabling it to write a majority-rule constitution.
Conversely, the ANC objected to the party-convention idea,
on the ground that the existing non-white parties were apartheid puppets with no support. And given the presence of the
old homeland parties at such a convention, it would amount
to little more than the co-opting of the ANC into P.W. Botha's
old idea of a "national forum" of selected black leaders to
discuss the future of the country with the National Party
government. To have legitimacy, the ANC argued, the new
constitution had to be written by authentic representatives of
the people, who could be determined only by an election.

The two diametrically opposed concepts – the one clearly
leading to power sharing, the other equally clearly to
majority rule – seemed irreconcilable. Both sides argued,
with justification, that the procedure advocated by the other

would decide the outcome of the negotiations before they began. All talks until now had been to remove obstacles in the way of negotiations; now the question became whether the negotiations themselves could ever begin if there could be no agreement on how they should take place.

The breakthrough was made, perhaps characteristically, by Mandela. In January 1991, he called for "an all-party congress" to negotiate the route to a constituent assembly. This offered a basis for compromise: first there would be the multiparty convention the National Party was calling for, to negotiate an interim constitution under which one-person, one-vote elections would be held for a constituent assembly such as the one the ANC wanted, which then would negotiate the final constitution for a new South Africa. But this constituent assembly would not have a free hand in drafting the final constitution; the multiparty convention would also have the power to lay down a number of binding principles restraining it – including the requirement of special majorities on certain issues.

The ANC's national executive committee endorsed this compromise on October 22, adding that no more than eighteen months should elapse between the end of the multiparty convention and the election, during which time South Africa should be ruled by an interim Government of National Unity. The logjam was broken, and a preparatory meeting of all the participating parties ensued.

But there were still setbacks. The PAC, which had joined forces with the ANC to form a Patriotic Front just a few days before, withdrew from the preparatory meeting and the convention that followed. It insisted that the convention should be held outside South Africa, and under a neutral chairman, and it rejected the two judges who had been appointed to chair it on the ground that they were functionaries of the state. When the ANC joined with the National Party in overriding this objection, the PAC walked out, accusing its Patriotic Front partner of colluding with the forces of apartheid. But in what was to become a pattern from that moment onwards, once the two major players had agreed, the process went ahead. It was decided that the first phase of the negotiations should take place within a forum to be called the Convention for a Democratic South Africa.

CODESA ASSEMBLED AT an improbable place at an improbable time. The World Trade Centre, a cavernous exhibition hall alongside a highway near Johannesburg airport, is about as far removed as it is possible to imagine from the gracious Pennsylvania State House in Philadelphia where the Founding Fathers of the United States gathered for their constitutional convention in the summer of 1787. But the two major parties had promised that negotiations would begin before the end of 1991, so the meeting was convened hastily and the exhibition hall was available and conveniently located. That also accounted for the time: December 21 and 22, the weekend before Christmas, at the height of the summer holidays, when South African politicians, and most everyone else besides, are usually at the beach or mountain resorts with their minds disengaged from anything more weighty than fishing or golf or organizing a family gathering.

It was almost two years since Mandela had been released, much longer than anyone had anticipated, but the atmosphere was optimistic and the occasion seemed to herald a new beginning. There were two hundred and twenty-eight delegates representing nineteen political parties – the broadest cross-section of the country's leaders ever to meet. One conspicuous absentee, apart from the PAC, was Chief Buthelezi. In a foretaste of fractiousness to come, he had insisted that a single delegation representing what he now called his Inkatha Freedom Party was not enough: he wanted two others, representing his KwaZulu homeland administration and the king of the Zulus, Goodwill Zwelithini, and when the CODESA organizers refused he stayed away in protest, leaving the IFP delegation to be led by its chairman, Frank Mdlalose. Buthelezi, a prickly man quick to take offence, was the only political leader in South Africa never to attend any session of the negotiating conventions, which, as we shall see, had a bearing on some of the major problems which later arose.

The chief justice, Michael Corbett, opened the convention and the two judges presided over it: Petrus Shabort, a white Afrikaner, and Ismail Mohamed, South Africa's first non-white judge, who had distinguished himself as a civil-rights lawyer. This first session was intended to be mainly a ritualistic event, a television spectacular to impress the country and the world, but such were the wounds still suppurating in this riven society that even it erupted in anger.

At the first plenary session, speaker after speaker went ritually to the podium to read prepared speeches, the last being De Klerk. After the usual bland utterances wishing the negotiators well, the president inserted a passage accusing the ANC of failing to honour an agreement to dismantle its guerrilla force, saying this called into question its ability to enter into binding agreements at the convention. Mandela was furious at this attack, and requested time to respond. The government and the ANC had in fact entered into a secret agreement, known as the D.F. Malan Accord, in February 1991, which stipulated that Umkhonto we Sizwe need not be disbanded until the transition to a democratic government was completed, and that in the meantime the regime would not officially regard it as a "private army". It would give the government details of the arms under its control, and these would be placed under the joint control of a transitional authority once an interim government was formed. The public knew nothing of this at the time of De Klerk's accusation, of course, and Mandela felt the president had double-crossed him to take a cheap shot at the ANC in this high-profile forum.

Accusing De Klerk of "abusing his position" by launching the attack after requesting the negotiation organizers to allow him to be the last speaker, Mandela turned on the president with an ice-cold fury that stunned the audience. Speaking in measured tones and referring to De Klerk in the third person without looking at him, though he sat only a few feet away, Mandela declared, "He thought I would not be able to respond. He was completely mistaken. I respond now." Gesturing towards the president but still looking straight ahead, Mandela accused De Klerk of being "less than frank" and of breaking confidence on negotiations between them on the subject of the guerrilla force. "Even the head of an illegitimate, discredited, minority regime, as his is, has certain moral standards to uphold," he said. "If a man can come to a conference of this nature and play the type of politics he has played, very few people would want to deal with such a man."

The normally unflappable De Klerk was visibly rattled. Hyperventilating and struggling for words, he launched into an angry rebuttal of Mandela's accusations, saying it was a vital matter of principle that no party should have a private army. This was a spectacular start to the convention, and set the scene for a crisis-driven negotiating process.

11
A Chain of Crises

DESPITE THEIR COMPROMISE agreement on a two-phase negotiation, the two sides were still divided by fundamental differences. The ANC wanted a short, sharp CODESA that would decide as little as possible about South Africa's new constitution, and leave most of the drafting of it to the elected constituent assembly. The government wanted CODESA to be drawn out as long as possible, putting off the evil day when it would have to relinquish exclusive power, and letting the ANC twist in the wind as its followers became disillusioned at the failure of Mandela's release to bring about a quick improvement in their lives. The government also wanted CODESA to decide as much of the new constitution as possible, leaving little for the elected constituent assembly to do.

So when CODESA reconvened in May after its December launch – the second session was called CODESA 2 – the ANC tried to hurry things along and the government stalled. Trying for maximum agreement without allowing small parties to obstruct progress, the participants had settled on a novel decision-making procedure which they called "sufficient consensus": the convention should seek consensus, but if this proved impossible the chair had to judge whether there was sufficient agreement among the parties to allow negotiations to move ahead. In practice this meant that if the ANC and the government agreed, the issue was considered settled; if not, there would be a deadlock. This proved a useful tool for the government as it sought to slow things down.

A whites-only referendum, which De Klerk called in March 1992 to deal with a challenge from his right wing that he was acting without a mandate, complicated matters further. Blacks were insulted by the poll that once again excluded them on racial grounds, but Mandela urged his supporters not to disrupt the referendum and even called on white ANC supporters to vote yes, showing a sensitivity to De Klerk's constituency problems that the president did not reciprocate. Thus with the help of white liberals traditionally opposed to him, De Klerk won the referendum with a thumping two-thirds majority; then, in a triumphant mood, the National Party toughened its negotiating stance at CODESA. It seemed that the referendum had boosted De Klerk's confidence that he could indeed build a winning anti-ANC alliance, and with international applause indicating that there would be no adverse reaction from abroad, he sensed that now was the time to start playing hardball with his opponents.

The results were disastrous. CODESA had been divided into five working groups to cover different issues; Working Group Two had to deal with the central issues on which a settlement depended, and it was here that the parties had concentrated their most senior negotiators – Cyril Ramaphosa, Mohammed Valli Moosa, and Joe Slovo on the ANC side; Gerrit Viljoen and his deputy minister of constitutional affairs, Tertius Delport, on the government side. Immediately after the referendum the ANC members noticed a hardening of Viljoen and Delport's stance, which raised their ire and increased their suspicions that a trap was being set.

Reporters covering CODESA became aware that, while the other working groups were moving ahead fairly smoothly, Working Group Two was bogged down in wrangling. The issue delaying it was the core one, of course, which the two-phase agreement had papered over but not resolved: when and where the critical decisions would be made between power sharing and majority rule. The government had accepted that an elected constituent assembly would draft a final constitution, but it had extracted a concession from the ANC that CODESA should agree on some binding basic principles. Now the government's aim was to get as many issues as possible accepted as "basic". In effect, it wanted to entrench the essentials of its power-sharing model as a binding principle, so that the constitutional assembly would be powerless to reject it. The ANC would not agree.

A week after the referendum, the government introduced another proposal – that there should be an interim constitution with an interim Parliament serving concurrently as the constitution-making body. The catch here was that it would be bicameral, much the same as in the original government model, with a Senate where the National Party and its homeland allies would have a veto power. The wrangling then focussed on percentages – the size of the majorities that the constitutional assembly would need to adopt particular decisions.

Matters came to a head on May 15. That had been set five months before as the date for CODESA 2, to which the working groups were supposed to submit their reports for endorsement. As the day dawned it became clear that Working Group Two was in trouble: it was still deadlocked over the percentages. The plenary session was delayed until noon to allow the group to try to resolve their differences; then until 2 p.m., then 4 p.m. Finally it was clear that agreement was not going to be reached.

To outsiders the issue of the percentages seemed arcane, but in fact it went to the heart of the problem that five months of negotiating had failed to resolve. The ANC proposed that ordinary clauses in South Africa's new constitution should require a two-thirds majority in the constituent assembly, which, it argued, was the international norm; but the government insisted on an effective 75 per cent majority. Eventually the ANC increased its 66.6 per cent figure to 70 per cent, and to 75 per cent for clauses of a Bill of Fundamental Human Rights that was to be entrenched in the constitution; but the government stuck to its demand for an overall 75 per cent.

Coupled with this was the issue of a deadlock-breaking mechanism. With the percentages required for agreement so high, the ANC feared that the constituent assembly would be deadlocked indefinitely and there would be no final constitution. As its delegates put it at the time, South Africa would have "a permanent interim constitution" – which happened to be the government's power-sharing model. The ANC smelled a trap. So it coupled its 70 per cent concession with a requirement that if the assembly could not agree on a constitution within six months, a popular referendum should be held to decide the issue by a simple majority. To the government, this looked like an ANC trap: all the ANC would have to do was to deadlock the assembly deliberately for six months and then have its majority-rule constitution adopted by the referendum at which the black majority vote would obviously prevail.

So the argument in Working Group Two swung back and forth ever more acrimoniously, while the plenary was delayed and scores of delegates hung around anxiously waiting for a breakthrough that never came. A complicating factor was the absence of Viljoen, the government's chief negotiator, who had withdrawn shortly before this critical day and who announced his retirement from public life soon afterwards. This meant the government team was led by his deputy, Tertius Delport, a hardliner with known ties to "securocrats" in his home region of the Eastern Cape. Delport's junior status made it doubly difficult for him to be flexible: he periodically withdrew from the room to telephone De Klerk for instructions. To make things worse, he had a bad bout of flu and his voice faded to a croak as the wrangling continued; he looked sick and irritable by the end of the day.

By evening Ramaphosa announced the ANC's withdrawal from Working Group Two. It was pointless, he said, to con-tinue in the face of what he called Delport's "total unwillingness to drive this working group towards an agreement." This meant the collapse of CODESA 2: the plenary was summoned to receive a report of failure and then adjourn. It never reconvened. The convention's working committee tried for several months to find a compromise where Working Group Two had failed, but events overtook it.

FRUSTRATION WITH CODESA had built up outside the World Trade Centre as well as within it. The working groups met behind closed doors, and the expectant masses in the black townships grew restive at the lack of information about what was happening in the smoke-filled rooms. The ANC's regional branches felt excluded from a process that seemed closed and secretive. Such news as they gleaned from the newspapers made them suspicious that their leaders were giving away too much; in any event the whole thing had become an elitist exercise that excluded the masses, and was it not the masses who had spearheaded the struggle against apartheid and forced the government to the negotiating table?

Even before the collapse of CODESA 2, groups within the liberation movement had started arguing the case for some kind of "mass action", both to consolidate a support base that was becoming restless and to put pressure on the negotiators. This came most strongly from the trade-union movement, which was part of the ANC alliance. Members of the Congress of South African Trade Unions, or COSATU, believed they had a better understanding of the dynamics of negotiation than the ANC politicians did. To them it was fundamental to shop-floor bargaining that there should be a demonstration of strength outside the negotiating forum to strengthen the hand of the negotiators within. Moreover, with the referendum over, there was no longer any need to avoid the kind of action that might scare whites into voting no.

So the centre of political gravity within the ANC alliance shifted in mid-1992 towards its militant wing. A number of militants, particularly those who had been involved in the guerrilla army, had been lukewarm about negotiations anyway: in a sense they were resentful at having their dream of a revolutionary victory snatched from them. Now they saw a chance at least to get back to the streets, if not to the barricades.

Pressure for a more activist campaign grew as political violence in the black townships increased. Since before Mandela's release there had been clashes in the province of Natal, as ANC supporters and Buthelezi's Inkatha members fought over political turf. Inkatha had long been the dominant movement among the Zulu tribe, which is based in Natal, but with the legalizing of the ANC, young Zulus in particular had flocked to the more glamorous liberation movement and civil war had erupted between the factions. In mid-1990 this regional conflict had leapfrogged into the crowded black townships of the Witwatersrand, the industrial heartland of South Africa, centred on Johannesburg. Here there is no dominant black tribe: it is South Africa's melting pot, a polyglot urban society with no history of ethnic conflict among black groups. Now that changed.

On July 14, 1990, Buthelezi had relaunched Inkatha, until then a self-styled "cultural and liberation movement", as a political party that, he said, would seek to establish a nationwide support base. Eight days later, violence erupted in the Witwatersrand: more than thirty people were killed in fighting between supporters of the new Inkatha Freedom Party and the ANC in Sebokeng, a black township thirty-five miles south of Johannesburg. Sebokeng residents reported seeing busloads of rural Zulus arrive in their township and seize control of migrant workers' hostels, expelling the occupants.

A rash of similar clashes had followed, again accompanied by local reports of Zulus being bussed in and taking over the migrant workers' hostels, then using them as bases from which to launch attacks on residents. This provoked reprisals against the hostels, starting a cycle of violence that raged up and down the urban belt of the Witwatersrand, with sporadic outbursts in more distant townships. In September random attacks in commuter trains began, with armed men rampaging through the cars, stabbing and shooting passengers and hurling them from the moving trains. Then there were attacks on minivan taxis used by blacks, drive-by shootings in township streets, random bombings and machine-gun attacks on bars, night clubs, and private homes.

No arrests followed these terrible outbursts. Again and again there were allegations of the police either standing by and allowing attackers to do their work, or sometimes joining in the attacks. As the death toll mounted, the ANC began accusing the government of conducting a systematic campaign of destabilization. Although conclusive proof was never forthcoming, more and more people in the black community believed that a "third force" within the military-security establishment was instigating and directing the violence to weaken the ANC and prevent it from being able to organize and electioneer effectively.

This is what soured relations between Mandela and De Klerk. Reluctantly at first, but more emphatically later, Mandela turned on the president with accusations of bad faith. While never accusing De Klerk of actively instigating the violence, Mandela blamed him for failing to end it and hinted at a degree of complicity. Privately, he spoke with anger about a man he felt had betrayed his trust. Publicly, he maintained a cordial relationship, recognizing the mutual dependency of black and white South Africans which he saw as essential to the country's future.

All this was part of the reason for the serious disillusionment in the black community when CODESA 2 collapsed, and Mandela could not ignore it. His position, far more than De Klerk's, required him to respond to the mood shifts among his supporters. The ANC had always been more a coalition than a tightly-knit political party, including people of various ideological hues who shared the common goal of liberating their country from apartheid; now it was in an even broader alliance with other organizations which shared that objective. Mandela had to read the mood carefully to hold this diverse body together. Moreover, unlike De Klerk, Mandela had no patronage with which to bolster his leadership position. De Klerk was elected by his parliamentary caucus, and once in office his electors were totally dependent on him for job security and career advancement. Mandela, on the other hand, like all office-holders in the ANC, was elected by the hundred-member national executive committee, which meant he had constantly to ensure his continued support in a body that itself depended on branch-level votes.

Despite his commitment to negotiation, therefore, Mandela had to accede to the demand for more militancy that was now sweeping through the liberation movement. Two weeks after the collapse of CODESA 2, a special ANC strategy conference decided to launch a campaign of "rolling mass action" – a continuous series of strikes, boycotts, and street demonstrations. It appointed a commission to map out the campaign strategy, and significantly chose Ronnie Kasrils, the former chief of intelligence of the guerrilla forces who had been part of Operation Vula and had a reputation for gung-ho adventurism, to head it.

The campaign began on June 16, the anniversary of the 1976 Soweto uprising, observed as a heroes' day by the black community. There were rallies all around the country and a mass stayaway from work that brought the industrial cities to a standstill. This was the factor De Klerk had overlooked before taking that bold step on February 2, 1990. He had imagined then that from his position of power he could control the transition, but South Africa's black population is also its working class, and by unbanning the blacks' political movements De Klerk enabled them to mobilize their mass support and literally paralyze the country. Short of reverting to old-style states of emergency and security crackdowns, which would ruin the image of moderation he had been at such pains to cultivate internationally, there was little the president could do to counter this formidable new prospect. This was the genie he had let out of the bottle.

But before events could go any further in this direction, something else happened that shook South Africa even more profoundly. On the night of June 17, a posse of armed Zulus crept out of a migrant workers' hostel near a township called Boipatong, south of Johannesburg, and in an orgy of slaughter hacked, stabbed, and shot thirty-eight people to death in their homes. Among the dead were a nine-month-old baby, a child of four, and twenty-four women, one of them pregnant. After the massacre, residents refused to give statements to the police because they were convinced the authorities were involved. Some claimed police had escorted the attackers into the township and out again; several told reporters they had seen white men in tracksuits directing the attackers. Tapes from the police central control room that day were tampered with and destroyed, according to British experts who were called in later to help with the investigation. Weapons found in the hostel were never checked for fingerprints and were thrown together into the back of a police truck so that it was impossible to tell later who owned them. The British experts were scathing about the inadequacy of South Africa's own police investigation.

Whatever the truth of the residents' allegations, there was an absolute conviction in the minds of nearly the entire black community that the police were involved in the attack by Inkatha supporters, and that this was part of a government plot to weaken the ANC and its supporters. Posters openly accusing De Klerk of murder appeared at mass rallies. When De Klerk tried to make a conciliatory visit to Boipatong three days later, a crowd turned on him in a chilling display of hostility.

I WAS IN BOIPATONG the day the mob drove De Klerk out. It was a Saturday and I had driven with my wife, Sue, and our eleven-year-old son, Julian, to a ceremony at a school in a nearby black community where Sue worked as an adviser. After the ceremony we decided to stop by Boipatong to check on De Klerk's visit, which had been widely publicized. As we drove into the township we could see pandemonium in the street ahead.

De Klerk had arrived only moments before. As he entered the township a mob swarmed around his silver BMW, yelling abuse and waving posters saying things like, "To Hell with De Klerk and Your Inkatha Murderers", "We Want Police Protection Not Murders", and "De Klerk Kill Apartheid, Not Us." Sitting ashen-faced in the back, De Klerk gestured to his driver to back out. With difficulty the driver did so, easing the big car through the angry crowd as aides and security men ran for their vehicles behind a line of heavily armed police. But that was only the beginning.

Two hours later I watched as the police opened fire on the still seething crowd, and now another twenty bodies lay sprawled and bleeding on an open stretch of dry winter *veld* on the outskirts of Boipatong. At least three were dead.

This is how it happened. As De Klerk drove away, the big police personnel carriers called Casspirs nosed their way out of the township, past a hastily called street-corner meeting where a speaker was thundering accusations against De Klerk and his government. A group of youths dragged a heavy branch across the road, snarling up the last of the Casspirs. As men leaped from the vehicle to drag the branch away, the crowd surged towards them, waving posters and shouting insults. This brought armed men pouring from the other Casspirs and forming a line in front of them. There were clicks as they loaded their pump-action shotguns. Several carried light machine guns. The two sides faced each other in a state of brittle tension for about ten minutes. Then the moment passed. The crowd backed off, turned, and began to drift off down the street back into the township.

It looked as though the crisis was over. But inexplicably the Casspirs started up their motors and began driving back down the road after the retreating crowd. Reporters who were there were aghast at the provocation. "What the hell do they think they're doing?" asked a *New York Times* man incredulously.

My family and I followed on foot, as the crowd, with the Casspirs only a few feet behind, moved slowly down the road, through the township, and out onto an open stretch of ground on the far side that looked like a makeshift soccer pitch. There the crowd began assembling again, and I saw a number of big yellow police paddy wagons parked on the field. The Casspirs joined them, forming a square of armoured vehicles.

The crowd was agitated. A man who said he was a monitor from the township's civic association ran up to me stammering excitedly that a youth had been shot dead. He took me by the arm to lead me through the crowd to where a body lay, but a police sergeant ordered me back, saying I could not look at the body "until the investigation has been completed". When later I was able to slip through the police cordon and see the body, I saw a machete lying beside his clenched left hand in a pose that seemed too precise to be natural.

People in the crowd were accusing the police of shooting the youth, then planting the machete on him to make it look like self-defence. They were trying to reach the boy to take his body away for their own community funeral, and a cordon of about thirty policemen, in camouflage battledress and with their shotguns held across their chests, strained to keep them back. It must be said that the provocation was intense. Furious black men and women yelled abuse in the faces of the young white policemen. I saw one man prod a stick into the face of a policeman, who took a step back and cocked his shotgun. From time to time some daring person would try to push his way through the police cordon, only to be pushed back roughly. Each time this happened an angry buzz would run through the crowd and there would be a surge of pressure at that point. It seemed crazy to me for the police to continue trying to hold the line and keep the crowd from retrieving the body: sooner or later there was bound to be a disaster.

The young white policemen tried to keep a stolid expression, refusing to respond to the taunts as they confronted the crowd, hostile faces literally only inches away, but one could see their muscles twitching and their hands shaking. They were under tremendous strain. As the tension continued to rise, I edged my way to one end of the police column to be sure I was out of the line of fire should any shooting begin.

Sue and Julian were somewhere in the crowd – I hoped at the back, where they might be safe – but it was impossible to get to them through the seething, angry crowd. I was standing alongside the policeman at the end of the police line, less than a yard from the front of the crowd, when I heard a shot ring out from the other end. Instantly the whole line opened fire, pumping their heavy-gauge, twelve-bore buckshot into the crowd at point-blank range. There was no order to shoot, nor was there any warning to the crowd.

I dropped flat to the ground. As I lay there, my head to one side pressed against the stubbly *veld* grass, I could see the policeman beside me, down on one knee, loading and re-loading his pump-action shotgun as he fired round after round into the fleeing people. I saw the face of a man only two or three yards away disintegrate. Beyond, people were falling and rolling in the dust.

Sue and Julian ran for their lives along with the rest. Sue told me later how she had seen bodies falling around her as she fled with the stampeding mob. One man near her was hit in the back and she looked back desperately as he writhed in agony. She ran on, but came back later to drag him to safety behind a parked car. Julian, more fleet of foot, outpaced her and reached a cluster of houses where the local black people gave him refuge indoors.

When the shooting stopped there was an eerie silence. I lifted my head and saw a field of carnage. A pile of bodies lay in a tangle about twenty yards from me. Beyond them were more, strewn haphazardly across the field for about a hundred yards. They lay still for a moment, then some of them moved. I heard groans, and screams from the shocked people who had fled to the houses beyond the field. Cautiously I stood up to get a better view. The police were still in a line, down on one knee in their firing positions. Ten paces away one of them rose to his feet and began yelling in Afrikaans. "Who told you to shoot?" he screamed at the policemen. "I told you not to shoot without orders." He was clearly the officer in charge, and he was in a frenzy of agitation.

I walked among the fallen people counting them and trying to offer what little help I could. The police made no move, either then or later, to go to them or to offer assistance. They stayed in their line, guns at the ready. I counted twenty people lying on that makeshift soccer field. Most had gaping wounds. One, the man whom I had seen hit, had half his face shot away. A young woman press photographer was kneeling next to him, crying as she cradled his shattered head and tried to take his pulse. He groaned and died in her arms. Another man who was hit at longer range also died. With the first boy, whose disputed body was still lying there, forgotten now in the mayhem, that made three dead.

As I moved among the wounded I heard a shot coming from the houses and the angry hiss of a bullet passing nearby. Someone in the township was starting up a retaliatory fire. "Get down!" cried a voice from the police line, and I dived for cover beside four black men who were tending the injured. As we lay there we could hear a police officer about thirty yards away calling instructions to his men as they tried to identify who had opened fire on them. He seemed to spot someone, and the police line opened fire again. As they did so more shots rang out from the opposite side, and I heard the zip zip of bullets above us. The police fired off a volley in that direction, too, then at an order from their officer they ran helter-skelter for their armoured personnel carriers.

"Stay down!" the officer called to us over a bullhorn, and I clung to the ground wondering how I was ever going to get out of this incipient civil war. The trigger-happy police were on one side, and my white skin gave me the wrong kind of identification to the other. But my black companions who had hit the dirt beside me proved wonderfully accommodating. After a while, when the shooting seemed to have stopped, we rose cautiously, lifted up one of the wounded men who had been groaning beside us, and together carried him across the open field to a car.

The police were still huddled in their Casspirs. A spotter helicopter in the yellow-and-blue police colours hovered overhead, apparently searching for the snipers. It landed in a cloud of dust nearby, then took off again. I linked up with Sue and Julian; all around us were township residents in a state of shock and almost inexpressible anger. An old man came up to us shaking with distress. "Do they have the right to shoot our people like that?" he demanded. "Do they have the right?"

Others began showing signs of belligerence towards us, and I realized it was time to leave. But how? I had left my car on the far side of Boipatong and for a white family to walk through this traumatized black township seemed unwise. Just then a Nigerian journalist, Dele Olojede, whom I had met a few days before, pulled up in a car. "Do you want a lift?" he asked. His dark skin seemed the most beautiful thing I had ever seen. Gratefully, we climbed in. Olojede was shaking with shock. "I have never been so scared in all my life," he confessed, making me realize that every skin-uniform is a perilous thing in this racially obsessed country.

As we drove back to Johannesburg, our route took us past Sebokeng, the biggest of the black townships in this industrial complex known as the Vaal Triangle. I could see Casspirs, with men holding guns at the ready, speed along one of the rim roads. Heavy boulders formed barricades across the township streets, and black smoke rose from burning tyres. There was trouble there, too. Indeed, with the constitutional negotiations deadlocked, it looked as though all South Africa was in trouble.

Two days later the shock wave of black anger hit Mandela full in the face. While he was addressing a rally in Evaton township, near Boipatong, angry voices yelled at him: "You are like lambs while the government is killing us." It was clear that the ANC had to respond to this anger. Soon afterwards Mandela announced the ANC's formal withdrawal from negotiations, listing fourteen demands the government would have to meet before talks could resume – the critical ones being an end to "the regime's campaign of terror" against ANC supporters, and the implementation of earlier agreements to secure the migrant workers' hostels, which were seen as Inkatha fortresses, and to halt the carrying of so-called "cultural weapons" by Inkatha members. These weapons were the clubs, spears, and machetes that Inkatha members claimed they had a traditional right to bear and which had been used in the township butchery.

Not surprisingly, in the heated atmosphere of the conflict the government rejected these demands, and for three months the two sides waged what Cyril Ramaphosa described as "a war of memoranda", as they exchanged letters and documents heaping blame on each other for the collapse of the talks. The verbal jousting might have continued indefinitely were it not for another crisis that shook the country, and the contestants, even more profoundly.

THE OUTRAGE OF BOIPATONG, coming on top of the collapse of CODESA, further strengthened the militant wing of the ANC, who had been accusing the negotiators of giving away too much and wanted the government to be put under maximum pressure. Just as the referendum had caused the government to toughen its stance, now the balance of influence in the ANC swung sharply to the radicals. Encouraged by the popular response to the mass-action campaign, and still feeling cheated out of their revolution, some of the radicals began talking of a "Leipzig option" – a reference to the mass demonstrations in the streets of Leipzig and other cities that had toppled Erich Honecker's East German regime three years before.

One of the ANC's main sources of grievance was that it was unable to hold meetings and organize branches in the self-governing homelands, where De Klerk was busily building his anti-ANC alliance. The local potentates simply prohibited such activity. On August 23 the ANC leaders accepted a discussion paper drafted by a group of radicals which suggested that the governments of three particularly obstructive homelands – Ciskei, Bophuthatswana and Kwa-Zulu – be targeted for mass action.

Over the next few weeks Ciskei emerged as the prime target. The ANC's inability to hold meetings and organize branches there was especially galling, since Ciskei lay in the heart of its stronghold area, the Eastern Cape. Opinion polls showed that support for the territory's military ruler, Oupa Gqozo, was negligible, but with the backing of a white-officered army and police force, he ruled with a rod of iron and kept the ANC immobilized and unable to prepare for elections. On September 3, the ANC sent a memorandum to De Klerk demanding that Gqozo be removed as ruler of

Ciskei and replaced by an interim administration that would permit free political activity in the area. De Klerk refused, on the legalistic ground that Ciskei was considered an independent territory under South African law.

While a flurry of further memos shuttled between Mandela and De Klerk, the "Leipzig school" built up its case for launching a campaign to oust Gqozo. If it succeeded, they believed, it would have a domino effect on the other two territories. The "Leipzig option" might not work against Pretoria itself, but perhaps it could against the satellites. In any event, the ANC moderates had to agree that these territories should be opened up for free political campaigning.

Members of the radical group travelled to Ciskei and pronounced it ripe for a popular insurrection; they were sure that Gqozo's unpopularity was such that the Ciskei army and civil service would switch allegiance rather than crush a "people's revolt." Ronnie Kasrils, one of the most enthusiastic advocates of the "Leipzig option", told a reporter, "I have just spent a week in Ciskei and I have never encountered such hatred for a despot."

The plan was to stage a march on Ciskei's capital, Bisho, just outside the city of King William's Town, which lay technically in "white" South Africa, and occupy it with a "people's assembly" until Gqozo agreed to resign. When Gqozo issued a warning that he would meet any attempt to march on his capital with force, the planners ignored him, confident that his soldiers would not fire on the marchers.

The march was set for September 7, a Monday. Esther Waugh, a political reporter of *The Star*, Johannesburg's leading daily newspaper, had spent the previous weekend touring villages in Ciskei, and she reported that there was a wave of enthusiasm for the demonstration. "The hills rang with the chant of *Phantsi Gqozo* – Down with Gqozo," she wrote. "It was clear that the activists were ploughing fertile ground."*

On Sunday night Gqozo sought an urgent court order prohibiting the march. (The ANC announced that since it did

---

* *Saturday Star*, September 12, 1992.

not recognize Ciskei's independence, which had been granted under the apartheid system, it would not recognize any ruling from its courts.) That evening a bizarre court hearing took place in the dining-room of magistrate D.B. Tali's home, while reporters waited for the outcome in his sitting-room. At 1.50 a.m., the nervous magistrate delivered a compromise ruling, granting permission for the march to take place but ordering that it should not go beyond the homeland's independence stadium some one and a half miles outside the capital, on the very edge of the unmarked border between "white" South Africa and "black" Ciskei. That meant the marchers could not enter Bisho itself, as they had planned.

But Kasrils had other ideas. He had reconnoitred the area and spotted a gap in the stadium fence. It would be a simple matter, he thought, to lead the marchers into the stadium, then dash through the gap, across a highway, and into the capital. Kasrils managed to get the ANC leadership to approve his scheme, but they had not reckoned on the heedless violence of Gqozo's ill-trained troops.

September 7 dawned clear and hot. A huge crowd gathered on King William's Town's Victoria cricket ground. There was a carnival atmosphere as they sang, danced, and chanted the ANC's freedom slogans. But at the same time hundreds of soldiers of the Ciskei Defence Force, with their white officers seconded from South Africa's Military Intelligence, were taking up positions around the stadium and near the highway between the two towns. They set up a razor-wire barrier across the highway at the unmarked border point.

A crowd of about eighty thousand people set out from the cricket ground, singing and chanting as they marched along the highway, up a steep rise towards the stadium. Esther Waugh, standing near the entrance to the stadium, described the scene:

> The mood on the other side of the border was very different. There was no carnival. Soldiers lay in position, most of them behind tripods on which were balanced menacing light machine-guns.

Ronnie Kasrils appeared, ahead of the march, and fingered the razor-wire barrier. It would be easy to cross, he joked. The ANC would be marching into Bisho.

The heat was stifling as we waited for the last march- ers to bring up the rear. Flippantly, I pointed to a small heap of hard sand on my left and said to a colleague that I would take cover there in the event of shooting. He laughingly pointed out a better hiding place.

By then the march had reached the border . . . At that moment the deadly crackle of automatic gunfire burst out behind me, at the far side of the stadium. Still uncom-prehending, I turned and saw people running in a dusty blur. I stood frozen at the fence for a moment, quite still. Then more soldiers opened up. They were 50 metres from where we stood. I fell on to the road heavily. At first I thought the soliders were firing blanks . . . then I became aware of others falling, running, and I saw bullets thud-ding into the dirt. I crawled to the heap of sand I'd seen before. I wanted to tell people to stop running, that they'd be shot if they didn't, but I made no sound. There was no other sound, no screaming, just the long death-rattle of the rifles.*

What had happened is that Kasrils had moved into the stadium at the head of the main body of marchers, then sprinted for the gap with part of the crowd following him. His aim was to lead them across an open field, moving to one side to outflank the line of Ciskei soldiers lying in position immediately ahead of them, then to swing back again, cross the highway, and enter Bisho a mile and a half away. "By not charging in their [the soldiers'] direction," Kasrils wrote later, "by giving them a wide berth, we would avoid con-frontation."

It was a grievous miscalculation. "One moment I was running, my comrades with me," wrote Kasrils. "The next instant, without warning, the soldiers opened fire." Kasrils

---

* Ibid.

hit the ground, but the bullets cut into the crowd running behind him. His bodyguard, Petros Vantyu, was among those hit. "As I began to crawl towards him, the gunfire broke out again, as angry and prolonged as before, and I froze where I lay. The sinister whirr of projectiles overhead, followed by four dull thuds, made me realize with horror that they were firing grenades as well."*

An official investigation revealed that the first fusillade had lasted a minute and a half, the second a minute. More than four hundred and twenty-five rounds were fired. Kasrils and the other ANC leaders survived, but twenty-eight marchers were killed and more than two hundred wounded. It was another outrage, but this time not only the regime was held blameworthy. Even before an official commission of inquiry censured both the soldiers for firing without justification and Kasrils for behaving recklessly, the incident discredited the radicals in the ANC, and the balance of influence in the movement swung back the other way.

A week after the massacre, Mandela gave an interview to *The Star* in which he held out an olive branch to De Klerk. Saying he was concerned at the steep decline of the South African economy since the breakdown of the talks, he compressed the ANC's fourteen preconditions for resuming talks to three – the release of two hundred disputed political prisoners, the effective securing of eighteen migrant workers' hostels in the Witwatersrand area that had been identified by a United Nations mission as focal point of violence, and a ban on the carrying of "cultural weapons". "If Mr. de Klerk can just say to me, 'You have expressed your three concerns, I give you my undertaking that I will address them,'" Mandela said, "then I will be able to go back to my people and say, 'Look, he has met us. Let us meet him.'"

Two days later De Klerk issued a public invitation to Mandela to join him at a summit meeting to find a way of ending the spiral of violence. Mandela responded positively.

---

* Ronnie Kasrils, *Armed and Dangerous: My Undercover Struggle Against Apartheid* (1993), p. 354.

Once again, South Africa's black and white leaders had had to stare into the abyss in order to recognize their mutual dependency. If the violence went out of control, both would be losers. As Frederik van Zyl Slabbert, the former white opposition leader, put it, they were like two squabbling drunks: they could threaten one another with much shouting and finger-wagging, but neither could land a knock-out blow and, in the end, they had to lean on one another to stay upright.

12
Behind the
Violence

W AS PRESIDENT DE KLERK involved in the violence? Most black South Africans are convinced that he was. Why, they asked at the time, was a regime that had been so successful in tracking down undergroud elements during the years of the black resistance suddenly so incapable of arresting anyone in connection with such widespread and ongoing violence? They also found it hard to believe that such an extensive and sophisticated campaign could be conducted by officials alone without the political leadership knowing anything about it. At what level there might have been such knowledge, however, is still unclear.

In June 1991, a former Military Intelligence officer, Capt. Nico Basson, made a series of startling claims that he had been part of a dirty-tricks campaign against the South West African People's Organization (SWAPO) during Namibia's 1989 independence election, which, he said, was a dress rehearsal for a similar campaign to defeat the ANC in South Africa. Captain Basson, who said he had undergone a change of heart and now wanted to expose Pretoria's trickery, claimed that the campaign, run by Military Intelligence, was called Operation Agree. Its purpose was to destabilize SWAPO with violence and disinformation while the Pretoria government secretly aided a coalition of ethnic parties called the Democratic Turnhalle Alliance (DTA).

According to Basson, the campaign was headed by Gen. Kat Liebenberg, chief of the South African army then, who had just been promoted to chief of the Defence Force at the time he made his allegations. The captain suggested the promotion was to enable Liebenberg to head a similar operation in South Africa. "When Operation Agree began," Basson said, " General Liebenberg told us our objective was to prevent SWAPO from winning a two-thirds majority in the election [the margin needed to have a free hand in writing the national constitution]. He said we should assume its lead at that time was 70 per cent. By the time the election was held, SWAPO won with only 55 per cent."

The campaign planners were delighted, according to Basson. He claimed a senior government delegation flew to Namibia after the election to study the results, and reported back to De Klerk's *bosberaad* at D'Nyala in December 1989. "They decided that if they could run a bigger, better operation in South Africa they could defeat the ANC, where the DTA had only come close," Basson said.

None of the people I spoke to who had been at the *bosberaad* could confirm this, however. Roelf Meyer and Leon Wessels could not recall the Namibian election campaign being discussed at all. Basson promised that other military officers would come forward to corroborate his allegations, but none did. His allegations must therefore be considered unsubstantiated.

They gained some credence a month later, however, when a Johannesburg newspaper, the *Weekly Mail*, disclosed that the South African security police had secretly funded the Inkatha Freedom Party to help it organize rallies and other activities to counter the ANC shortly after Mandela's release from prison, and to help Buthelezi found a new labour movement, the United Workers Union of South Africa (UWUSA), to rival the pro-ANC COSATU. At a press conference called to deal with a public outcry over this "Inkathagate scandal", De Klerk revealed that the South African government had also helped the DTA with secret funding during the Namibian elections in 1989.

When I questioned De Klerk at the July 30 press conference, he denied that he had known anything about the payments to Inkatha and UWUSA which had been made out of a security police slush fund. "I was not aware until it was disclosed [by the newspaper], and the procedures prevalent did not require me to know," he said. Yet in a speech that evening he made a statement which showed this could not be true. "I remind you," he said, "of my speech in Parliament on March 1, 1990, when I disclosed information about an investigation of secret projects which I had instituted in November 1989. As a result of it, numerous secret projects were cancelled. UWUSA is an example. . ." So, by his own account, he knew of the UWUSA part of the scandal. And since he instituted the investigation in November 1989, it must have included a report of the first payment made to Inkatha on November 5, 1989 – unless his own police commanders kept the information from him and from his investigators.

De Klerk's reply about the Namibian payments was equally unsatisfactory. I asked whether, as president or acting president, he had been aware that his government was secretly funding an anti-SWAPO party, in violation of an international agreement it had entered into not to interfere in the Namibian election. He fudged the answer by focussing on when the agreement was signed, not when the election was held, ducking the question of his responsibility for what happened while he was head of state. He then added: "In international ethics there is nothing wrong with governments, if they support the principles of a party and if they think it is in the best interests of their own country, to support financially parties outside their borders." He ignored the core issue of violating an international agreement. "Tricky Frickie", a Johannesburg newspaper later called him, for De Klerk periodically revealed sleights of hand which caused more and more people to suspect that a hidden agenda lay behind his public image of Mr. Integrity.

Five months later the *Weekly Mail* revealed that the police had again secretly funded Inkatha in January that year – contradicting an assurance by De Klerk that all funding to Buthelezi's party had been stopped by March 1990.

De Klerk's repeated denials that elements of his security forces were involved in what the media began suggesting was a shadowy "third force" behind the intensifying violence became less and less convincing. There is no evidence that De Klerk himself knew at the time about the criminal activities that have since been revealed within his security forces, but the fact is that he failed to take action to weed out these elements when it was clear to people all over the country what was happening. Even some members of his own cabinet were no longer in doubt. Leon Wessels, a key National Party negotiator and always the frankest of the ministers, told me he was satisfied, from what he had himself witnessed, that there had been police complicity in at least two massacres in areas he had visited. But De Klerk remained heedless of all appeals to act.

As early as December 1990, Mandela had expressed his concern about just this problem. "I still regard De Klerk as a man of integrity, and I think he feels the same about me," he told me in an interview. "We have developed enormous respect for each other. I can call him at any time, I can get him out of bed or out of cabinet meetings. I believe he, and perhaps the majority of his cabinet, are still as committed to the peace process as we are. But he has problems with elements inside his government – especially his security establishment, which is riddled with right-wingers who are not with him at all – and he is not being frank with me about that."

Not only was he not frank, but at times he seemed to be deliberately trying to protect the culprits. When in January 1990, he had appointed a judge, Louis Harms, to investigate disclosures of widespread death-squad and dirty-tricks activities, De Klerk set such limits to the commission's terms of reference that a thorough probe was impossible. He barred the commission from investigating operations in neighbouring countries and left the way open for senior officers to refuse to testify and for vital documents to be shredded before Harms could see them. De Klerk then hailed the inconclusive results as an exoneration of his security forces and said he hoped this would put an end to "witch-hunts on individuals".

It did not, of course. Press investigations continued, eventually compelling De Klerk to appoint a more effective commission under another judge, Richard Goldstone. Even then, when Goldstone raided the secret headquarters of a renegade element of Military Intelligence and seized documents showing them to be carrying out clandestine anti-ANC operations, De Klerk fired or suspended twenty-three senior officers but not the head of Military Intelligence, Gen. Joffel van der Westhuizen – and the suspended officers retired with full pensions.

Yet it is difficult to believe that De Klerk himself had a hand in these shabby activities. Certainly, he had a political interest in weakening the ANC as his main adversary in South Africa's first democratic election, but he did not have any in either destabilizing the negotiating process or the country itself. His entire reputation and future depended on the success of the process he had started.

How, then, does one explain De Klerk's half-hearted attempts to clamp down on the renegade elements in his security forces? The most likely explanation is that De Klerk, never sure of the extent of his control over Botha's old securocrat establishment, did not want to put it to the test. As the pithy Frederik van Zyl Slabbert puts it: "What do you do if you confront your top generals and say, 'You're fired,' and they reply, 'No we're not'?" In Lyndon Johnson's phrase, De Klerk tried to keep the securocrats inside the tent pissing out, rather than outside the tent pissing in.

But if De Klerk was reluctant to act against the renegades, did he know what they were doing? Again we can only conjecture. An official who was closely involved in investigating the violence says: "He was like someone whose spouse is having an affair – everyone else knows about it and he is the last to find out because he doesn't want to know."

The evidence is now overwhelming that there was indeed a third force, consisting of elements of Inkatha, the police force, and Military Intelligence. Thabo Mbeki believes its aim was to sponsor sufficient chaos to justify the armed forces taking over the country to restore order – and halt the transition to democracy. My own belief is close to this. I believe a military-security underworld was established during the Botha years to destabilize the frontline states bordering South Africa and to discourage them from allowing their territories to be used as springboards for anti-apartheid guerrilla attacks against the South African regime, and that this underworld, structured on a need-to-know basis, took on a life of its own. It was able to operate independently and pursue its own agenda. During the De Klerk years that agenda was to derail the transition. Instead, it alarmed the fractious negotiators into reaching agreement.

To COMBAT THE liberation movements, President Botha had established an elaborate National Security Management System, directed by the State Security Council with himself as chairman. This super-cabinet had the power to intervene at every level of South Africa's civil administration. It was also the brain centre of a security network whose nerve ends reached into some five hundred regional, district, and local Joint Management Centres. From the standpoint of this militarized structure, white South Africa was engaged in a total war for national survival against the forces of communism, spearheaded by the ANC. The securocrats of the NSMS were granted almost limitless power to do whatever they considered necessary to neutralize these "enemies of the state". Any behaviour was considered legitimate in such a survivalist struggle.

In the culture of the "total onslaught", as it was perceived by the military-security establishment, South Africa was facing a multidimensional assault on the diplomatic, economic, propaganda, social, spiritual, and military fronts. Consequently, the enemies of the state had to be countered wherever they were, at home or abroad, with a "total strategy" that operated on all these fronts. That meant, in the first instance, keeping the enemy at a distance: a massive campaign was mounted to destabilize the black neighbouring states so as to keep them weak and dissuade them from giving sanctuary to the liberation movements. Commando raids were launched against ANC targets in these countries, hit squads crossed borders to abduct or assassinate ANC operatives, and rebel organizations were used as surrogates to keep the neighbouring countries in a state of degenerative instability.

When Ian Smith's white minority regime collapsed in Rhodesia and the country became independent Zimbabwe under black-majority rule in 1980, the South African Defence Force took over control of the Mozambican rebel movement, RENAMO, from the Rhodesian Central Intelligence Organization.* South Africa continued to supply and support RENAMO as it laid waste to Mozambique, long after Botha signed a mutual non-aggression pact with that country in March 1984. Jonas Savimbi's UNITA rebel movement against the government of Angola was another foreign surrogate. Support for UNITA began in 1976, though it was formally acknowledged only ten years later when this was made easy by the fact that the United States was then also supporting Savimbi. Raids were launched into Lesotho, Botswana, Swaziland, and Zimbabwe. In January 1986 South Africa clamped a border blockade on tiny Lesotho to topple the government of Prime Minister Leabua Jonathan because it continued to allow black refugees to pass through its territory, and brought in a surrogate military ruler, Maj. Gen. Metsing Lekhanya. A Commonwealth report published in 1989 estimated that South Africa's destabilization operations inflicted a death toll of 1.5 million on its neighbours and cost them $45 billion.**

As the 1984-87 uprising developed, the NSMS launched a parallel campaign against the government's internal political opponents. Again it was a multidimensional attack in line with the "total onslaught" theory. A campaign of formal repression, enforced under the umbrella of two states of emergency, was backed up by a campaign of informal repression, using many of the techniques and instruments that had been

---

* See Ken Flower, *Serving Secretly: An Intelligence Chief on Record* (1987), p. 262.

** Phyllis Johnson and David Martin, *Apartheid Terrorism: A Report on the Devastation of the Frontline States Prepared for the Commonwealth Committee of Foreign Ministers on Southern Africa* (1989), p. 161.

employed against the neighbouring states – only this time to destabilize the United Democratic Front and its component organizations that were opposing the apartheid structures which the regime was trying to put in place.

James Selfe, a researcher for the liberal Democratic Party, who has made a major study of this informal repression, describes some of its methods. There was extensive use of infiltration, disinformation, and *agents provocateurs*, he says. And again there were surrogates to do the dirty work. These were often "vigilante" groups – African traditionalists and other collaborators who had been included in the apartheid structures and had a vested interest in defending them against the young "comrades" who were spearheading the uprising. "The activities of the surrogate had to be deniable," Selfe explains, by which he meant the government had to keep enough of a distance from them so that it could convincingly deny any collusion with them. "In practice, a third feature was present – genuine ignorance of the exact day-to-day actions in the campaign of destabilization the further up the system one went. For want of better words this might be described as 'the need not to know'." This also explains why it has been so difficult to obtain conclusive evidence of the third force. As Selfe says: "Because of the secrecy and cut-outs required to promote deniability, it is probable that no single decision-maker in the NSMS knew the full extent of operations performed in its name, or in terms of its mandate."*

Gradually, however, a combination of investigative reporting, confessions by insiders, Goldstone's commission of inquiry into political violence, and various court hearings produced a partial picture of the covert operations. They involved operatives from Military Intelligence, the SADF's Special Forces, a clandestine unit of the security police, and a motley collection of veterans from southern Africa's various colonial and civil wars – Selous Scouts from Rhodesia,

---

* James Selfe, "The State Security Apparatus: Implications for Covert Operations", contained in *The Hidden Hand: Covert Operations in South Africa*, Eds. Anthony Minnaar, Ian Liebenberg and Charl Schutte (1994), pp. 109-10.

elements of RENAMO from Mozambique, remnants of South Africa's allies in Angola formed into units called Koevoet (meaning crowbar) and 32 Battalion, and former mercenaries from the Congo wars of the 1960s. All these "dogs of war" found their way into South Africa's Rambo units, together with captured ANC guerrillas who had been "turned" by their interrogators and were now called *askaris*, an East African name for a black policeman.

Early in the 1980s a special covert unit of the SADF's Special Forces had been formed under the code name D40. It underwent several name changes, to Barnacle, then 3 Reconnaissance Regiment, and finally the Civil Co-operation Bureau. The CCB's trick was to masquerade as a private company, giving a new twist to the concept of privatization. Its commander was known as "the chairman", its chief officer as the "managing director", and the government was referred to as the "controlling trust". It formed front companies whose task was to disrupt "enemies of the state" – the liberation movements – by means of "continuous offensive actions".

Operating under this civilian cover, CCB agents had assassinated, harassed, and intimidated opponents of apartheid both inside and outside South Africa. They planted car bombs, slashed tyres, severed brake cables, poisoned clothes, and on one occasion tried to kill a leading civil-rights lawyer, Dullah Omar, who is now minister of justice in the Government of National Unity, by substituting other pills for his heart medicine so as to induce a heart attack. By the end of 1989, a commission of inquiry was later told, the CCB had undertaken more than two hundred projects. After the disclosure of its activities, it was formally dissolved in July 1990.

Another limb of the covert network had been revealed on the night of October 19, 1989, when a black hit-squad member, Butana Almond Nofomela, who was awaiting execution in the morning for the murder of a white farmer that was unrelated to his hit-squad activities, sent for his lawyer. Senior police officers had promised Nofomela that they would save his life if he kept silent about his hit-squad activities, but when the last day passed and they had done nothing, Nofomela realized they were going to let the gallows silence him. When his lawyer arrived, he made a sworn affidavit giving details of his involvement in eight political assassinations. Nofomela was granted a stay of execution so that his allegations could be investigated.* When his former commanding officer, Capt. Dirk Coetzee, heard that Nofomela had talked, he decided the only way to save himself was to make a full confession of his own involvement. He contacted a small, independent Afrikaans-language newspaper, *Vrye Weekblad*, which had built a reputation for courageous investigative reporting, and offered to tell them everything.

What followed was the most comprehensive disclosure of South Africa's death-squad activities yet to emerge. To save Coetzee from being murdered to silence him, *Vrye Weekblad* flew him first to Mauritius, then to London, where he gave their reporter, Jacques Pauw, a mass of detail not only about his own involvement in twenty-three serious crimes, including six murders, but about the special counter-insurgency unit he had commanded for nine years.**

The special unit, Section C1, had been based at a secluded police farm called Vlakplaas, west of Pretoria. Coetzee had been seconded from the Security Branch of the South African police to take command of the unit in August 1980. His task was to train a group of *askaris*, the so-called rehabilitated terrorists, and former RENAMO fighters into a hit squad. These he led on a number of operations both inside South Africa and in the neighbouring states. Coetzee gave chilling details of the assassinations his squad carried out, the most gruesome being the murder of a civil-rights lawyer, Griffiths Mxenge, whom they stabbed to death on a sports field in Durban on the night of November 19, 1981.

Coetzee's disclosures, together with those about the CCB,

---

* Together with seventy-seven others on death row, Almond Nofomela's sentence was commuted to life imprisonment by the new South African government on September 24, 1994.
** See Jacques Pauw, *In the Heart of the Whore: The Story of Apartheid's Death Squads* (1991), for a detailed account of Dirk Coetzee's disclosures.

led to the Vlakplaas unit also being formally disbanded in July 1990. But as we shall see, the dissolution turned out to be more theoretical than real. The hit squads had acquired a life of their own.

NATAL HAS ALWAYS been South Africa's most violent province. From the days of the Zulu kings Shaka and Dingaan, the clashes with the Voortrekker pioneers and the imposition of British colonial rule, its history has been one of blood and heroism. More recently it has been plagued by endemic fighting between clans and family groupings. But the violence that began in the 1980s was of a different order, reaching a level of destructiveness that exceeded even the worst years of warfare. The Western media, always too ready to accept simplistic explanations out of Africa, swallowed and regurgitated the government propaganda line that this "black-on-black" violence was just another African tribal conflict between Zulus and Xhosas whom, it claimed, had traditionally been at one another's throats – the implication being that South Africa needed continued white rule to prevent its black population from self-destructing.

All of this was nonsense. Not only do the Zulus and Xhosas have no history of conflict, but the black population of Natal is homogeneous, consisting almost entirely of the 7-million-strong Zulu tribe. What was happening in Natal was in fact a Zulu civil war – and it was overtly political, with considerable involvement of South Africa's security forces.

The feud between Inkatha and the ANC had grown steadily worse after Mandela's release. During his early years as chief minister of KwaZulu, through the 1960s, Chief Buthelezi had seemed willing to act as an internal voice of the silenced ANC, as his old friend Oliver Tambo had asked him to do; sometimes he even alluded to Inkatha as "the internal wing of the ANC", and the exiled body as "the external wing". The souring of the relationship started in the mid-1970s, when young blacks began denouncing Buthelezi as a "collaborator" and the ANC leaders failed to halt these insults. Buthelezi, deeply embittered, turned against them and began exploiting the pride of the Zulu people in their famous tribe's military history in an effort to build Inkatha into a rival political movement equal in status to the ANC.

For two decades Inkatha was unchallenged in its dominance of black politics in Natal. But with the formation of the United Democratic Front in 1983, that had changed. Young blacks in particular identified with the more progressive movement, while Inkatha found its main support among tribal traditionalists in rural areas. With millions flocking to South Africa's overcrowded cities in search of work, clashes erupted between the younger UDF supporters and the older vigilantes who identified with Inkatha – clashes exacerbated by the competition for living space and jobs.

The conflict had peaked in 1987. The UDF made spectacular gains that year, particularly in the Natal Midlands area, around the provincial capital of Pietermaritzburg, and Inkatha began to fear that its claim to represent the Zulu nation was threatened. Its aggressive recruitment drives led to charges of intimidation, and communities began organizing themselves into defence committees to resist its recruiters. The Inkatha vigilantes retaliated – and the turf war spread like a bushfire. "The cycle of attack, revenge, retaliation and retribution became embedded in the social fabric of the region," says Anthony Minnaar, head of the Centre for Conflict Analysis at Pretoria's Human Sciences Research Council."*

It would be wrong to give the impression that Inkatha alone was responsible for the violence, or that it was the only political organization that used hit squads to eliminate its opponents. Activists of the UDF, and after 1990 the ANC, did likewise, both in Natal and in the townships of the Witwatersrand. Indeed, ANC militants in Natal did not disguise their willingness to meet violence with violence. "How can you negotiate with a man who has a sword if you have no sword

---

* Anthony Minnaar, "Patterns of Violence: An Overview of Conflict in Natal during the 1980s and 1990s", contained in *Patterns of Violence: Case Studies of Conflict in Natal*, Ed. Anthony Minnaar (1992), pp. 10-13.

yourself?" said the ANC's Midlands leader, Harry Gwala, in early 1990. Gwala, an unrehabilitated Stalinist and unrepentant militant, was deeply embroiled in the violence in his region, and in July 1994 the Communist Party suspended his membership following allegations that he had been involved in hit squads. But the critical difference was that the UDF and ANC activists did not operate with the collusion and encouragement of elements of the state's armed forces. Their "self-defence units" were usually ragtag groups of untrained and often undisciplined youths, not part of an organized attempt, backed by sinister government forces, to stop history in its tracks and halt South Africa's transition to democracy.

Heavy police reinforcements had been moved into the Natal Midlands in 1987, and in November, Brig. Jac Buchner was appointed head of the police security branch in that area. Buchner was later seconded to head the KwaZulu police force under Buthelezi, who was the homeland's minister of police as well as chief minister. Police officers held key positions in the local Joint Management Centres, the nerve ends of the vast National Security Management System, and again and again there were reports of partisan police involvement in the violence – of police standing by while armed Inkatha men attacked a UDF community, of police escorting the attackers home again, and of police ensuring that there was no effective investigation of the massacre. Father Tim Smith, a Roman Catholic priest at a mission station there, recalls an incident he witnessed on New Year's Day, 1988, when he personally called in the riot police to prevent a mob of Inkatha supporters from attacking a UDF settlement after a rally. "They did not," he says. "Instead they assisted the attackers in searching the UDF area, after which a young boy, Makhithiza Ndlovu, was arrested and handed over to Inkatha for the night. His blood-stained body was found next to the road the following day. The murderers have never been brought to trial."*

Of the scores of cases reported, none epitomized what was

---

* *Weekly Mail*, May 15-21, 1992.

happening more vividly than a massacre in a small rural settlement called Trust Feed, twenty miles northwest of Pietermaritzburg, on the night of December 3, 1988. As one researcher puts it, the incident "illustrates the covert collusion between Inkatha and the South African Police, a partnership which extends far beyond the boundaries of Trust Feed."*

The little community lived on land bought by black farmers at the turn of the century; under the rules of apartheid the land was now regarded as a "black spot" in white territory and so its occupants were subject to forced removal. A local activist, Phillip Shenge, formed an organization to fight the removal, which he called the Trust Feed Crisis Committee (TCC). The TCC won its battle to stop the removal but soon ran into trouble from another quarter. Trust Feed was predominantly an Inkatha area, and the local Inkatha leader, Jerome Gabela, wanted it incorporated into the KwaZulu homeland. The TCC opposed this – and a bitter conflict ensued.

The local police chief, Lt. Brian Mitchell, was also chairman of the local Joint Management Centre, and, as he confessed at his subsequent trial, he saw himself as a soldier in a civil war in which organizations such as the TCC and the UDF were enemies of the state trying to make South Africa ungovernable. He helped Gabela form a Landowners' Committee, consisting of nine local Inkatha members, which demanded that Trust Feed be placed under the control of tribal structures. More seriously, Mitchell decided that Gabela was not being tough enough in dealing with Shenge and the TCC. He needed "jacking up", Mitchell said.

In November, Mitchell took Gabela to a meeting at Inkatha headquarters in Pietermaritzburg. There he met a riot unit commander, Maj. Deon Terblanche, who told him riot units were being used in various parts of Natal to help Inkatha take over UDF-controlled areas. Terblanche undertook to send six "special constables" to Trust Feed to deal with the UDF supporters there.

---

* Deneys Coombe, "Of Murder and Deceit: The Trust Feed Killings", contained in *Patterns of Violence*, p. 229.

At three o'clock on the morning of December 3, Mitchell, accompanied by four special constables, crept up on what he thought was Shenge's house. He was mistaken: Shenge lived next door. The house Mitchell had targeted was crowded with men, women, and children gathered for a wake. As one of the women opened the door in response to a police knock, Mitchell and the constables opened fire. Survivors told how the attackers first blitzed the house, then came inside, and while one man shone a flashlight on those still living, another shot them. When the shooting stopped, eleven people were dead, including a child of four and a woman of sixty-six.

What followed was an elaborate police cover-up. Capt. Patrick Wattrus was put in charge of the investigation. When he began to suspect Mitchell, he referred the case to Brig. Christo Marx, divisional head of the Criminal Investigation Department in Pietermaritzburg, who passed it on to two deputies. No one ever questioned Mitchell thoroughly, and the four special constables were drafted into the KwaZulu police: two of them later confessed they had been advised to go into hiding there. As the stalling continued for more than a year, Mitchell was promoted to captain and Marx to major general. It might have ended there, just one more of the many unsolved murders in Natal, but for a police officer of integrity and courage, Capt. Frank Dutton, of a special investigation unit based in another area. While investigating an unrelated case, Dutton stumbled across the Trust Feed case, and within two weeks he had arrested Mitchell and the four special constables. It was two and a half years after the massacre.

The trial judge not only found a mass of evidence pointing to a police cover-up, but also that the massacre was "a final event in a planned operation to disrupt a community, oust the residents' association, and give Inkatha control of the area." He sentenced Mitchell to death eleven times over for ordering the massacre, and the special constables to fifteen years' imprisonment each.*

---

* Mitchell's sentence was commuted to thirty years' imprisonment in September 1994.

The government tried to brush off Trust Feed as an isolated case, saying no wider implications should be drawn from it about police involvement in the violence. But few who lived through the violence or reported on it would agree. As Father Smith puts it, "The evidence of my own experience and that of many others is that the police were deeply involved from the beginning. Their aim has been to support Inkatha and weaken the United Democratic Front and its allies. The Trust Feed case is only one example of many."

DE KLERK HAS TRIED to draw a line between events such as these, which occurred before he unbanned the liberation movements in early 1990 and initiated the formal negotiations to lead to a new constitution, and what happened after, suggesting that the earlier phase was a time of confrontation and conflict that should now be considered past and forgotten. "Don't rake up the past," he keeps saying.

Yet the evidence is overwhelming that the hit-squad and destabilization activity, and the collusion between elements in the security forces and Inkatha, not only continued but intensified after the negotiating phase began. The ANC-aligned Human Rights Commission reports that political assassinations, which averaged about ten a year during the 1980s, reached twenty-eight in 1990, sixty in 1991 and ninety-seven in 1992. And violence in Natal scaled new heights of intensity after Mandela's release.

I travelled to the Natal Midlands in late March 1990, six weeks after Mandela's release, when the area was being convulsed by what became known as the Seven-Day War. It was the most prolonged and systematic campaign by armed Inkatha warriors on a series of pro-ANC settlements of the whole decade of strife, and what I saw and heard there was clear evidence that the police were as deeply involved as ever in the region's turf war.

The road that runs westwards from Pietermaritzburg passes through the beautiful Edendale Valley, flanked by rolling hills. At that time of year, after late summer rains, it was idyllic, with grass and bracken just becoming tinged with the shades of autumn and its little clusters of houses dotting the hillsides. Yet it became a killing field.

In the front part of the valley, closest to Pietermaritzburg, lies Edendale itself, a black freehold area with a number of villages along the slopes and on the floor of the valley, all of them ANC strongholds. Beyond them, deeper in the valley, are various rural communities – Vulindlela, Sweetwaters, Taylor's Halt, Elandskop – which fell under the authority of the KwaZulu homeland administration, where Inkatha held sway. To travel to and from the city, the people of these villages had to pass through Edendale, where they claimed their buses were often stoned. That became the pretext for the attacks which began on March 25, 1990.

The scale of these attacks, some of which took the form of set-piece battles, seemed to lift the violence to a new and more ominous plane. Thousands of armed men assembled near the home of a local Inkatha "warlord", David Ntombela, and were then transported in vehicles along an upper road above the valley. There they regrouped and descended in battle formations on selected targets in Edendale. The assembling and provisioning of an army of that size in itself required major logistical preparation: there is no way it could have been a spontaneous response to the stoning of buses.

Pierre Cronje, a local farmer and member of parliament for the liberal Democratic Party, was there on the first day.* He had received a report from his party's crisis-monitoring office in Pietermaritzburg that an Inkatha *impi* (a warrior regiment) had entered Edendale in buses, a six-ton truck, and a number of smaller vehicles and was heading towards the settlement of Caluza. When Cronje got there the *impi*, which he estimated at between two and three thousand men armed with assegais, shotguns, and rifles, had already been

---

* Pierre Cronje has since joined the ANC, influenced largely by his experiences monitoring the violence in Natal, and was re-elected to Parliament in the 1994 election.

engaged by a group of local defenders and had withdrawn a short distance up the hill.

"I watched them regroup on a ridge above Caluza," Cronje told me. "A police armoured personnel carrier drew up across their path. The police did not disarm the attackers, but they did stop them moving on Caluza again." The *impi* then divided in two, and moved right and left behind ridges to attack a settlement called Ashdown in the east and three other ANC settlements to the west.

Next day a force of some twelve thousand Inkatha warriors attacked the same communities, wreaking havoc over the next five days and causing at least thirty-five deaths. Again and again the warrior *impis* swarmed across the hillsides in battle formation, plundering and killing and burning. The battles were fought by day in an area within sight of the provincial capital, yet the security forces did nothing to repel the attackers or seal off the villages under attack. Monitors recorded a few retaliatory attacks by the communities, but it was an overwhelmingly one-sided battle that left a hundred and thirty people dead, hundreds more wounded, and two hundred houses destroyed. An estimated twelve thousand five hundred people fled to makeshift refugee centres.

IT WAS SHORTLY before midnight, Philemon Malinga recalls, that he heard a heavy vehicle pull up in front of his house and a voice inquire in Afrikaans: "Is this the place?" He peered through his kitchen window and saw a big police personnel carrier, a Casspir, offloading men. A white Volkswagen minibus pulled up behind it, and Malinga saw more men get out. Some he recognized as policemen, others as local members of the Inkatha Freedom Party. Moments later a policeman kicked open his front door and stormed in with others behind him.

There followed what can only be called the sacking of the Malinga household in the small black township of Kwadela, a hundred and fifty miles east of Johannesburg. In a bedroom Malinga's pensioner mother, Belesia, scrambled in terror under her bed, but the attackers found her and shot her dead. Malinga's younger brother, Sibusiso, climbed on top of a cupboard, where he was skewered with a spear. As he fell to the floor he was stabbed again. Miraculously, he survived. Malinga himself managed to escape from the house and run for his life.

It was August 16, 1991, a year and a half after the Seven-Day War in Edendale, and the government was deep in negotiation with the ANC, initiated by De Klerk, yet here again was evidence of police collusion with Inkatha in an act of political violence. I had travelled to Kwadela with a young lawyer's clerk from Johannesburg, sent there by his firm to collect statements from community members about the attack on the night of July 26. The statements were to be attested later before a registered commissioner of oaths and sent to the attorney general to initiate a prosecution.

The lawyer's clerk took eleven statements from members of the little community, all of whom told the story of how the Casspir had driven around Kwadela that night, dropping off armed men to attack the homes of ANC branch committee members, then picking them up again. Jeremiah Mashinini, the local ANC chairman, described how a brick bearing a note warning of an impending attack had been thrown through his window a few nights before. His house was burned down, his son was injured, and his daughter-in-law was killed in the attack. Others told how a police car with a loudhailer had driven around the township, warning that a curfew was being imposed and that everyone should remain indoors after 9 p.m. That made the residents sitting ducks and ensured that no witnesses were on the streets to see what was happening.

But Kwadela is the kind of small community where everyone knows everyone else, and so the statements did in fact name the people who did the attacking: the policemen involved and those who fired the fatal shots. A number also mentioned a local policeman, a Constable Swart, whom they said they had seen with the Casspir. The lawyer's clerk noted that the official police record of the case named Swart as the investigating officer.

At the end of the day the lawyer's clerk had to find a commissioner of oaths to attest the statements as sworn affidavits. We drove first to the local post office, hoping the postmaster could perform the task, but she was a new appointment and not yet a commissioner of oaths. That left only the police station. Reluctantly the group made its way there – and swore their oaths before Constable Swart. No court action ever materialized.

EVENTUALLY, IN LATE 1992 and early 1993, the Goldstone Commission produced the most damning evidence of security force involvement in "third force" activities. The commission had begun hesitantly. Richard Goldstone is a fine lawyer and a man of liberal instincts, yet those two characteristics threatened to paralyse him for a time, as he brought an excessively legalistic mind to bear on his task and shrank from making decisive findings unless these could be proved beyond all reasonable doubt, as in a court case. With time and experience, however, he became more in tune with the political environment and began to act more boldly and proactively.

After the botching of the investigation into the massacre at Boipatong in June 1992, Judge Goldstone requested and was eventually given his own small investigative team, which included several foreign detectives – an insurance against the growing sense that South African policemen were suspect. On November 11, 1992, this team made a dramatic noonday raid on a building in the fashionable Pretoria suburb of Lynnwood Ridge, which they found was being used as the operational headquarters of a secret Military Intelligence unit that was running a dirty-tricks campaign, code-named Project Echoes, to discredit ANC leaders. At least forty-eight Military Intelligence officers were involved in the covert unit. Several had been transferred to it from the CCB, when that dirty-tricks outfit was supposedly disbanded in July 1990. Five files seized by the commission showed that a notorious former CCB agent, Ferdi Barnard, had been hired to head a task force whose job was to implicate ANC leaders, especially members of the guerrilla arm, in criminal activities by using "a support agent network of prostitutes, homosexuals, nightclub managers and criminal elements." Barnard, a six-foot-six-inch giant with a bull neck, concrete-slab shoulders, and a shuffling, muscle-bound walk that would fit him for the lead role in *Terminator 2*, had an ugly record: two convictions for murder, one for attempted murder, and three for theft. In 1984 he had been sentenced to twenty years in prison, but was released on parole after only four and soon afterwards joined the CCB. Now he had been transferred to the covert Military Intelligence unit with the personal approval of the chief of staff, intelligence, Lt. Gen. Rudolph Badenhorst.

The files also showed that another member of the unit was Leon Flores, who had been detained by British police on suspicion that he was involved in a plot to murder Capt. Dirk Coetzee while that former hit-squad informant was in hiding in London. Equally sinister was that the clue which led Goldstone's investigators to the secret headquarters had come from a former Mozambican soldier who said he had been employed by a policeman to murder township residents in Natal. The man had paid his hotel bill in Pietermaritzburg with a credit card which, the commission discovered, was for the account of a front company for the covert Military Intelligence unit.

All these disclosures occurred while De Klerk was on a state visit to Great Britain, and the president's immediate reaction was one of anger at Goldstone for making them public. He complained of a "plethora of insinuations, allegations, and accusations" and of "continuous propaganda", which, he said, "threatened the credibility of the security forces." On his return, De Klerk appointed the chief of the South African air force, Gen. Pierre Steyn, to investigate Goldstone's findings. A month later he either fired or suspended twenty-three senior Defence Force officers, including two generals and four brigadiers. But he never revealed the contents of General Steyn's report, and he never took any action against the chief of Military Intelligence, Gen. Joffel van der Westhuizen.*

Again this raised the question of De Klerk's reluctance to act even in the face of compelling evidence. Another former Military Intelligence officer, who emulated Dirk Coetzee and went to the newspapers with his story around that time, suggested a possible reason. Col. Gert Hugo, who resigned his commission in July 1991 after undergoing what he described as a religious awakening, claimed De Klerk was constrained in acting against officers involved in third-force activities because Military Intelligence was in a position to blackmail members of his cabinet. "The most powerful reason why he can't act is that he and his ministers don't know even the half of what is still going on today, but they're still implicated because many of them were part of the system under P.W. Botha. If he were to go after Joffel he would send a message to other senior officers with dirty hands, and the spin-off would be that all would open up, all the beans would spill. The top brass simply have got too much dirt."**

Two years later Judge Goldstone's commission released another, even more devastating bombshell. In January 1994, a senior police officer whose name is still being kept secret called on the director of a politial institute in Pretoria to tell him he had information about a "third force" that he was not prepared to give to any South African, only to an appropriate foreign person. The director, Ivor Jenkins, referred the officer to the Danish embassy. After several discussions with a senior diplomat at the embassy, this "deep throat" who has become known as "Q", was eventually persuaded to meet with Judge Goldstone personally. There followed the disclosure of what Goldstone described in his report to De Klerk as "a horrible network of criminal activity" among senior

---

* General Van der Westhuizen retired from the Defence Force "for health reasons" shortly before South Africa's democratic election on April 27, 1994.
** *The Star*, August 25, 1992.

South African police force officers who helped to sponsor violence. "Q" named the second-in-command of the police force, Lt. Gen. Basie Smit, and the chief of police counter-intelligence, Maj. Gen. Krappies Engelbrecht, who in fact was in charge of investigating all acts of political violence, as key figures in the network. "Q" testified to Judge Goldstone under oath at two separate meetings and in a written memorandum. Goldstone also spoke with two of the informant's trusted colleagues, Maj. P. du Plessis and Maj. E. van Vuuren, of the police Efficiency Services Department, who were later seconded to the commission to help with its investigation.

Like a grand-jury finding in the United States, Judge Goldstone's report does not amount to a trial and conviction. The charges are not proved. But the evidence constitutes what lawyers call a *prima facie* case that a "third force" was operating within the military-security establishment to try to destabilize South Africa, make holding an election impossible, and halt the nation's transition to democracy.

The story that emerged went like this. After Dirk Coetzee left the hit-squad unit stationed at Vlakplaas in 1984, the unit was renamed C10 and placed under the command of Col. Eugene de Kock. It continued its destabilizing activities. When the unit was formally disbanded in July 1990, its members were transferred to other police units – but police headquarters in Pretoria issued them with false identity documents and passports and they continued to operate in "third force" projects. De Kock was given a golden handshake of R1,200,000 ($350,000), specifically approved by De Klerk's cabinet, yet he, too, remained active in covert operations and was given seven passports, all in false names.

At the instigation of the two generals, Smit and Engelbrecht, the C10 unit established a plant on the East Rand for manufacturing homemade guns. At the same time a large quantity of arms – AK-47 asault rifles, RPG-7 rocket launchers, mortars, and hand grenades – that had been used by the Koevoet unit in the Namibian bush war against SWAPO were brought to Vlakplaas. From there they were taken to the East Rand gun plant to be cleaned with acid and have their serial numbers removed.

Both the Koevoet weapons and the homemade guns were packed in black bags and distributed to the Inkatha Freedom Party through two of its provincial leaders in the Transvaal, Themba Khoza and Victor Ndlovu. "Q" claimed that Khoza and Ndlovu were given false identities and that De Kock paid them as informants out of a secret fund. He said Khoza, who was chairman of the Transvaal region of the IFP, was also given a car. Weapons were also distributed directly to Inkatha members in Natal by C10 agents in that province. "Q" said that Gen, Jac Buchner, commissioner of the Kwa-Zulu police, was involved in the project in Natal.

According to "Q", the C10 unit had also been implicated in the violence that had occurred on commuter trains. He named an East Rand Security Branch officer as the organizer, saying he used C10 operatives, black policemen, *askaris*, and IFP members employed as security officers at a Johannesburg bank to carry out the vicious attacks on hapless commuters.

When Judge Goldstone met with the generals they denied all allegations of criminal conduct. So did De Kock. Khoza and Ndlovu have also denied the gunrunning accusations. As this is written, a massive investigation into "Q"'s allegations is continuing, and a major trial is in prospect. De Kock is in custody, charged with eight counts of murder, one of attempted murder, and other charges of sponsoring murder, terrorism, and the illegal possession of arms and ammunition. Eight other members of C10 also face charges. Further arrests are expected.

Meanwhile, Goldstone has also called for a probe into evidence that hit squads were operating within the KwaZulu police force, and that senior commanders were blocking police investigation of the murders these squads were committing.

The trail of this evidence is as damning as the Vlakplaas allegations. It begins in 1986, when a Military Intelligence unit secretly trained two hundred Inkatha members at a base in the Caprivi Strip, a remote part of northern Namibia. Namibia was still under South African control at that time, and the thirty-year bush war with SWAPO had not yet ended. When word leaked out in 1990 that the Defence Force had been training members of a political party, President De Klerk insisted the men had merely been trained as body-guards for Inkatha leaders. In fact they were trained in techniques of guerrilla warfare, sabotage, and assassination – and on their return were incorporated into the KwaZulu police force. Later they were deployed to form and train hit units in various parts of Natal and in the migrant workers' hostels of the Witwatersrand. It is these units that were supplied with the weapons from Vlakplaas.

Judge Goldstone first touched on this in December 1993, when he announced that he had found credible evidence that a KwaZulu police death squad had murdered at least nine ANC members during 1992 and 1993. In a detailed statement made in prison and sent to him, an alleged Inkatha assassin, Brian Mkhize, stated that the deputy commissioner of the KwaZulu police, Gen. Sipho Mathe, knew all about the death-squad operations. As Goldstone observed in his final report to De Klerk in March 1994, General Mathe's name has "regularly and over years been linked with improper conduct", yet he remains in his job.

Certainly someone high up in the KwaZulu police force has ordered the quashing of investigations into political violence. Phillip van Niekerk, a journalist who had dug deeply into the murky crevices of official involvement in the violence, found startling evidence of this when he investigated a massacre in the northern Natal settlement of Nqutu.*

Eleven friends and relatives of Chief Elphus Molefe, an ANC supporter, were slaughtered in an attack on the chief's home on November 7, 1993. Within forty-eight hours an alert KwaZulu policeman, Lt. Westleigh Mbata, arrested two suspects and extracted confessions from them. They told how, when the ANC planned to hold a rally in their IFP stronghold area, their local leader decided to enlist the support of the IFP in Johannesburg to drive out the ANC.

---

* Phillip van Niekerk's detailed report of the Nqutu massacre and its cover-up was published in *The Observer*, London, on March 6, 1994.

According to the confessions, Themba Khoza, the Transvaal IFP chairman, personally selected four hit men from a migrant workers' hostel in an East Rand township, issued them with weapons, and sent them to Nqutu, where they attacked Chief Molefe's house.

Armed with these confessions, Lieutenant Mbata asked his commander, Col. B.L. Ndlovu, for permission to travel to Johannesburg to arrest Khoza and the four hit men. Instead, he was put on sick leave, the two suspects were freed, and the case was put into the hands of another investigating officer, who allowed it to lapse.

These allegations seemed to gain further credibility when the retiring commissioner of the KwaZulu police, Gen. Roy During (he had succeeded Jac Buchner as the homeland's police chief), said in a newspaper interview as he left office in July 1994 that hit-squad murders had almost certainly been committed by members of his force. During said the killings had probably been ordered from a "high level." His own decision to retire, he said, was due in part to the attitudes and activities of a small but powerful group of right-wing radicals within the KwaZulu police force.*

Whatever their motives, these radicals not only failed to stop the government-ANC negotiations but, paradoxically, spurred it to success. For this was always a crisis-driven process. From the moment De Klerk made his fateful announcement on February 2, 1990, there could be no turning back. There was no way he could ban the ANC or any other black movement again, return Mandela to prison, or revert to apartheid. With his political opponents in the same boat, he had embarked on a one-way voyage, and they could either arrive at a new shore together or sink together. There were no other options. So as each new crisis reminded these squabbling voyagers afresh of their mutual dependency, they leaned on their oars with renewed effort and pulled for the shore.

---

* *The Star*, July 26, 1994.

13

The Roelf and Cyril Show

THE SUMMIT MEETING, held in Johannesburg on September 26, 1992, was the turning point, but in fact there had been progress towards it for some time. Behind the miasma of blood and rhetoric that was enveloping South Africa and giving outsiders the impression that it was sliding down the Sarajevo road, a series of secret meetings had been taking place between two men who were ultimately to emerge as the heroes of the political agreement.

Roelf Meyer, forty-five, and Cyril Ramaphosa, forty, both youngsters in a political arena well trodden by veterans, had forged their bond of trust – if not actual blood brotherhood – during Sidney Frankel's fishing weekend in August 1991. Ten months later, as the ANC walked out of CODESA, Meyer was appointed minister of constitutional development and took over as head of the government's negotiating team – Ramaphosa's opposite number. Outwardly, they presented a character contrast: the burly, outgoing Ramaphosa, who had risen through the mineworkers' union and become what Bobby Godsell of the giant Anglo American Corporation called "the most skilled negotiator I have ever met"; and the lean, boyish-looking Meyer, a quiet, buttoned-down politician descended from a three-hundred-year line of Afrikaner farmers. Yet they were alike in their tolerant, unflappable personalities and their willingness to compromise. The two were careful to keep each other at arm's length: they maintained a strict working relationship, never socializing, so as not to compromise their parties. But they had a high level of mutual trust and an almost intuitive understanding of one another's minds. Through the grim months from June to September, when the negotiations were officially broken off, Meyer and Ramaphosa went on meeting, one on one, unnoticed, in hotel rooms several times a week, meticulously trying to pick up the pieces. Those months were a formative time in other ways, too, with a subtle change of political chemistry taking place in both camps.

Doubts began to arise within the National Party about De Klerk's strategy of trying to build a winning anti-ANC alliance. The violence and the suspicions of government complicity in it were hurting the party's image, not to mention the national economy. In addition, Buthelezi's erratic behaviour, and opinion polls indicating that Inkatha was losing support among the Zulus, raised doubts about his value as an ally.

Meanwhile, a group of upwardly mobile young Afrikaner politicians – Roelf Meyer and Leon Wessels among them – began reassessing their own career prospects. While older members of the De Klerk cabinet were preoccupied with justifying their past activities and ensuring that not too much was changed, these younger people began facing the inevitable truth that their futures lay in what would be a nonracial South Africa and they did not want the albatross of apartheid around their necks. Building a dubious alliance to fight the major black political movement made less and less sense to them. Coming to terms with it seemed more rational. So a fault line developed in the cabinet – the pro-Buthelezi faction, still committed to the original strategy, on one side, and the younger bloods, keener to link up with the ANC, on the other. The division widened as the younger ministers gained the ascendancy after Boipatong and Bisho.

Ironically, Kobie Coetsee, the man who started the whole transition process with Nelson Mandela, emerged for a time on the side of the cabinet Old Guard – the "antis", as an Afrikaans newspaper called them. Unlike De Klerk, Coetsee failed to keep pace with the evolution of events and grew distressed as he saw the constitutional agreement moving beyond the National Party's original model, with its emphasis on power sharing among ethnic groups. "It has taken a different direction, which I think may cost the country dearly," Coetsee told me in an interview after the final agreement was reached. But he retained a warm relationship with Mandela; the two lunched together regularly. Some months later, after the election, when he was president of the Senate, he appeared mollified and he told me his moment of doubt had arisen only because he feared a right-wing revolt. At that critical juncture in the southern spring of 1992, however, he was clearly in the "anti" camp.

While the cabinet was dividing between its Old Guard and Young Turks, a similar change was taking place in the liberation movement, where some of the moderates were exploring how they might bridge the vital gap between power sharing and majority rule. Surprisingly, the lead came from Joe Slovo, for so long Pretoria's bugbear whom De Klerk had tried to exclude from the Groote Schuur summit but who now, as chairman of the Communist Party, was playing an increasingly conciliatory role. "A sheep in wolf's clothing," I called him in an article for the *The Observer* in London. Writing in the August issue of the *African Communist*, Slovo suggested a "sunset clause" that would provide for compulsory power sharing for a fixed number of years, then fall away. Pointing out that "we are not dealing with a defeated enemy," Slovo argued that it was not possible to force the regime's unconditional surrender across the table. Compromise was inevitable, and the trick was to distinguish between what he called "qualitative" and "quantitative" compromises – a strategic retreat as against a surrender of principle. A temporary commitment to share power on a basis of proportional representation would be a strategic retreat, he argued. So, too, would a general amnesty and an offer of security to the predominantly white civil service to stop it from obstructing change.*

The hard truth Slovo had recognized was that the ANC had no civil service waiting in the wings to take over the running of the country. Like it or not, a new black-majority government would have to work through the old, pre-

---

* Joe Slovo, "Negotiations: What Room for Compromise?", *African Communist*, Third Quarter, 1992, pp. 36-40.

dominantly white Afrikaner bureaucracy – so the liberation-ists had better make sure that it did not sabotage their new regime. As Slovo put it in a conversation at the time, "We can win political office, but we won't have political power."

The article caused a storm of controversy within the ANC and in Slovo's own Communist Party, but since it came from someone with impeccable revolutionary credentials, it was hard for the militants to discredit it. The ANC's negotiating commission developed Slovo's ideas into a strategy proposal, which the leadership accepted, to defuse resistance to a black takeover by offering De Klerk a coalition partnership in "a government of national unity and reconciliation" for three to five years, and giving civil servants, police, and military personnel guarantees that they could keep their jobs. It was an offer that the younger members of De Klerk's cabinet found irresistible.

Another ANC policy shift also appealed to them. A study trip to Germany by a group of ANC strategists finally allayed the organization's fears that federalism would emasculate its power and enable apartheid to live on through ministates ruled by ethnic parties. On the group's return, the ANC produced a policy document advocating a new South Africa "that is unified but not over-centralized", and a distribution of powers at national, regional, and local levels. "We have no problem with the democratic principle that different parties can hold office at national and regional levels," it declared. To the National Party, still conditioned by its portrayal of the ANC as a communist front committed to a centralized political system enforcing a command economy, this was a revelation. "When we explained our regional policy to members of the government they were taken aback," Ramaphosa told a press briefing.

The Mandela-De Klerk summit took place in this changed and chastened atmosphere – but not before some tough one-on-one negotiating between the two principals themselves. The ANC had boiled its fourteen conditions for resuming negotiations down to three, but even these De Klerk found hard to accept: releasing a number of disputed political prisoners, included several on death row for murders committed during the years of the "armed struggle", fencing Inkatha hostels, and banning the carrying of "cultural weapons". Releasing the death row prisoners was a highly emotive issue in the white community, while the other two conditions required action against Inkatha that would strike at the rift in De Klerk's cabinet. The president was reluctant, but Mandela was adamant – all three demands had to be met in full or there would be no deal. "He was tough as nails," says Ramaphosa, who confesses that there were moments he feared Mandela was overplaying his hand and would blow the whole deal that he and Meyer had painstakingly stitched together.

Mac Maharaj, too, worried about his leader's intransigence. The one-on-one meetings had by now broadened into what became known as the "Cyril-Roelf channel", with additional men on both sides joining in the discussions to try to get the negotiations back on track. The old Operation Vula hand was one of those, and Maharaj recalls meeting with Mandela and Ramaphosa in the ANC's Johannesburg headquarters building, Shell House, on the Sunday before the summit. De Klerk wanted to release the death row prisoners in phases, to lessen the impact, but Mandela insisted that they all had to be released at once if the summit was to be held. "He got on the phone several times to De Klerk and spoke to him so bluntly that both Cyril and I told him we thought he had gone too far. But he was quite relaxed. He laughed and said, 'No, chaps, we hold the line here.' Next thing a call came from De Klerk to say OK, he would release them all." Both Ramaphosa and Maharaj believe that was a critical moment. Mandela not only got the concession he wanted, but, as Maharaj puts it, he established a psychological ascendancy over De Klerk. "From then onward there was a different balance in the relationship," he says.

The summit itself was a tricky affair for De Klerk. Members of the "channel" had agreed on a draft "Record of Understanding", but when De Klerk ran it past his cabinet some of the Old Guard raised objections. As the two sides faced each other at the World Trade Centre on the morning of September 26, De Klerk cunningly let the "antis" – notably Kobie Coetsee and the minister of law and order, Hernus Kriel – lead the argument against Mandela, putting them in the position of having to yield in order to get agreement. When the issue arose of fencing the Inkatha hostels, the touchiest of all as far as the pro-Inkatha ministers were concerned, De Klerk claimed he had not had time to study the draft properly and could he do so at a later date? "Very well, Mr. de Klerk, you can have the time," Mandela replied coolly, "provided you understand that when we leave here to have a press conference I shall say that this meeting has been a total failure." Again De Klerk blanched. Eventually it was agreed that a "working committee" should study the draft during the lunch break, and De Klerk slyly ensured that only Young Turks were on the committee. When the nego-tiators reassembled, De Klerk casually announced that the working committee had approved the document and he would sign it. He had bypassed the Old Guard – and they were furious. When I spoke to Coetsee about it months later, he was still resentful. "It's too contentious – you musn't ask me about that," he said.

The summit ended with the signing of a Record of Understanding that committed the two sides to resume multiparty negotiations. It was acclaimed nationwide. "The channels of communication are open again," De Klerk enthused. "This is what our people want, this is what the economy needs, this is what our country yearns for," Mandela said. But Buthelezi rightly saw that it meant the government was dumping him as a partner to strike a coalition deal with the ANC. Angrily, he broke off relations with De Klerk. At the start of the negotiating process, the president had offered Buthelezi a unique open door, reserving dates in his diary for an entire year so that the two could resolve their differences in private and not clash publicly. Now Buthelezi cancelled that arrangement. From then on he became increasingly irascible and, in the view of both Meyer and Wessels, marginalized himself.

This was an extraordinary feat of political self-immolation. Buthelezi had started out with every advantage: extensive international support, considerable domestic support, and most-favoured leader treatment by the South African government. Within a year he had thrown it all away. Why?

Leon Wessels, who dealt with him closely as the National Party's chief negotiator (Meyer represented the government), offers two explanations. First, he says, Buthelezi was the only political leader who never participated in the negotiating councils. "He never had his feathers ruffled or got cut down to size at the World Trade Centre, and so he kept on acting like a prima donna." Added to that, says Wessels, Buthelezi was not used to being opposed and didn't like it. "He is accustomed to being treated like a chief minister, like a boss, like a chief of his tribe. If he doesn't get his way, he throws his toys out of the playpen. Buthelezi is not used to exchanging punches with people in the arena, and then making friends with them again. That is something you have to learn in politics – it is the art of persuasion, you have to convince people. But if Buthelezi doesn't get his way he takes it as a personal affront and nurtures a grievance."

Nor was it only the Young Turks in the cabinet whose attitude towards Buthelezi soured. De Klerk, too, became exasperated at what he saw as Buthelezi's obstructiveness. By contrast, government negotiators found the ANC leaders easier to get along with. Wessels describes the difference: "We would arrive at a bilateral meeting with the ANC, and they would be well prepared. They would be properly mandated, and we would always find a spirit of compromise, of seeking solutions. They would say, 'No, we can't entertain this idea, but let's look for a way around it. What is your position? Why can't you move? Let's see if we can understand the situation better.' The personalities blended, they came to understand one another, and there was really a spirit of co-operation among us. That was not the situation with Inkatha. They would listen, they would be divided, they would not always be mandated properly. They wouldn't explore ideas with us. Sometimes they would read a lecture that sounded as though it had been written by Buthelezi, attacking all our people. Other times we would seem to reach agreement, and then we would adjourn to go back to our principals, and the next day we would be back to square one. It was very exasperating."

The government and the ANC cemented their new understanding at two *bosberaad* meetings in December and January 1993. For four days and nights they talked, lived, ate, and relaxed together in the seclusion of D'Nyala. Some went jogging together in the mornings, and in the evenings they sat around a campfire under a tamboti tree getting to know each other. Old animosities thawed and a certain *rapprochement*, if not actual friendship, developed. Wessels recalls going for an early-morning swim and meeting Slovo in the pool. "We chatted for an hour and I got an altogether different perspective on him," he says. Meyer remembers a night game-viewing trip when he and Ramaphosa rode together on the back of a Land Rover. "It was damn cold and we were sitting there – Cyril, his wife and I – and we were talking, not about the game we were seeing but about what lay ahead for us. We were reaching out to each other, sharing common values about what we wanted to achieve. It was one of those rare moments of Cyril and I finding each other."

I first became aware of new thinking in government circles during a long conversation I had with Meyer at the president's annual *Tuynhuys* cocktail party for the media in February 1993. Most of the press corps was crowded around De Klerk in the middle of the long banquet hall when I spotted the unobtrusive Meyer alone at one end of the room. He told me of his confidence that the government and the ANC would reach a workable compromise soon. When I asked him what possible compromise there could be between power sharing and majority rule, he indicated that the government was moving away from the idea of an enforced coalition. "I'm having trouble convincing some of my colleagues of this, but it is a fact that entrenched coalition indefinitely is not a defensible position," he said. Did that mean the government was moving away from its commitment to power sharing? No, Meyer replied, but power sharing could take many forms. Federalism was one. Clearly the National Party was shifting ground in a significant way.

The following month a new Negotiating Council convened at the World Trade Centre, with twenty-six parties participating. From day one the government and the ANC cruised towards agreement, carrying most of the negotiating parties with them. As sticking points arose, one would see Meyer and Ramaphosa slip quietly from their seats to meet in a corner. A compromise proposal would follow. Or there would be an adjournment to allow for a longer consultation. The media dubbed it "The Roelf and Cyril Show," and it became the hub around which the entire negotiation turned.

But still it was not a smooth ride. Buthelezi in his anger formed an alliance with the right-wing Conservative Party and two nominally independent homelands, Ciskei and Bophuthatswana, which he had previously despised. They called themselves the Concerned South Africans Group (COSAG) and began talking ominously of civil war if their demands for a federalism that sounded suspiciously like secession were not met. Again Buthelezi pulled Inkatha out of the Negotiating Council. And again acts of political violence, this time perpetrated by the left as well as the right, shook the country and threatened the process.

ONE MONTH AFTER the negotiations resumed, there occurred the most shattering act of all. On the morning of Easter Saturday, April 10, Chris Hani, general secretary of the Communist Party and the most charismatic of the black leaders, pulled into the driveway of his home in the Boksburg suburb of Dawn Park on the East Rand. As he stepped from his car, a man in a red Ford Laser parked across the road leaned out the window and fired two shots from a nine-millimeter Z88 army-issue pistol, and Hani staggered against his garage door and slumped to the ground. Casually the man walked across the road, fired two more shots into the prostrate body, then leaped back into his car and drove off.

Hani's neighbour in the middle-class suburb, a white Afrikaner woman named Retha Harmse, had set out for the local shopping centre a few moments earlier, but she found she had forgotten her purse and turned back. As she drove past Hani's gate she heard the shots and saw the red Laser pull away. In a flash she memorized the registration number, PBX231T, shouted to her husband as she ran into their home, and dialled the police flying squad. Fifteen minutes later the police stopped the red Laser on a highway and arrested a thirty-eight-year-old Polish immigrant, Janusz Waluz. The smoking gun was still in his car.

The news of Hani's assassination hit South Africa like a thunderclap. Anyone wanting to ignite an inferno of rage in the black community could not have chosen a better target, for Hani was a hero particularly to the militant young "comrades" who had spearheaded the black revolt. As a guerrilla commander he had built a reputation for courage by always leading his units on their strike raids, never ordering them forth on their own. He had risen to become chief of staff of the guerrilla army, and for the angry young "comrades" he had become a living legend. He was, besides, a powerful orator, the most potent of all the liberation movement leaders, who could bring the crowds cheering to their feet. Now he was dead, murdered by a white racist who, it soon turned out, had political links on the far right: a leading member of the Conservative Party, Clive Derby-Lewis, and his wife, Gaye, were also arrested. The murder weapon turned out to have been part of batch of arms stolen from the South African air force armoury in Pretoria by a well-known right-winger, Piet-Skiet Rudolph, in April 1990.

The funeral was set for Monday, April 19, and South Africa held its breath. Surely this would precipitate the apocalyptic bloodbath that so many people had predicted. There was an ominous prelude on the Sunday night, when four unknown gunmen killed nineteen people in Sebokeng township. A hundred thousand people packed the giant football stadium

where the funeral service was held, and twenty thousand
followed the coffin to the cemetery in Boksburg thirty-five
miles away, but the event was not as catastrophic as feared.
The early morning saw some running battles between youths
and the police outside the stadium; a few cars and houses
were set on fire; some windscreens were smashed; one
youth, in a demented moment, unleashed a burst of AK-47
gunfire at a police helicopter; and the air was filled with an
acrid mixture of smoke and teargas. But when the coffin was
carried into the stadium, the raucous crowd rose as one and
stood in respectful silence for their hero. There was more
trouble later at the cemetery, and by the end of the day six
people had been killed and fourteen injured, but this was far
fewer than the catastrophe that had been feared.

As with all the previous crises, this national trauma
strengthened rather than weakened the political centre and
spurred the negotiating parties to speed up their work. It also
enhanced Mandela's stature as a national leader. As the crisis
swelled, there was little De Klerk could do to calm the nation;
but Mandela could, for they were his people who were
aggrieved. He went on national television at the height of the
furore and issued a moving appeal to whites and blacks to
close ranks and prevent their emotions from destroying their
joint future. "A white man, full of prejudice and hate, came
to our country and committed a deed so foul that our whole
nation now teeters on the brink of disaster," he said. "But a
white woman, of Afrikaner origin, risked her life so that we
may know, and bring to justice, the assassin." He sounded
presidential, and from that moment onwards Mandela seemed to assume the mantle of national leadership that would be
bestowed on him formally a year later.

At the World Trade Centre, Ramaphosa called a press
conference to announce that the ANC-led alliance had
decided the negotiations should be speeded up, not delayed,
because of the assassination. At his side, Joe Slovo chimed in:
"Any suggestion of calling off the negotiations would be
playing into the hands of the murderers, whose purpose is to
stop the process. We must defeat them." Meyer's deputy,

Fanus Schoeman, concurred: "I think it is important that we get a democratically elected government installed as soon as possible so we can solve the problem of violence."

The assassins were duly brought to justice. Walusz and Clive Derby-Lewis were found guilty and sentenced to death on October 14. Gaye Derby-Lewis was acquitted: the judge said it could not be proved beyond reasonable doubt that she was part of the conspiracy.

SIX WEEKS LATER the Negotiating Council experienced a crisis of a different sort. As the delegates gathered for their morning session on June 25, a raucous mob of some three thousand Afrikaner right-wingers made their way towards the gates of the World Trade Centre. There were farmers in floppy hats, women with children in tow, and young men in khaki carrying placards calling for an independent Afrikaner *volkstaat* and banners bearing the swastika-like insignia of the Afrikaner Weerstandsbeweging, the Afrikaner Resistance Movement (commonly known by the initials AWB). Some wore the black uniforms of the AWB's Ystergarde, or Iron Guard, with SS-style shoulder flashes and cap badges. A few were in business suits. Many had holstered pistols on their hips, long hunting knives dangling from their belts, and shotguns and rifles sheathed in quilted bags. They also carried picnic hampers, cooler bags, and barbecue equipment.

The mood was festive at first, but it turned ugly as the mob came through the gates into the spacious grounds outside the exhibition centre. They rocked cars, ripped off rearview mirrors and yelled insults at reporters and clerical staff hurrying to the centre. Police guarding the building did nothing.

As the mob swarmed around the building, chanting AWB slogans, a yellow armoured vehicle called a Viper edged its way through them and with a surge of low-geared power crashed its way through the plateglass frontage into the foyer. The crowd surged in behind it. Within seconds the place was overrun. Uniformed AWB men raced up the stairways yelling, "Where are they? We want them." Others scrambled over the balustrades and also ran through the corridors looking for delegates. "We don't want kaffirs in here. Kaffirs, we are going to shoot you dead today," they shouted. They made their way into the negotiating chamber and sat in the seats. They emptied the delegates' bar, poured fruit juice on the carpets, and urinated on the desks. When an Indian delegate tried to remonstrate with them, he was punched in the face.

Gen. Constand Viljoen, a former chief of the South African Defence Force who had recently been elected to head a new Afrikaner Volksfront to unite right-wingers in their quest for a separate Afrikaner state, ran among the crowd with a bullhorn trying to restrain them – but the unruly AWB mob was in no mood to heed orders. Its leader, burly Eugene Terre'Blanche, revelling in the occasion, marched triumphantly into the foyer flanked by members of his Ystergarde and delivered a fiery address. Incongruously, in the midst of the mayhem there suddenly came the sounds of a prayer over the loudspeaker system. The wreckers stopped in their tracks, bowed their heads, and stood silently for a moment – before running riot once more. It was a token gesture to the claim of this thuggish lot that they were engaged in a Christian crusade to save their country from godless communism.

Eventually the intruders withdrew, to light their barbecue fires on a stretch of ground near the exhibition centre, open their picnic hampers, and quaff gallons of beer. It was their finest hour, Terre'Blanche claimed. They had shown that the Boers were a tough lot, determined to fight for their rights and prevent the De Klerk government from selling out the Afrikaners' birthright. Others were less sure. "Today I divorce myself from these lunatic Afrikaners," declared Fanus Schoeman, the deputy minister of constitutional affairs. Ramaphosa was coldly angry. "I say to the Conservative Party, to the Afrikaner Volksfront, we will defend this process. We will not be driven out. We will reach a settlement that will be good for all our people, including Afrikaners." General Viljoen looked uncomfortable and admitted that the demonstration had probably not done his *volkstaat* cause any good – but he refused to condemn the AWB.

THE NEXT SHOCK came from the left, or so it seemed. July 25 was a Sunday, and that evening the St. James's Church in Cape Town's Kenilworth suburb, a large, semi-circular building, was packed with more than a thousand worshippers, all of them white, including one hundred and fifty Russian sailors. As the service began, five masked black men stormed in through a side door and began firing burst after burst of automatic gunfire into the congregation. They ended by hurling in several hand grenades, slamming the door, and leaving.

The carnage was terrible. Limbs were blown off and bodies torn apart. Twelve people were killed and fifty-six injured, many of them maimed for life. Never before had white South Africans suffered so grievously from the violence that had long racked the black townships. A few black voices sneered at the white cries of outrage because of this, but for the most part the shock was universal. Archbishop Tutu denounced the massacre as "a devilish deed – low and despicable," and the ANC said it would launch its own search for the killers.

Suspicion centred on the Pan-Africanist Congress, which still refused to suspend its own armed struggle and whose military wing, the Azanian People's Liberation Army (APLA), had claimed responsibility for a spate of attacks on whites during December: a grenade attack on a Christmas party at the King William's Town Golf Club in Eastern Cape Province that left four dead and seventeen injured; a bomb thrown into a steakhouse in nearby Queenstown, injuring seventeen; and a machine-gun attack on a crowded Cape Town bar that killed four and injured five. But this time APLA denied responsibility, and although the police found the getaway car in a coloured township outside Cape Town they got no further in their efforts to track down the St. James Church killers – leaving open the possibility that it may have been the work once again of *agents provocateurs* using black surrogates.

Whatever the truth of it, anger at the PAC intensified in the white community and a new threat of racial polarization loomed. Young PAC activists had popularized the chilling slogan "One Settler, One Bullet," and although the parent organization tried to explain that the term "settler" did not necessarily mean white but only meant someone who did not identify with Africa, the racist connotation remained. Feelings were further aroused when a group of PAC youths attacked and killed a young American Fulbright scholar, Amy Biehl, when she gave three black friends a lift home to Cape Town's Guguletu township on the evening of August 26. The youths had yelled racist insults at Biehl and called her a "settler" as they chased and stabbed her to death.

True to form, the security forces then made a bad situation worse. Just two weeks before a scheduled meeting between APLA and the government, at which APLA – which had come in for a roasting from the United Nations and the Organization for African Unity – was expected to announce the formal suspension of its armed struggle, an army commando unit raided a house in the Transkei capital of Umtata which, it claimed, was "a springboard for APLA attacks on unarmed South Africa civilians." The house turned out to be occupied not by guerrillas but by a group of schoolchildren home for the holidays. Five of them, aged twelve to nineteen, were blown to pieces in the predawn raid. The army said the youngsters had "offered resistance", but the evidence showed they had been shot in their beds. APLA cancelled the meeting with the government as counter-accusations and threats filled the air once more.

Again the negotiations survived. "Perversely, the APLA attacks – if indeed they were APLA attacks – have had a salutary effect on the diseased negotiations process," wrote Shaun Johnson, political editor of *The Star*. "The more outrageous the behaviour from the periphery, the more the centre coheres. And the more the centre coheres, the more pressure there will be on the peripheries to play the game to the new rules, or relegate themselves to the sidelines."

THE LAST CLAUSE of the new constitution was adopted just be-fore dawn on November 18, 1993. The agreement ended eight years of negotiating that had begun in Nelson Mandela's hospital ward, continued through prison cells and a cabinet minister's home, through intelligence networks and secret brotherhood channels, through undergound communication systems and covert couriers, and finally concluded in a formal diplomatic forum involving as many as twenty-six political parties and government bodies. Now at last it was all wrapped up in a one-hundred-and-forty-two-page constitution that ended the odious system of apartheid and ushered in the promise of democracy; that in a symbolic way finally brought to an end half a millennium of white colonial domination over the dark-skinned people of the earth.

Its strange origins aside, the negotiating process itself had been a remarkable phenomenon. An authoritarian country with no history or experience of interracial dialogue had engaged in what David Welsh of Cape Town University called "a gigantic and ongoing seminar" on South Africa's future. And it had reached concurrence. People as far apart as the Communist Party and the Old Guard of the National Party had agreed on the essential shape of that future. Moreover, it was all done without the help of outsiders. There was no United Nations brokerage or Lancaster House conference or Vance-Owen plan, no meeting of old adversaries on the White House lawn. These widely divergent elements had thrashed out a new constitution for themselves, much as the Founding Fathers of the United States did in 1787 – except that, unlike the Founding Fathers, they did it in public, in a forum that was reported and televised to the nation.

Much of the new constitution was devoted to reassuring the white minority that the tables would not be turned on them in a regime of vengeance. It promised cabinet seats to minority parties for the first five years, and it protected the jobs and pensions of white soldiers, police and civil servants. It assigned important powers to nine provincial governments, and included an entrenched Bill of Fundamental Rights, safeguarded by a powerful constitutional court, guaranteeing freedom of speech, of the press, of movement, of the right to fair trials and the right to life, which means that never again may the state kill its dissenters. There was consensus on a new flag and on a new national anthem, "Nkosi Sikelel iAfrika" (God Bless Africa) – which had long been the battle hymn of the liberation movements – to be sung together with the old Afrikaans anthem, "Die Stem van Suid-Afrika" (The Voice of South Africa).

There would be a House of Assembly of four hundred members and a Senate of ninety, ten from each province. The two-chamber legislature would also sit as a constituent assembly to draft a final constitution within two years – but, except for the coalition agreement, nobody expected this to differ much from the interim charter, since the fundamental principles were already agreed.

The grand compromise between power sharing and majority rule was embodied in clauses which stipulated that the minority parties would share in executive power on a proportional representation basis until the next general election in 1999, and that there would be a president and two deputies – one from the party running second in the election, the other from any third party that gained more than 20 per cent of the popular vote, failing which it would also go to the winning party.

But for all the checks and balances, it was clear that in the end the winning party would hold most of the power. In fact, it was a last-ditch dispute over a critical aspect of this which delayed agreement on the final clause until nearly 4 a.m. De Klerk had held out for a formula that would require the new president to obtain a two-thirds majority in the cabinet on major issues, but in the end he had surrendered on this, too. The final version merely required the president to consult the cabinet in a "consensus-making spirit" before making decisions. In practice, power-sharing would depend more on the goodwill and pragmatism of the winning party, and on the economic and bureaucratic power of the white community, rather than on constitutional provisions.

It was a workable deal, and as the negotiators broke up for the last time there was a mood of exhilaration. As the first light of the new day began to filter through the windows that the AWB had smashed five months before, the delegates opened the bar to toast the new nation being born. It was Ramaphosa's forty-first birthday and Meyer presented him with a candled cake. "I want to propose a toast to Cyril," he said. "I want to wish our country a happy birthday," Ramaphosa replied. A band struck up with "In the Mood" and the two principal negotiators swung onto the dance floor together.

The bonhomie was high and reconciliation was in the air. Hardly anyone noticed the ominous absence from the celebrations of Inkatha and the other delegates of the COSAG alliance.

14

The Battle
of Bop

A LL THAT REMAINED now was to bring in the COSAG
parties to make the founding election of the new South
Africa as inclusive as possible. Five non-participants out of
twenty-six was not a bad record for such an extraordinarily
wide-ranging agreement, particularly since two of them, Ciskei and Bophuthatswana, were known to have negligible
support and both the ANC and the government had decided
that if necessary they would go ahead without them. Still,
getting access to the territories the COSAG parties controlled
would pose logistical problems, besides which there was a
strong feeling that a founding election should have full participation to give the new constitution maximum legitimacy.
Every effort should therefore be made to bring in the recal-
citrants. What nobody realized at the time, and most South
Africans still do not, is that this meant overcoming an armed
operation that threatened a massive secessionist rebellion,
perhaps even a civil war. It was the last and most serious
threat to the democratic transition.

The source of the threat was an opportunistic alliance between political parties and organizations that had nothing
in common except a shared sense that the ANC-National
Party accord made them losers. Chief Buthelezi had spent
his whole life fighting apartheid. At one time he was the
sole internal black figure openly campaigning against it and
blocking the regime's attempts to declare all the tribal
homelands independent and so provide the justification for
denationalizing the entire black population. Yet here he was
forming an alliance with the country's worst white racists,
the last-ditch defenders of apartheid, and threatening to
wage a civil war rather than participate in the first one-
person, one-vote election. It made no sense, except in the

crude calculation of who would get power once the old regime was gone. When Buthelezi found he was being dumped by his major ally, he sought other partners regardless of their racial records. It was partly expediency, partly vengeful anger. But it had a potent imagery. The idea of a Boer-Zulu alliance, of a coming together of the old warrior enemies of the past to fight for a common objective, had a certain romantic appeal. It also posed a significant military threat.

The white right, meanwhile, were a disputatious lot. Once Afrikaner solidarity, which had kept the National Party firmly in power since 1948, began to break up under P.W. Botha, the dissenters had quickly fragmented into more than twenty different political and "cultural" organizations. These ranged from the crude racist Rambos of the AWB to a larger population of *ordentlike mense*, ordinary decent people, who, though conservative in matters of race, were stern, upright, God-fearing Calvinists who would not countenance loutish behaviour but at the same time saw anything aimed at changing the social order, communism especially, as the work of the devil. Then there were the ideologues who had absorbed the propaganda of apartheid and the "total onslaught" and become locked into its mindset. Running through all these groups was the theme of apartheid as a civil religion – a self-image of Afrikaners as a special people with a divine right to rule themselves in their own homeland in Africa. Finally, there were racist fanatics from other white groups – English-speakers like Clive Derby-Lewis, anti-communist zealots from Eastern Europe like Janusz Waluz, and white fugitives from black rule in Zimbabwe, Angola, Mozambique, and other African ex-colonies.

Straddling all this was the Conservative Party, which had broken from Botha's National Party in 1982 and was itself a discordant body. It had been held together by its founding leader Andries Treurnicht, a theologian turned politician who had spelled out the old doctrine of the Afrikaner civil religion with new force in a book called *Credo van 'n*

Afrikaner. Treurnicht was a heavyweight in the Afrikaner political establishment and a man of Old World courtesy, which helped contain the more brutish elements in his party, but he died in April 1993, and Ferdinand Hartzenberg, rough and hardline, took over the leadership. Hartzenberg was much closer to Eugene Terre'Blanche and his AWB, and as the party lurched further to the right the fractiousness within it increased.

At this point an enigmatic new figure appeared on the scene. Gen. Constand Viljoen, a retired chief of the Defence Force who had led South African troops on a number of incursions into Angola and acquired a reputation as a soldier's soldier, stepped out of the obscurity of a bushveld cattle ranch to become an instant hero to the wild men of the right. He did so at a time when their blood was up in the overcharged atmosphere following Chris Hani's assassination, the arrest of three Conservative Party members for the murder, and a series of random attacks on white farmers around the country. To make matters worse, the farmers were struggling through a severe drought and the government had cut agricultural subsidies. On the morning of May 7, 1993, fifteen thousand of them, some armed to the teeth, gathered in a rugby stadium in the Western Transvaal town of Potchefstroom to vent their feelings. The deputy minister of agriculture, Tobie Meyer (younger brother of Roelf Meyer), tried to address them, but they shouted him down. "Shoot him," the farmers yelled. "Send him home. Get rid of the traitor." Then Viljoen, who was sitting in the crowd, was called on to address them.

The dapper little general, white-haired at fifty-nine and with piercing blue eyes, had no speech prepared. He spoke off the cuff, perhaps a little recklessly, but he quickly had the crowd roaring its approval. He told them that he believed the ANC was still pursuing a revolutionary strategy and that the attacks on farmers were part of this. The government should stop the negotiations and deal first with the security situation; otherwise it would be weakened and intimidated into yielding too much. "Lead us! Lead us!" the crowd roared, and Viljoen found himself elected by acclamation to a leadership role that was to prove critical in the delicate balance between the forces of violence and of reason in the white right. It was clear at that meeting that the farmers who acclaimed Viljoen wanted him to lead them into an apocalyptic "Third Boer War" to save the Afrikaner *volk* from being sold out by the ethnic traitor, De Klerk.* But when I interviewed the general a few days later, it seemed that the farmers at Potchefstroom may have misread their man. "I'm not for fighting," Viljoen told me. "I'm not available for that role – for the moment."

That little addendum, tossed in almost as an afterthought, expressed the enigma of the man. If the *Boerevolk's* position were ignored, he said, if they were not given more time to present their case for "self-determination", well then, who knew what might happen? But for the moment, no. "I have accepted the fact that we have switched from a military strategy to that of negotiation." Viljoen used the right-wing term *Boerevolk* in preference to Afrikaner, but in other respects he differed sharply from the main extremist groups. He told me he thought De Klerk had been right to release Nelson Mandela when he did and begin negotiating with the ANC, but that things had gone awry since then. It was hardly war talk – for the moment.

Swept forward on a new surge of enthusiasm, representatives of all the squabbling right-wing groups, including Hartzenberg and Terre'Blanche, met at the Pretoria headquarters of the Transvaal Agricultural Union and formed a united front, the Afrikaner Volksfront, to campaign for a separate Afrikaner *volkstaat*, or homeland. A Volksfront Council was formed: Hartzenberg cunningly secured agreement that all right-wing parliamentarians should be members of the

---

* Many Afrikaners regard the 1881 Battle of Majuba Hill, at which a posse of seventy-eight Boers defeated a regiment of seven hundred British troops sent to quell their resistance to Britain's annexation of the Transvaal Republic, as the First Boer War, and the main conflict with Britain from 1899 to 1901 as the Second Boer War.

council, thereby ensuring that the Conservative Party would control it. He was elected chairman. The Volksfront also appointed a directorate of four retired generals, headed by Viljoen and including a former chief of Military Intelligence, Gen. Tienie Groenewald. Part of the generals' task was to form a "Boer People's Army" drawn from farmers, miners, and a large pool of Citizen Force reservists who had undergone two years of military training and served in some of South Africa's border operations.

Tensions soon arose between Viljoen and the Conservative Party leadership. As the government and ANC raced towards agreement at the World Trade Centre, both spurning the idea of a separate Afrikaner *volkstaat*, Hartzenberg, who was there as a representative of the Volksfront (he would not allow his Conservative Party to take part in its own name), withdrew from the Negotiating Council. The Inkatha and KwaZulu government delegations followed soon after, but Ciskei and Bophuthatswana remained. Viljoen disagreed with Hartzenberg's decision. Although he had called on De Klerk to halt the negotiations until the security situation had been stabilized, he thought it was strategically wrong for the white right to withdraw from the process. That way it could only marginalize itself. "My role," Viljoen told me at the time, "is to convince these people that to stay out of the negotiations will leave only one option, the military option – and I don't believe in that. They must be given time to act responsibly."

He and Hartzenberg finally settled on an uneasy compromise: the Conservative Party would stay out of the negotiations, but the Volksfront generals would begin direct bilateral talks with the ANC outside the Negotiating Council. And so began yet another round of secret negotiations – this time between the ANC and the right-wing generals who were supposed to lead the Boer People's Army into a Third Boer War.

YET ANOTHER new figure in the widening character cast of the South African drama appeared on stage at this point. Braam

Viljoen is Constand Viljoen's identical twin brother, so alike that their closest friends confuse them, yet widely different in his political views. Braam Viljoen, a former theology professor turned farmer, had long been a tribal dissident and was one of the first Afrikaners to meet with the exiled ANC, even before members of the brotherhood held their meetings at Mells. Yet he also retained good relations with the conservative farming community, and as he watched the conflict grow between the white right and the ANC he tried quietly to arrange some informal contacts through the farmers' associations.

Now as the Volksfront generals decided to make contact with the ANC, Constand Viljoen turned to his twin to help facilitate the meetings. It was not easy. Both sides needed to keep the meetings secret – the Volksfront because its supporters would be enraged if they learned that the generals whom they expected to lead them to war were fraternizing with the enemy; the ANC because its followers would take exception to such a meeting so soon after right-wing fanatics had murdered Chris Hani. That meant Braam Viljoen could not be seen in the company of ANC people as he set about making arrangements for the secret meetings. "Because of my face I couldn't go into the ANC headquarters at Shell House," he explains. He would instantly be mistaken for his brother. "I had to make arrangements to drive into the parking basement, and the ANC people would come and talk to me in my car."

The first meeting was in a private home in Johannesburg's affluent suburb of Houghton. Constand Viljoen, Tienie Groenewald, and a third general, Kobus Visser, represented the Volksfront. Mandela was there for the ANC, together with the commander of the guerrilla force, Joe Modise, and its chief of staff, Joe Nhlanhla. It was a tense occasion and Braam Viljoen decided to break the ice with a gentle dig at the military enemies he had brought together. "I'm no good at telling jokes," he says, "but I had to do something." So he told a story, which he swears is true, of a Boer general who calls his troops together for a prayer meeting on the eve of a battle to defend their capital, Pretoria, against the invading British army. In the midst of their prayers a scout rides up with the news that he has just spied out the British camp, and they, too, are praying for victory. The perplexed Boer general turns to his troops. "Men," he says, "let us now ask the Lord to stand back for a while until we have settled this fight." The military men in the room chuckled and the atmosphere thawed.

What followed was a meeting that surprised both sides. "They were much more reasonable than we had expected," says Constand Viljoen. "There was an honesty between us. In fact, we agreed afterwards that we could get along better with the ANC than with the National Party." Douw Steyn, head of the Volksfront's defence committee, who attended subsequent meetings, concurs. Steyn commanded a force of farmers, all army trained, who called themselves Boerekrisis-Aksie (Boer-Crisis Action) and who formed the core of the Volksfront's military capability. He is a large, fierce-looking man with a big black beard, a veteran of the Angolan bush war who has cast himself consciously in the romanticized image of the tough Boer commando fighters of old, and he says matter-of-factly that he was included in the Volksfront negotiating team "to scare the ANC a little". As he puts it in a voice that rolls up from his barrel chest, "If you have a guy like me there, then you are saying to the other side you'd better give us what we want or we're going to push you around." Yet he, too, was surprised at the ANC's flexibility. "My overriding recollection of the talks," he says, "is of the ANC's willingness to accommodate us, compared with the National Party's total unwillingness to do so." This troubled him at the time: why should fellow Afrikaners be so much more hostile than the black enemies he had been taught to hate? Now he thinks he knows the answer. "We rightists and the ANC can never be political rivals," he reasons. "Our people will never vote for them and theirs will never support us, so we can talk practically about the future of South Africa. But when we talk to the National Party we are really talking about the future of that party rather than the future of South Africa."

Mandela's appraisal of the situation they both faced was frank. "If you want to go to war," he told the generals, "I must be honest and admit that we cannot stand up to you on the battlefield. We don't have the resources. It will be a long and bitter struggle, many people will die and the country may be reduced to ashes. But you must remember two things. You cannot win because of our numbers: you cannot kill us all. And you cannot win because of the international community. They will rally to our support and they will stand with us." General Viljoen was forced to agree. The two men looked at each other, and like Meyer and Ramaphosa on their fishing outing, they faced the truth of their mutual dependency.

More than twenty meetings followed. Braam Viljoen was joined by two other co-facilitators, Jurgen Kögl and Ivor Jenkins, who had been involved in separate efforts to bring the white right and ANC together. Mandela did not come again, but Thabo Mbeki, with his easy manner and long experience of allaying white fears, led the ANC team. At first Mbeki assumed that reassuring the Volksfronters point by point that their fears of black majority rule were groundless would remove the underlying cause of their desire for a separate homeland, but he soon realized that their sense of ethno-nationalism ran deeper than that. As he told the generals one day: "If claiming the right to govern yourselves is the issue, then we have to address that."

This is easier said than done, since the Afrikaner community is scattered throughout South Africa and does not constitute a majority of the population in any region that could be demarcated as a *volkstaat*, but the ANC negotiators accepted the principle of "self-determination" if not the exact form. They agreed to set up a joint working group to study the feasibility of creating a *volkstaat*, stipulating that there would have to be proven support for it and that it should not conflict with the national principle of non-racialism. In return, the Volksfront undertook to discourage any action to destabilize the political transition. A memorandum of agreement was drafted, but it promptly ran into trouble.

First, Hartzenberg refused to sign it, since he was not prepared publicly to accept the principle of non-racialism. Then the National Party objected that it had not been party to the negotiations. This caused the ANC to back off so as not to damage its new relationship with the government. The memorandum remained unsigned. Still, it represented an agreed position between the ANC and the Volksfront, and the talks between the two continued. The question of whether the right wing would participate in the election remained unresolved: the Volksfronters wanted their *volkstaat* to be granted first, but the ANC insisted its feasibility had to be established first. When the Volksfront produced a proposed map, it was so outrageously large that it chilled the negotiations. The ANC also insisted on proof that a significant number of Afrikaners supported the *volkstaat* idea. The Volksfront proposed a special Afrikaner referendum, but it was too close to the general election for this to be feasible. Mbeki suggested that votes for the Volksfront in the election could be regarded as a test of support for the *volkstaat*, which seemed like a workable compromise, but again the National Party objected, fearing that this would swing significant numbers of Afrikaners away from it in the election.

Mbeki seemed to score another breakthrough when he proposed that a Volkstaat Council be established as a statutory body to negotiate the establishment of a *volkstaat* with the Constituent Assembly after the election. The Volksfront accepted this, but then, inexplicably, the negotiations stalled. The ANC got caught up in anniversary celebrations in January, and in the launch of its election campaign. Meetings were postponed and priorities changed. "We couldn't pin anyone down and morale in the conservative movement slumped," says Braam Viljoen.

Pressure built up in the white right to revert to the original idea of military action. Then, suddenly, the opportunity for it arose.

WHAT PROMPTED THE Volksfront army to ride to the rescue of Bophuthatswana's President Lucas Mangope in the fateful second week of March 1994 remains a matter of dispute. Constand Viljoen and his fellow generals say it was just a matter of answering a call for help from their COSAG ally, and had they succeeded in stabilizing Bophuthatswana in its time of trouble they would have left quietly within days and the election could have taken place there without bloodshed. Members of the ANC believe there was a much larger and more sinister game plan – that the Volksfronters were to link up with Bophuthatswana's five-thousand-strong army, get equipped from its well-stocked armoury, link up similarly with the army of Ciskei and thousands more trained in secret camps in KwaZulu, plus untold numbers of South African Defence Force members who would defect at the call of the generals. The COSAG alliance would then have itself a formidable fighting force, plus a territorial base with an airport from which to operate. Given that, and the reluctance of the SADF to engage such a white rebel army, there was no knowing what they could have done. "They could have taken over the country," says one key figure. "There was nothing that could have stopped them."

"Absolute nonsense," says Constand Viljoen. "There was nothing like that. We never had any greater plan to start a joint military operation." He sounds emphatic, but there is no denying that had the operation succeeded it would have meant a radical change in the balance of political power. As Douw Steyn, who led the Volksfront army into Bophuthatswana, admits: "If we had succeeded in our objctive of stabilizing Bophuthatswana in twelve hours, the whole picture would have been different. Then we could have declared a UDI and ten-to-one nobody would have touched us" – an allusion to Ian Smith's 1965 unilateral declaration of independence. "One must understand that our alternative to taking part in the election was not necessarily going to war," Steyn adds, "it was also the possibility of a UDI with a military power base so strong no one would have been able to do anything about it."

Steyn insists, too, that this was not the motive for going into Bophuthatswana, but agrees that the territory, once secured, could have served as a useful base for further military operations. "Not that we ever visualized an externally based operation," he adds. "It wasn't necessary. We would simply have staked out our territory, said here is our *volkstaat*, here we make the rules, here we will hold our own election, leave us in peace." The importance of a successful Bophuthatswana operation in his mind is that it would have demonstrated a military capability that would have made such a unilaterally declared *volkstaat* untouchable. Inevitably, too, it would have triggered similar declarations in Ciskei and KwaZulu, which the Volkstaat army would doubtless have backed, and South Africa's transition to democracy, so close to completion, could have collapsed into ethnic fragmentation and civil strife.

As it turned out, it was the operation itself that collapsed ignominiously. It turned into a fiasco that humiliated the Volksfront forces, broke the back of COSAG's resistance to the election, and split the white right into squabbling factions once more. The reason for the failure was the inter-vention of Eugene Terre'Blanche and his AWB roughnecks, whose loutish behaviour provoked a Bophuthatswana Defence Force mutiny that screwed up the whole operation. Which brings us to the ultimate irony in this tale of paradoxes – it was the very worst white racists who finally cleared the way for South Africa's first one-person, one-vote election.

A strike by Bophuthatswana's twenty-two thousand civil servants began the chain of events that led to the Battle of Bop. President Mangope announced early in March that he would not participate in the April election: his government would stick to the independence granted it in 1977 under the apartheid system. This decision was based on shaky ground, for all the indications were that the seventy-one-year-old Tswana tribal chief had little popular support. Only fifteen thousand of the territory's 2.5 million eligible voters had cast ballots in the homeland's last election in 1985, a pathetic 0.6 per cent turnout. The South African Defence Force had rescued Mangope from a coup attempt in 1988, and since then he had ruled autocratically over the thirteen thousand five hundred square miles of landlocked territory spread over seven enclaves across three of the old South Africa's four provinces. Dissent had grown but Mangope kept it suppressed. In February 1994, Lawyers for Human Rights reported that there were serious violations of civil rights in the territory: political opponents of the regime were detained without trial, political meetings were prohibited except for Mangope's Christian Democratic Party, people were prevented from attending voter education classes, and police shootings were commonplace.

Mangope's defiance posed a direct challenge to the South African authorities. In terms of the agreement reached in the Negotiating Council, all black people living in the tribal homelands had their South African citizenship restored on January 1, 1994. The homelands themselves were due to be absorbed into the country's nine new provinces on election day, April 27. Their administrations would disappear. Yet here was the Bophuthatswana president saying he would have none of it and standing stubbornly on a law that had granted him legal independence seventeen years before. De Klerk didn't know what to do: after all, his party had created the man and the territory. And the ANC was in something of a jam, since it was now part of a new Transitional Executive Council working in tandem with the government to prepare the ground for a free and fair election. Mangope was making that impossible in the region he controlled, but what could be done about it as long as the government was reluctant to crack down on the obstructive old president?

While the authorities dithered, the people of Bophuthatswana took matters into their own hands. It seems likely that ANC agents got to work among them. Constand Viljoen insists they did, and even claims he had evidence of Umkhonto we Sizwe guerrillas being infiltrated into the territory to start an insurrection – a claim ANC leaders deny. Whatever the truth of this, within days of Mangope's announcement that he would not participate in the election the territory's civil servants began striking. Their demands were simple enough: since the homeland was scheduled to disappear on April 27, they wanted their wages and pensions paid out in advance. Mangope, lacking the funds, did nothing and the place ground to a halt. Worse, when the police began joining the strike, anarchy spread. Looters rampaged through Mmabatho, the capital, plundering Mega City, its main shopping mall (of which the Mangope family were the chief shareholders). Television cameras showed people pouring through stores as though at a mass clearance sale, making selections and hauling away refrigerators, electric stoves, and entire lounge and bedroom suites.

By Wednesday, March 9, the place was in chaos. Staff had seized control of the Bophuthatswana Broadcasting Corporation and taken its chairman, Eddie Mangope, one of the president's sons, hostage; students had taken over the university; and the civil servants had escalated their demands to include participation in the election and Mangope's deposition. At this point Mangope appealed to the Volksfront for help. Constand Viljoen flew to Mmabatho to see him; he says that Mangope sought the Volksfront's assistance because he did not trust the South African Defence Force. But, says Viljoen, Mangope stipulated that there should be no AWB men among the Volksfront forces. "He made it clear that the AWB was politically unacceptable and that there would be trouble with his own forces if any of them came," Viljoen explains.

Next day the Bophuthatswana minister of defence, Rowan Cronje, sent a formal request for help to the Volksfront executive – of which Terre'Blanche was a member. He, very excited, promptly despatched an aide to Radio Pretoria, the AWB's clandestine radio station, ordering it to broadcast a call for all members of his commando units to head for Bophuthatswana. When the Volksfront executive instructed him to keep his men out of the homeland, Terre'Blanche replied petulantly that they were already on their way. Viljoen and Hartzenberg were adamant: he should assemble his men outside the homeland and hold them there, awaiting further instructions. Viljoen then called on Gen. Georg

Meiring, chief of the South African army and an officer who had served under him for most of his career, to tell him of the coming Volksfront operation and make sure there would be no clash with the SADF. That done, Viljoen telephoned Douw Steyn from Meiring's office and asked him to mobilize a force of his Boerekrisis-Aksie men to move into Mmabatho that night and establish itself at the town's airport. They were to go without arms. "I didn't want to put them in a situation where they would have to mutiny by taking their own commando-unit weapons," Viljoen explains, "so I arranged with President Mangope that when they reached the airport the Bophuthatswana Defence Force would arm them." Gen. Jack Turner, chief of the BDF, would issue them with automatic weapons, armoured vehicles, and rations.

By Thursday evening Steyn had one thousand five hundred men ready and another three thousand on standby. He is cagey about how he was able to mobilize such a force so quickly. "The Volksfront has never had a private army," he says. "It has the loyalty of trained Citizen Force people, men in commando units. It is a mixture of the political ideal of the Afrikaner to be free, on the one hand, and, on the other, the loyalty which the whole army owes to Constand." Getting them together was simply a matter of making contact with these trained supporters through the Boerekrisis-Aksie network. "I can do it again in a day to show you," Steyn boasts.

Steyn's job was to mobilize the force and get it to Mmabatho, where Col. Jan Breytenbach, a retired commando leader with a reputation for daring exploits, would take over. As things turned out, the operation had collapsed by the time Breytenbach arrived, so the burly Steyn remained the hapless commander throughout. "My men were in place by six o'clock on Friday morning," he says with some pride. The one thousand five hundred men had driven through the night in their farm pickup trucks, bringing only a few sidearms with them. There were one hundred and fifty R4 automatic rifles waiting for them at the airport, and Steyn was told more would arrive soon from a nearby BDF armoury. But they never came. Not long after he had pitched camp, Steyn learned that despite the orders and appeals to Terre'Blanche, some six hundred AWB men were already in Mmabatho and creating mayhem. They had gathered on Thursday night at a hotel ten miles from Mmabatho, ready to move in at daybreak. When General Turner heard this, he sent an aide to tell Terre'Blanche to keep out of the territory, but the AWB leader dismissed the man contemptuously. Next morning Turner tried again to reason with Terre'Blanche, and after several hours of argument eventually agreed to let his men stay provided they came under Douw Steyn's command. "It was not a very good decision," says Steyn ruefully. "You can't take men from one unit and put them under someone else to whom they may feel no loyalty."

Even as the argument dragged on between Turner and Terre'Blanche, more AWB groups arrived in Bophuthatswana in response to the Radio Pretoria broadcasts. They, too, came in their farm trucks, armed to the teeth with hunting rifles, shotguns, and pistols. Others broke away from Steyn's command at the airport. They drove through the streets of Mmabatho yelling racial abuse at the locals and taking potshots at groups of people, killing and wounding several. As the Afrikaans newspaper, *Beeld*, reported angrily the next day, for these crass racists it was a *kaffirskietpiekniek* – a nigger-shooting picnic – and it so outraged the already shaky Bophuthatswana Defence Force that it mutinied. By mid-morning on Friday, March 11, Mangope's army had joined the rebellion against him. The men boarded their troop carriers and rode through the town shouting ANC freedom slogans and opening fire on the AWB raiders, while the townsfolk cheered. There was no question of the Volksfront army getting its promised weapons now. When Steyn went to the armoury himself, the guards refused to open up. With only 10 per cent of his men under arms and the local army and population turned hostile, Steyn realized he had better get out – and ordered his army to withdraw. Leaving his one hundred and fifty armed men to hold the airport until they could hand it over to the South African Defence Force, Steyn and his Volksfront volunteers went out the way they had come, with a few rearguard skirmishes on the way.

Not so the AWB rabble. Some lost their way and went roaring through villages and township suburbs, still blazing away at bystanders. Several encountered journalists along the way, beat them up, and seized their cameras. A convoy of twenty trucks and cars came barrelling along a road towards Mmabatho's twin town of Mafikeng. Ahead was a roadblock, with a police barracks nearby. A group of people, including some soldiers, stood near the roadblock and waved their fists as the convoy raced towards them and burst through the barrier. The soldiers yelled obscenities and fired shots at the speeding convoy, while the AWB men cursed and fired back. The last car in the convoy was an old, light blue Mercedes-Benz, and a bearded man in the passenger's seat was firing through the window. There was a blast of gunfire from the soldiers, the car's windscreen shattered, and it slewed to a halt. As the shooting continued the passenger's door slowly opened and the bearded man slumped into the dust with blood pumping from his neck. His two companions crawled out and squatted beside his body, their hands in the air.

For twenty minutes Alwyn Wolfaard and Fanie Uys, both from the northern Transvaal town of Naboomspruit, lay slumped in the dirt while the crowd taunted them and a series of Bophuthatswana policemen from the barracks watched menacingly over them. Uys was propped against the back wheel of the Mercedes; Wolfaard was stretched out on his stomach. Both were bleeding. Behind them Nic Fourie, a building contractor from Natal, looked dead. Several reporters arrived, among them Phillip van Niekerk of *The Observer*. TV cameras trained on the cowering men. "Please, God, help us, get us some medical help," Wolfaard begged. A reporter spoke to a Bophuthatswana army colonel who came by and who said an ambulance was on its way – but it never arrived. A young policeman walked up to Uys and screamed at him: "Who do you think you are? What are you doing in my country? I can take your life in a second, do you

know that?" When a reporter tried to calm him, the policeman snapped back. "We want to shoot these fucking dogs.
They have killed women. They are animals, not people."*

Minutes later, they were indeed shot like dogs. While the
TV cameras rolled, another frenzied policeman stepped up
to Uys, pointed his assault rifle at him and fired a single shot
into his body. Phillip van Niekerk, who moments before had
been talking to the men, describes the scene. "There was a
loud pop and the man (Uys) slumped. His head fell on to his
chest. Seconds before he had been answering questions.
Now he was dead . . . The man who shot him tugged at the
breech of his rifle, then turned to look at the second white
man (Wolfaard), who lay helpless on his stomach in the road.
The officer walked over to him and pointed the gun at the
back of his head. Again the pop, a firecracker. The head fell
lifelessly forward. One more shot to each, just to finish them
off . . . then the man with the gun held it up triumphantly,
like a trophy."**

Back in Naboomspruit, Ester Wolfaard and her eight-year-
old daughter, Annalise, were watching television that night.
Alwyn had been dead for more than six hours, but the AWB
had not called, and his wife and daughter knew nothing of
his fate until they saw him executed before their eyes on the
six o'clock news. For them and for white rightists everywhere this traumatic experience made a tremendous impact.
The image of the execution, in all its awfulness, had blown
away an ancient myth that had grounded generations of
colonialism and racial domination – the myth that the white
race, with its superior arms and training, could always and
everywhere command indigenous people of colour. That
was the rationale behind the existence of the AWB and Volksfront armies. Now everyone had seen on their television
screens that it no longer held; that black people, too, had
lethal weapons; and to go to war against them was not a
hunting expedition, a jolly adventure with one's mates

---

* *Sunday Times*, Johannesburg, March 13, 1994.
** *The Observer*, London, March 13, 1994.

where one could demonstrate one's dominance. The bubble of adventure, the heroic re-enactment of historic Boer myths, was punctured in a day of blood and humiliation.

But the crisis of Bophuthatswana was not yet over. There was still a political battle to be fought over who should control this substantial chunk of territory whose administration appeared to have collapsed. With the election less than six weeks away, the government wanted to keep President Mangope in place – provided he would agree to participate in the election and allow free political activity in Bophuthatswana. On Friday morning, as things began running out of control in Mmabatho, Constand Viljoen and Rowan Cronje flew by helicopter to the Union Buildings in Pretoria to see De Klerk, and they seemed to reach an understanding with the president along these lines.

The ANC had decided differently, however. During the early stages of the crisis it had gone along with De Klerk's view not to send troops in too soon, but when news came through on Thursday night that right-wing forces were moving into the territory, the ANC grew alarmed. The prospect of a powerful insurrectionary force establishing an operational base there, with the latent support of large sections of the South African Defence Force, loomed frighteningly in their minds. Key leaders meeting at Nelson Mandela's home late one night decided it was time to push for more decisive action, and in particular that Mangope should be removed from office. He was obstructing the election, he had precipitated the crisis, and the ANC was determined he should go.

There was a flurry of meetings next morning – of the De Klerk cabinet, the ANC's National Working Committee, the Transitional Executive Council's Working Committee, and De Klerk's private meeting with Viljoen and Cronje. At one point the TEC meeting was being held in a committee room of the Union Buildings while a bilateral meeting between the ANC and the government was taking place in a hallway outside, with people shuttling between the two. The atmosphere grew more tense as the news from Mmabatho grew more alarming. Around noon Roelf Meyer suggested to Cyril Ramaphosa that Mac Maharaj and Fanie van der Merwe (the civil servant whose experience went back to the committee of officials that had met with Mandela in prison) be sent to Mmabatho as emissaries of the Transitional Executive Council. Ramaphosa agreed. This critical decision put the canny Maharaj in a position to make the running in the events that followed.

The two men, together with General Meiring, Police Commissioner Johan van der Merwe, and the director general of foreign affairs, Rusty Evans – sent along as a token gesture to Bophuthatswana's nominal status as a foreign country – landed at Mmabatho at 3.30 p.m. and went directly to the South African embassy, now protected from the surrounding anarchy by six hundred SADF soldiers. In the adjacent home of Ambassador Tjaart van der Walt, they met General Turner, head of the Bophuthatswana Defence Force. Asked for a situation report, the Bop general gave it straight: "I've lost control of my forces," he told them. "My officers are refusing to take orders from me." Looking agitated, Turner appealed for help, saying he had ordered the AWB out, and if Viljoen's men and the SADF would assist him he believed he could regain control of his army and secure Mangope's position.

Meiring briskly drafted an action plan – to stabilize the Bophuthatswana Defence Force, then with them re-establish law and order and take over the police function. Maharaj intervened, leading to the first of several sharp exchanges. To him, reinstating Mangope was unthinkable, for it would allow the right wing to regroup and once again pose the threat of establishing a base for destabilizing operations, perhaps even a military coup. Pointing out that he and Van der Merwe were there as representatives of the Transitional Executive Council, Maharaj insisted that they had to report back to the Union Buildings and that De Klerk and Mandela had to give their joint approval before any action was taken. Meiring argued that the TEC men were there as observers, but Mararaj stood firm. "As I see it," he said, "the army has mutinied, the police force has lost control, law and order have collapsed, and there is no longer any effective administration in the country. Does anyone disagree?" No one did. "Well then," he said, "that is the report we have to send to the Union Buildings." With that, he and Van der Merwe crossed the yard to the embassy to telephone their separate reports to the TEC.

Viljoen, meanwhile, had gone from meeting with De Klerk to see Mangope, who by then had fled to his plush country home at Motswedi, fifty miles northeast of Mmabatho. "Mangope was very upset," Viljoen recalls. "He didn't know what had gone wrong, why we hadn't been issued with the weapons. I don't think his people were briefing him properly." Viljoen tried to calm Mangope, assuring him that he could do a deal with Meiring that would have the SADF secure the territory in return for an agreement to allow the election. "I said to Mangope, 'I promise you I'm going to go to Meiring now and I'll try to get him to assist, to consolidate the situation in co-operation with the Bophuthatswana Defence Force.' I said he would remain in charge, and I tried to convince him that he could accept that the Defence Force would act in a neutral way and not on behalf of the ANC or the government. I told him, 'You can trust Georg Meiring,'" Viljoen says.

Then Viljoen went by his helicopter to Mmabatho, touching down briefly at the airport to see the last of his forces still holding it while the bulk of the Volksfront army withdrew. With Bophuthatswana Defence Minister Cronje, he next went to the embassy. The helicopter swooped low over the trees just as Maharaj and Van der Merwe were stepping out of the embassy building, having phoned through their reports. Maharaj looked up, saw the white machine, and wondered who it was as they walked back to the ambassador's house. When he rejoined the other members of the group, he noticed Georg Meiring was not among them. Quietly he asked Rusty Evans to check where the general had gone.

Meiring, in fact, had left to join the new arrivals – Viljoen,

Cronje, Turner, and Jan Breytenbach, the man originally assigned to command the Volksfront army. Viljoen put the proposal he had discussed with Mangope to the South African army chief. "I put it to him and he said yes," Viljoen recalls. "That is what they were going to do. They were going to move in and work with Turner and try to stabilize the situation." According to Viljoen, Meiring agreed to accompany him and Rowan Cronje to see Mangope and give him a personal assurance about the role of the South African Defence Force. At that point Rusty Evans walked in, overheard the conversation, and advised Meiring that he should get De Klerk's approval first. When Evans returned to the ambassador's house and told Maharaj where the general had been, Maharaj promptly phoned the Union Buildings again: Ramaphosa told him the government had just received a request that Meiring, Viljoen, and Cronje should visit Mangope. "I told him this would be disastrous, that it was part of an attempt to reinstate Mangope and if that happened the right wing would be able to regroup in Bophuthatswana," Maharaj recalls. "Moments later Cyril phoned back to say Mandela had put his foot down and De Klerk had vetoed the trip."

Meiring then strode back into the room to announce that the light was failing and they would have to take off for Pretoria in half an hour. For Maharaj it was time for a final confrontation. "I said, 'Please sit down, general, I want to raise some matters with you,'" he recalls. Pointing out once again that he and Van der Merwe were representing the Transitional Executive Council, he objected that Meiring had "held meetings behind our backs", and insisted that they should be kept informed since no decision could be made without a proper report to the Union Buildings. "I take my orders from the State Security Council," Meiring protested. Maharaj snapped. "Fanie, tell your man he has made another mistake," he said, turning to an uncomfortable Van der Merwe. "Tell him he takes his orders from the state president – and that those orders from De Klerk have to be agreed to by Mandela."

This was the end of efforts to keep Mangope in office. Next morning the TEC's Management Committee, after some heated debate, agreed that Mangope had to go. Legally it was tricky, but the TEC decided that, since the new law made all homelanders South African citizens, it was legitimate for the South African government to intervene to protect them in a strife-torn region and ensure their right to vote – even to place President Mangope under house arrest for his own safety. In any event, South Africa was the only country in the world that recognized Bophuthatswana's independence, so if it withdrew that recognition, the independence itself surely ceased to exist.

At 4 p.m. Mac Maharaj, Fanie van der Merwe, and Georg Meiring were back in the air headed for Bophuthatswana – accompanied this time by Foreign Minister Pik Botha, whose unhappy task it was to tell Mangope he was deposed. They flew to Mmabatho, where the SADF had by now moved in and begun restoring order, then with an armed escort went on in three helicopters to Motswedi. It was dark when they landed, to be ushered in to Mangope's heavily draped sitting-room. The old president, with his doleful eyes and meltdown face, sat on a small throne dressed in a safari suit and patent-leather slippers. He was flanked by his sons, Eddie, the ousted broadcasting chief, and Kwena.

Slowly, awkwardly, Pik Botha told him his government was no longer recognized and he could therefore no longer continue as its head. Mangope tried one last gambit for more time: give him until Tuesday to address his people and see whether his parliament would accede to what was being done, he begged. Botha seemed about to assent, but Maharaj cut in sharply. "Your administration has collapsed," he told him. "There is no effective control, there are no hospitals, there is no TV, no radio, no functioning civil service, the security forces are divided, arms are being stolen and orders defied. The Transitional Executive Council has been petitioned by fifty-three senior civil servants from your territory who want reincorporation, free political activity, secure salaries and pensions, and security force control." As

Maharaj spoke, a half-smile flitted across the face of Eddie Mangope, who had been lounging alongside his father in a New Orleans T-shirt and slacks. Now he leaned across and spoke briefly to the old man in Setswana, telling him in effect that the game was up. With a sigh Mangope accepted the inevitable.

It was all over. That night Ambassador Tjaart van der Walt was installed as administrator of the territory (joined later by an ANC nominee, Job Mogoro, as co-administrator). Meanwhile, Constand Viljoen, his options shrunk to a stark choice between leading the right-wingers into a civil war or joining the election, had made a bold decision the night before and, with just ten minutes to go to the midnight deadline, registered a party, the Freedom Front, to participate in the election. He had tried earlier that evening to persuade Hartzenberg to register the Volksfront, and when the hardline leader refused, Viljoen decided to go his own way. Next day the committee of generals and several leading members of Hartzenberg's Conservative Party announced that they were following Viljoen.

THE EXAMPLE OF Bophuthatswana was duly noted in other homelands. Ten days later, on March 22, civil servants in Ciskei went on strike, demanding full pension payouts ahead of the April election. With signs of impending mutiny in his police and defence forces, military ruler Brig. Oupa Gqozo resigned before the end of the day and asked the Transitional Executive Council to appoint an interim administration. "Two down and one to go," Joe Slovo exulted when news of Gqozo's resignation reached ANC headquarters.

But Buthelezi was a tougher nut to crack. Unlike Mangope and Gqozo, he had substantial popular support in his region and there was less likelihood that his KwaZulu police force would mutiny. Still, he was now badly isolated: even Viljoen had registered for the election, leaving Inkatha and the Conservative Party as the only outsiders. Foreign pressures were also building up against Buthelezi. He had long presented himself to the Western world as the moderate alternative to the ANC, committed to non-violent struggle, anti-communism and multiparty democracy, but for some years – indeed, since Mandela's release – Western governments had begun questioning these claims. In September 1993, Africa Watch, a division of the respected U.S. organization Human Rights Watch, labelled KwaZulu a "traditional dictatorship", noting that it was "a one-party state" where freedom of expression, assembly, and association were not respected and expressing the view that its continued existence "threatens the transition to democracy".*

As Buthelezi found one reason after another to avoid participating in the election, even his closest supporters in the West began accusing him of playing a spoiler's role. Now there was the additional factor of Judge Goldstone's reports implicating Inkatha officials and the KwaZulu police in "third force" activities. These were particularly embarrassing for Buthelezi, because in addition to being KwaZulu's chief minister he was also its minister of police and therefore had direct line responsibility for the men Goldstone named. Although he denied knowing anything about the "third force" activities, or indeed that there was any truth in Goldstone's findings, critics were quick to point out that Buthelezi was the dominant figure in his party and was known to have a personal hand in even its smallest decisions.

The trouble was that as these pressures and criticisms mounted, Buthelezi became more aggressively recalcitrant than ever. This is what had estranged him from De Klerk; now he was backing himself ever more into a corner. His demands were unacceptable to the other parties, except for his COSAG partners, who had now collapsed. He insisted that the Zulu people had the right to self-determination, that they should be able to draft their own constitution, and that the KwaZulu homeland should not be dismantled until there was a constitutional dispensation acceptable to them. It was controversial from the start, though: the constitution Inkatha

* *Africa Watch*, Vol 5 No 12 (September 1993): pp. 1-45.

proposed for the KwaZulu-Natal region amounted to secession, making the territory a sovereign state whose laws would take precedence over those of South Africa. The state would have its own president, its own constitutional court, its own autonomous central bank, and its own army. The South African government would not be able to send armed forces there, nor levy taxes without the state's approval. Apologists argued that this was simply an opening position for negotiation, but at no stage did Buthelezi offer modifications. Instead, he withdrew Inkatha from the constitutional negotiations and insisted that his demands be met if he was to participate in the election.

A major factor underlying the KwaZulu problem was that Inkatha was not the embodiment of the Zulu people, in whose name it made these demands; it was questionable, indeed, whether it even commanded a majority of the tribe. Buthelezi tried to meet this difficulty by having the Zulu king, Goodwill Zwelithini, identify with the demands. He had not always got along with Zwelithini. In fact, the two had clashed bitterly in 1979 when the king tried to form a rival political party in KwaZulu, called Inala, and Buthelezi castigated him in front of the homeland's National Assembly, threatening to cut off his stipend and amending both the Inkatha and KwaZulu constitutions to prohibit him from taking part in politics. But now Buthelezi harnessed the king, his nephew, to his cause, and Zwelithini acted as though he was in the Inkatha leader's power.

The two men appeared together at a number of *imbizos*, or tribal rallies, which seemed aimed at whipping up Zulu paranoia with extravagant warnings that the negotiations were a "connivance" aimed at "obliterating the Zulu nation" and that they would have to stand together as never before in order to survive. Buthelezi also went out of his way to stress the blood relationship between his family and that of the king. At a rally in Johannesburg on July 25, 1993, he laid claim to hereditary political power. In addition to being president of the Inkatha Freedom Party and chief minister of KwaZulu, he said: "I, Your Majesty, am also your prime minister. I was born to follow a course in life which was fixed by nearly two centuries of Zulu history."

There was more in this vein. "The king and I," he said, "through our blood ties, go back to the very beginnings of our history as a nation . . . The king's family and my family, inseparably joined by history . . . The blood ties which bind us together . . . I have the right and duty to speak for the Zulu people which no power on earth will ever take away from me . . . I was born to lead, and I was also elected to lead." This was the litany of a man who was not disposed to let others take over the leadership of KwaZulu-Natal through the vagaries of a democratic election.

Efforts to coax Inkatha into the election culminated at Skukuza, a camp in South Africa's premier game reserve, the Kruger National Park, just eighteen days before the election. Deadlines for registration had long since passed, but Mandela and De Klerk had indicated they were prepared to bend all rules to have an inclusive election. So on April 8 they met with Buthelezi and Zwelithini in the game-park camp with a retinue of aides and advisers. Mandela had a package offer that he hoped would lure Zwelithini into an agreement. If the king were being kept in bondage through a sense of insecurity, then he had to be given assurances. His problem, after all, was not much different from that of the Bophuthatswana and Ciskei civil servants: who was going to pay him after the KwaZulu administration ceased to exist on April 27? Mandela proposed that Zwelithini would be the constitutional monarch of KwaZulu-Natal Province, he would sit in the provincial assembly, he would open the assembly sessions, he would have his own royal con-stabulary, his stipend would be secured, and all his rights and prerogatives would be entrenched in the provincial constitution. As Mandela said later: "I offered him the same constitutional status as the queen of England and the crowned heads of Europe."

Zwelithini, surrounded by Buthelezi's aides, did not respond immediately. He had to consult his advisers, he said. After being closeted with Buthelezi and his aides for ninety minutes he sent a messenger to say the proposals were unacceptable. When the group reassembled, Buthelezi explained that the king's requirements could not be addressed separately from Inkatha's demands. This impasse left the ANC and the government with very few options. They decided to go ahead and hold the election without Inkatha. A small joint committee was appointed to continue discussions, but as Ramaphosa puts it, from that point on, negotiating with Inkatha was considered hopeless and the two major players focussed on how to hold an election in hostile KwaZulu-Natal.

"Our main thrust now became a military one," says Ramaphosa. "We had to look at how to rein in the IFP, particularly the warlords and the hit squads, and we started identifying the camps where they were training people." A state of emergency was declared in Natal and troops began moving into the province. "I think that was salutary," says a government official. "Coming on top of what had happened in Bophuthatswana, it drove home the message to Buthelezi that the government was not going to shrink from physical confrontation."

When intelligence reports warned the government of increased activity in secret Inkatha training camps, the TEC appointed a special task force to investigate. Once again Mac Maharaj and Fanie van der Merwe took off on a helicopter expedition, accompanied this time by a police officer, Maj. Gen. Wynand van der Merwe, of Pietermaritzburg, and a member of the Goldstone Commission, Howard Varney. The general flew ahead with a small police support group and located a training camp called Mlaba deep in the northern KwaZulu bush. He tried to land, but a large group of men rushed towards his helicopter and forced him to take off again. General van der Merwe spotted a white man in the crowd whom he recognized as Phillip Powell, a former security police officer turned Inkatha official who, informants later said, was in charge of training at the camp. General van der Merwe returned to base and sent a message to Powell that he intended coming back to seach the camp. Instructions were given to set up army roadblocks around Mlaba, but when the general, Maharaj and Fanie van der Merwe arrived there that night the camp was deserted: the troops had allowed some five thousand Inkatha trainees to slip past the roadblocks. The search party found large quantities of arms and ammunition, including a homemade Vlakplaas shotgun hidden under the front seat of Powell's truck. The men had got away, but the training operation was disrupted. Inkatha's military option was over.

Buthelezi had one more card to play: he asked for international mediation. Mandela and De Klerk, still anxious to do everything possible to bring him in, agreed. Various distinguished foreigners, including Henry Kissinger, the former U.S. secretary of state, and Britain's former foreign secretary, Lord Carrington, were invited to form a mediation team. Their terms of reference were still being argued as they took off for Johannesburg. Buthelezi was insisting that the date of the election should be among the issues the mediation team would deal with. He wanted the election postponed, arguing that it was too late for Inkatha to campaign properly, but others saw it as a foot-dragging tactic. "He hoped that if he could get the election delayed the KwaZulu administration would be able to go on and on," says a government official. The joint committee that had been set up at Skukuza had in fact agreed that the election should be on the Kissinger-Carrington agenda, but when Cyril Ramaphosa and Roelf Meyer learned of this they both objected. "It was clear in my mind that if we fell into the trap of mediating the election date, the entire process could have been scuttled," Ramaphosa says. "Millions of people were geared up for their liberation, and if there had been any attempt to postpone the election I think the country would have blown up." Ramaphosa and Meyer got their leaders to endorse their view, but Buthelezi remained adamant that the election date had to remain on the mediation agenda. With the issue deadlocked, the mediators flew home again, mission unaccomplished.

Buthelezi had now run out of options. The election was going ahead without him; rumblings were starting among his civil servants about where their next pay cheques were coming from; and King Zwelithini sent an emissary to tell Mandela he was in fear of his life and was really interested in the deal offered at Skukuza.* In desperation Buthelezi turned for advice to an old Kenyan friend, professor Washington Okumu, who happened to be in South Africa at the time. Bluntly, the portly professor told Buthelezi what scores of others had been saying – that if he did not take part in the election, his Kwazulu administration would be dismantled and Inkatha would be marginalized and crushed. Better to participate and fight his case from within the new system, Okumu advised. This time Buthelezi listened. With only seven days to go to the first of the three election days, the Inkatha leader announced that he was ready to take part.

Was it still possible? Eighty million ballot papers had already been printed with the names of eighteen participating parties in the national and provincial elections: could Inkatha's name be added in time? It would be difficult but, well, yes, was the answer from the chairman of the Independent Electoral Commission, Judge Johann Kriegler. Eighty million separate stickers would have to be printed and attached to the bottom of the ballot papers by hand. If the printing company worked twenty-four hours a day, and if there were a special session of Parliament on Monday, April 25 – just one day before the first voting day – to pass legislation permitting a late registration, Kriegler reckoned they could just make it.

The deal was done. Inkatha was in. The COSAG rebellion had collapsed completely.

---

* After the election, when the king was freed from his dependency on the KwaZulu government, his feelings of resentment towards Buthelezi came into the open and in September 1994 he announced that he was severing relations with the IFP leader.

15

Another Country

The road to the future is
always under construction
– GRAFFITO IN A PORT ELIZABETH TOWNSHIP

APRIL 27 WAS more than just the main election day. On that day the new South Africa was born in spirit as well as constitutionally. The need to paste Inkatha stickers on 80 million ballot papers meant there were delays in delivering them to the thousands of voting stations, so voters had to wait, up to six or seven hours, in queues that wrapped around city blocks and stretched a mile or more. People tend to get irritable in such circumstances, tempers get frayed and racial friction may surface. But not on this day. Now, millions of South Africans stood patiently, good-humouredly, in the long queues, black and white together, hour after hour, sharing the tedium and the discomfort, sharing the sense of occasion, and for the first time in their lives discovering each other. White racists had made a last desperate bid to disrupt the election: a massive car bomb outside the ANC's regional office in downtown Johannesburg on Sunday demolished buildings, killed nine people and injured ninety-two; another at a taxi rank in nearby Germiston on Monday killed ten; bombs were hurled into six polling stations around the country; and now, on the morning of Tuesday, April 26, came news of yet another explosion at Johannesburg Airport. The intention, obviously, was to scare people into staying away from the polling stations. It failed utterly. There was no sense of anxiety in those long queues. People seemed to give the bombers no thought as they rejoiced in the mood of the occasion.

The nearest analogy was the mood of the great crowd at the Brandenburg Gate the day the Berlin Wall came down. Here once again was an event marking the collapse of an evil ideology that had inflicted misery on millions of people. Yet there was not the same spirit of exultation and triumphalism here. This was quieter, more reflective. Joyous but somehow more private, as though individuals were experiencing something profound within themselves. It was, I believe, a sense of personal liberation – for blacks, liberation from oppression; for whites, liberation from guilt.

Two centuries ago Hegel wrote of the relationship between lordship and bondage that holds both inextricably together. Slavery debases master as well as slave. The warder becomes a prisoner in his own jail; he is never free from the business of oppression and confinement. So, too, in apartheid South Africa where white and black had been bound together in a web of mutual destructiveness. Apartheid, brutalizing the whites as it destroyed the self-esteem of the blacks, robbed both of their humanity. Everyone had been victim of a system that was now being ritually exorcised. In some subliminal way the act of waiting in line together to vote in the country's first democratic election was a joint reaffirmation of their humanity. The spirit of it infused the air: everybody sensed it although they could not express it. It was the profound experience of a national rebirth.

It revealed itself in a multitude of ways: in the moving sight of an old black woman being propelled to the voting station in a wheelbarrow; in a young black woman who threw her arms spontaneously around a young white woman as she emerged from the polling station and planted a kiss on her cheek; and in the unemployed black man in the queue beside me who said simply: "Now I am a human being." Appreciation of the value of the vote may have become dulled in the jaded democracies of the North, but here, among people from whom it had been withheld for so long, it was new and vivid and real.

The results, when eventually they came out after complicated days of counting, held few surprises. The ANC won with 62.65 per cent of the national vote, enough to satisfy its grassroots followers but not enough to give it the unbridled dominance of a two-thirds majority. The National Party was second with 20.4 per cent, the Inkatha Freedom Party third with 10.5 per cent, followed by the Freedom Front, 2.2 per cent, the Democratic Party, 1.7 per cent, and the Pan-Africanist Congress 1.2 per cent. Under the proportional representation system, in a National Assembly of four hundred members, that translated into two hundred and fifty two seats for the ANC, eighty-two for the NP, forty-three for the IFP, nine for the Freedom Front, seven for the DP, five for the PAC, and two for a minor party called the African Christian Democratic Party.

The ANC won seven of the nine provinces. The National Party scored a breakthrough among the coloured population, giving it control of Western Cape Province and transforming the creator of apartheid itself into a multiracial party. The IFP won KwaZulu-Natal with 50 per cent of the vote, the only result that went against opinion-poll predictions. Although there were massive irregularities in the Natal voting these probably made little difference to the outcome, and the ANC abandoned plans to challenge the result. Cyril Ramaphosa believes many people voted for the Inkatha Freedom Party because they felt that was the only way to end the violence in the province. "They believed the IFP would not accept defeat, and they knew we would," he says. Just as likely is that the ANC and the opinion polls underestimated the number of people in the traditionalist rural areas where Inkatha's strength lay.

Two weeks later, on May 10, Nelson Mandela was inaugurated as president, with Thabo Mbeki as first deputy and F.W. de Klerk as second deputy president. Again there was a swelling of the ineffable spirit of national rebirth as a hundred thousand people gathered before the Union Buildings in Pretoria in a day of celebration that blended formal ceremonialism with the vitality of a Woodstock rock concert. The greatest array of international dignitaries ever to visit South Africa marked the return of the pariah state to the community of nations, and the old regime saluted the new as six air force jets flew overhead smoke-trailing the colours of the new South African flag. "They're ours now," murmured the ANC man next to me as he watched what only a few years before he would have regarded as the regime's weapons of oppression.

Yet there was no spirit of triumphalism. Reconciliation was the theme, and the voice of the new president, Nelson Mandela, slow and measured, boomed it out across the great crowd: "We enter into a covenant that we shall build a society in which all South Africans, both black and white, will be able to walk tall, without any fear in their hearts, assured of their inalienable right to human dignity – a rainbow nation at peace with itself and the world."

And then the pledge, from a man who had once told the judge who was about to sentence him to life imprisonment that he was prepared to die for the cause of non-racialism. "Never, never, and never again shall it be that this beautiful land will again experience the oppression of one by another, and suffer the indignity of being the skunk of the world."

A WONDERFUL PROMISE, but can it be fulfilled? In a world so riven by ethnic conflicts, and in a continent where tribalism and one-party dictatorships are endemic, is it realistic to expect South Africa, with its long history of racial intolerance, to buck the trend and become a truly non-racial, multi-party democracy? Is non-racialism in any event not a pipedream that ignores the hard realities of human nature, and is democracy not something that can exist only in a handful of developed countries with a high degree of homogeneity and what the social scientists call social balance?

There are many in the world and in my own country who believe this. They expect that the new South Africa will be just one more hopeful transition that will soon turn to ashes, that the country will sink into the economic decay and political oppression which seems to be Africa's destiny. I am not one. Though I hated apartheid, I never shared the view of the morally indignant who believed, even hoped, that it was bound to end in a bloodbath. Nor do I now share the view of the cynics that it is bound to become another African basket case, if not a Bosnia. And for the same reason. The unique balance of mutual dependency that made apartheid impossible and that drove its squabbling factions to a constitutional settlement against all the odds, will continue to bind the nation together and charge it with a creative tension.

Certainly South Africa is a country of great ethnic diversity and historical conflicts, but there are important countervailing factors. First among these is that ethnic dismemberment is not a practical possibility. We have just emerged from history's most determined effort to enforce ethnic partition: if it had been even remotely possible, half a century of apartheid would have achieved it. But it failed – totally. The country is too economically integrated; its races are too mutually interdependent, for ethnic separation ever to take place.

Another – indeed the chief – factor weighing against ethnically driven politics in the new South Africa, is that none of the major political parties (with the exception of Inkatha and the right wing) is ethnically based, as is the case elsewhere in Africa and in other countries where ethnicity dominates politics. From the day it was founded in 1912, the African National Congress has been a pantribal movement which today has members of all racial and ethnic groups in its leadership and proclaims non-racialism as its bedrock philosophy. The ANC's founder, Pixley ka Seme, was a Zulu, as was Chief Albert Luthuli who led it at the time it was banned in 1960. He was succeeded by Oliver Tambo, then Nelson Mandela, both Xhosas. The main contenders for succession now are Thabo Mbeki, also a Xhosa, and Cyril Ramaphosa, a member of South Africa's smallest black tribe, the Venda. Government propagandists tried, when the Natal violence began, to portray it as a tribal conflict, with the ANC described as a Xhosa party. The election results give the lie to that. The ANC won 84 per cent of the vote in the Xhosa heartland of the Eastern Cape, but it also won 92 per cent of the vote among the Venda and North Sotho people of Northern Transvaal, 83 per cent among the Tswanas of North-West province, 81 per cent among the Tsonga of Eastern Transvaal, and 77 per cent among the

South Sotho of the Orange Free State.

The same lack of ethnic identity goes for the ANC's alliance partners, the Congress of South African Trade Unions and the Communist Party, and for its main rival among the liberation movements, the Pan-Africanist Congress. The PAC, a breakaway movement from the older organization, is equally unidentifiable in ethnic terms. This means that none of the major contenders for power can mobilize support by appealing to tribal passions, as happens elsewhere in Africa. If Mandela were to whip up Xhosa ethno-nationalism, he would estrange all the non-Xhosas – by far the majority – in his movement.

Reinforcing this already strong disincentive is the fact that no ethnic group is in a position to dominate South Africa politically. The Zulus, with 7 million, are the largest black tribe, but even they number only one-sixth of the total population; thus any political party which defines itself in ethnic terms, as Inkatha has done, writes itself out of contention for national political power and can aspire only to regional power. Even the mother of all ethnic parties, the National Party, which fostered and rode to power on Afrikaner ethno-nationalism in the days of whites-only politics, has had to go multiracial to stay in the game. The founding election witnessed the remarkable sight of F.W. de Klerk and his erstwhile apartheidists campaigning hard for support in black, coloured and Indian townships.

This is not to ignore the reality of ethnicity. At the end of this terrible century, which has seen so much misery caused by explosions of nationalism, racism, and religious bigotry, that would be folly. Though ethno-nationalism may not again become the driving force in South African politics, it is a devil to be watched. In itself, a sense of national consciousness and pride in one's cultural heritage is harmless, even healthy, and there is no reason why a multiplicity of cultures should not coexist peacefully in a country like South Africa. But the lesson of history is that ethno-nationalism becomes inflamed and dangerous if it develops a sense of grievance or suffers some collective humiliation, either real or imagined.

Then it takes on an assertive aggression. The Oxford philosopher Sir Isaiah Berlin uses the vivid imagery of the poet Schiller to liken cultural nationalism to a bent twig. If the twig is bent too far, Berlin warns, it will lash back with an embittered and aggressive self-assertion.*

In other words, the cultural nationalism of a group like the Afrikaners can exist harmoniously in a multicultural South Africa, provided it is not put under pressure and made to feel threatened or suffocated. The danger is that it may feel culturally swamped, unable to express itself through its own "self-determination". The denial of a *volkstaat* to meet this need could bend the twig of bitterness and inflame the ethno-nationalism in a dangerous way. Much as the rulers of the new South Africa may recoil from anything that smacks of apartheid recidivism, they should be alive to this danger. The problem, of course, is that there is no Afrikaner Quebec, or Scotland, or Wales, or Basque provinces, or Suisse-Romande, or Ticino, or, for that matter, KwaZulu. There is no piece of land anywhere where Afrikaners, particularly Afrikaner *volkstaters*, constitute a majority – and it is unthinkable that South Africa could ever return to a system of removing citizenship rights from people of colour to create a white state.

The answer may be to place the onus on the *volkstaters* themselves by declaring a region where, on the precedent of Joe Slovo's sunset clause, they could be allowed an ethnically loaded vote to ensure Afrikaner control for, say, ten years, after which the special loading would fall away. In that time it would be up to the *volkstaters* to ensure that sufficient of their supporters resettled in the region to ensure a natural majority: the larger the region claimed, the more difficult this would be. If they failed, they would be outvoted at the next election. But they would have been given the chance to achieve their ideal and they would have no cause to feel aggrieved if their own efforts failed them. The twig of their ethno-nationalism would not have been bent.

---

* Isaiah Berlin, *The Crooked Timber of Humanity: Chapters in the History of Ideas* (1991), pp. 245-6.

THERE ARE AT least ten other reasons why I believe the new South Africa will not slide to disaster as other African countries have done. First, precisely because this is the last African country to go through the liberation process, it can learn from the mistakes of the others. Namibia is already showing that many of those mistakes can be avoided, and South Africa is much better equipped than Namibia to make a success of its future.

Secondly, the absence of racial animosity among the vast majority of black South Africans, epitomized by Mandela's own astonishing lack of bitterness after his twenty-seven years in prison, suggests that apartheid will not leave a legacy of counter-racism and a desire for vengeance against the white population.

Thirdly, black and white South Africans may still be deeply divided, but they share a strong mutual commitment to South Africa. This was startlingly evident at all those clandestine meetings in exile which I have described in this book, when political opponents who had been at war for years would suddenly wax nostalgic over the country they both loved and discover a common bond that left their facilitators feeling like outsiders.

Fourthly, the essential pragmatism of the ANC leadership should ensure moderate and sensible policies, and its unassailable credibility in the black population should enable it to carry those policies through the crisis of expectations it is bound to encounter.

Fifthly, that the ANC is an inclusive "broad church" containing many different viewpoints ensures that within its own structures all issues have to be debated extensively. This has inculcated a democratic culture that should counter any authoritarian tendencies that may emerge now that it is in power.

Sixth is the culture of negotiation that developed during four years of hard bargaining at every level of society, from the multiparty convention that drafted the new constitution to segregated sports bodies that negotiated unification, and labour and business organizations that hammered out co-

partnership deals. This means that South Africans have acquired an expertise and confidence in resolving even the
toughest issues around a table.

Seventh is the new constitution itself. While it is regarded
as defective by some liberal purists and is nobody's first
choice, it has the singular merit of being a contract born out
of a spirit of compromise between the major representatives
of all South Africans, and is therefore a workable charter for
a co-operative future.

Eighth, the new regime is having to work largely through
the bureaucracy of the old. While this has the disadvantage
of political incompatibility that can sometimes lead to ob-
structionism, it also compels co-operation across racial and
political lines which helps to heal woulds and build tol-
erance. Even more important, it means that, almost alone in
Africa, the black-majority government is backed up by an
experienced and efficient civil service, the absence of which
has been a major reason for the collapse of services and general decline in other African nations.

Ninth is the strength of South Africa's civil institutions –
from independent media and the judiciary to strong labour,
business, professional, church, sports, student, cultural, women's, and a multitude of "civic" organizations – all with
their own constituencies and interests to protect and over
which no government can ride roughshod. The lack of such
institutional strength led to many one-party dictatorships
elsewhere in Africa, where the liberation movement was
often the only institution of any consequence once the colonial power withdrew.

Lastly, and perhaps most importantly, South Africa is by
far the most developed country in Africa, the only one which
has undergone a fullblown industrial revolution, which has
a sophisticated economic infrastructure, and whose people
are accordingly at a higher level of development. This gives
South Africa a real chance to become the engine of salvation
for this mired continent.

Yet for all the new South Africa's advantages, there is one
overriding challenge facing it. Apartheid has left the country

with one of the world's widest gaps between rich and poor. This must be closed or it will become politically dangerous. At the same time South Africa is experiencing a population explosion, with its present population of 41,688,000 expected to reach 59 million within the next decade and a half. That means the economy must grow significantly faster than at any other time over the past twenty years if the already formidable unemployment rate of around 45 per cent of the economically active population is not also to become a political timebomb. So the government must walk a fine line between the conflicting needs to generate and to redistribute wealth. This is the challenge. Fail either way, and all the positive factors will be negated.

To complicate matters further, with shrinking ore reserves gold mining cannot long remain the prime earner of foreign exchange. South Africa must step up its rate of industrialization in order to export more manufactured goods. That will require a big increase in productive investment, which has been declining steadily for the past twenty years: Derek Keys, who was finance minister for the first five months of the Mandela government, estimated that South Africa needs to increase the amount of its economy that is devoted to investment from the present 16 per cent to between 24 and 25 per cent. That points to the need for significant amounts of foreign capital. How to attract those foreign investors? The fast-developing countries of southeast Asia have done so by following low-wage, high-employment policies, which has also helped them export competitively. The danger in South Africa is that the so-called crisis of expectations that inevitably comes with majority rule will assert itself on the factory floor, causing the powerful black trade unions to force up wages to a point where South Africa prices itself out of the investment market and makes its exports uncompetitive. This is likely to be the first big challenge for the ANC government, which has the trade union federation as its alliance partner. Yet precisely because of the partnership, it should be able to deal with the union pressure effectively.

WHAT WILL THIS new South Africa be like? I thought I caught a glimpse of it on a visit shortly before the election to a Boksburg suburb called Dalpark-6. It may seem an improbable place for a futuristic insight, for even by South African standards Boksburg is a name redolent of racism. It is an early mining town along the gold reef of the Witwatersrand, east of Johannesburg, but the gold is long since exhausted and the mines have shut down, forcing the town to turn to other forms of industry and leaving it with a has-been air and a population living lower on the income scale.

Through the unrest of the 1980s, Boksburg was frequently in the news as white extremists fought pitched battles with local blacks who began using the public parks. The town's notoriety reached a peak in July 1991 when the white residents of Dalpark-6, then one of its newer suburbs, built a "Berlin Wall" to keep blacks from a nearby squatter settlement called Tamboville out of their suburb.

Then a remarkable transformation began, illustrative of the social change taking place quietly behind all the drama of the political negotiations, and it has now turned Dalpark-6 into South Africa's most racially integrated suburb. It began, ironically, with the man who was responsible for building the wall. Frank Erasmus, whose house was closest to the encroaching squatter settlement, had taken a petition around the suburb and succeeded in getting the town council to build the wall. "I was angry at the time," Erasmus recalls, "but then I began to realize that these people were here to stay. I guess it was a matter of acceptance. And I decided that if they were going to live next to me I had better get to know them."

So Erasmus made contact with Abe Nyalunga, chairman of a residents association in Wattville, a black township adjoining the squatter settlement. Nyalunga, a savvy thirty-four-year-old, invited the whites to meet his community. Five whites drove into Wattville with some trepidation one Sunday night, to be welcomed in a church by a singing, cheering crowd of four hundred. What followed was a strange mixture of awkward paternalism and warm response that changed the lives of the whites who were there.

More meetings followed, and the two communities agreed to arrange a joint clean-up campaign, clearing litter from the hundred-yard stretch of land between them.

The day turned into an extraordinary lovefest across the colour line. After collecting the litter the residents planted a tree of peace, taking turns to dig in the hard-baked earth while the crowd formed a circle, held hands, and sang "Come together, people of Africa." Finally, everyone sat down together beside the wall for a beer and barbecue party.

That was in 1992. In the months that followed many of the hardline whites who had shunned the litter-clearing operation moved away. Property values dipped and young, upwardly mobile black, coloured, and Indian families snapped up the bargains. So the suburb changed. "We purged ourselves of our racists," says Andrew Loader, who with his wife, Annetjie, and their two children stayed on at 14 Tafelboom Street. "A few are left, but they keep to themselves. They are in a minority." According to the Loaders, the integration of the suburb took place without incident. In their view, it has been a change for the better. "There's a much better atmosphere here now," says Andrew, an extrovert who seems to know everyone in Tafelboom Street and lends his lawn mower to his black and coloured neighbours. "Then it was dead. People kept to themselves. Now everyone greets everyone else. It's much more friendly."

As I wandered about the streets of Dalpark-6, chatting with its residents of all races, I was struck by how similar they were – in age, in their lifestyle, in their jobs and attitudes and aspirations. This was an emerging multiracial middle class of bank clerks, teachers, computer programmers and factory supervisors, mostly in their early thirties, with Toyota Corollas parked in open carports, neatly tended gardens, and children attending the same multiracial primary school, kicking soccer balls together in the street and going to the local cafe for a Coke and a turn at the pinball machines. They all spoke of their hopes for the future, their children's education, how they hoped to better themselves and perhaps buy a bigger house one day – if their properties retained their value. And then one heard the words of concern. The wall had gone, but Tamboville was still there, grown closer now and more congested, and these middle-class people, black and white alike, were concerned about what its encroachment might do to their property values. And about the crime threat from its unemployed inhabitants.

Here was my glimpse into the future; of a new class stratification gradually beginning to overlay South Africa's old racial strata, never completely eliminating the old divisions but blurring them and adding a different dimension. At the top of this new class structure will be a predominantly white economic aristocracy, the present captains of industry who will be joined in time by a few black entrepreneurs. Then there will be a large multiracial middle class, followed by a working class of artisans, miners, and factory workers, a predominantly black proletariat with a significant white component (unskilled whites will lose the privileged status apartheid gave them). The working class will also rank as part of the economic elite, since its members will be people with jobs surrounded by a sea of unemployed. Which brings one to the large underclass, the outsiders – squatter-camp dwellers, landless peasants, and, increasingly, tribal traditionalists squeezed out by the industrialized society.

Over time, a political reformulation will surely take shape around this changed class stratification, for it is a fact of political life that parties form and leaders arise in response to constituency interests. It follows with equal logic, I believe, that the "broad church" of the ANC will eventually split into its component elements. True, this has long been predicted without coming about. The movement has shown an extraordinary cohesion, partly because its elasticity allows its component elements their own space within the broad alliance, but mainly because of the common objective of the struggle against apartheid. This will be replaced now by the power of patronage. A movement that held together in exile for so long is not likely to fragment when it comes to power and has jobs and privileges to dispense.

Still, the stresses of conflicting class interests will assert themselves over time, the different factions will respond to these in different ways, and when the towering figure of Nelson Mandela is no longer there as a binding force, fragmentation seems inevitable. When that happens I can foresee one element merging with the younger leaders of the National Party to form an African equivalent of the European Christian Democratic parties. It will appeal to the economic aristocracy and the more affluent echelon of the multiracial middle class. Another element is likely to align itself with the trade union federation and elements of the Communist Party to form a Social Democratic party that will appeal to the working class and the less affluent layers of the middle class. Finally, there will be a party that will appeal to the large underclass; a party that will exploit the failed expectations and the alienation of these outsiders. It seems to me this is a natural constituency for the radical Pan-Africanist Congress, but do not be surprised if it is joined by the Inkatha Freedom Party. It may seem an incongruous match, but both have a natural appeal to economic outsiders and Inkatha's traditionalism could strike a common chord with the Africanist philosophy of the PAC. For the PAC, which did badly in the 1994 election, it could mean a strong support base in South Africa's biggest tribe; for Inkatha, a way out of the tribal ghetto into which it has locked itself.

Thus the new South Africa as it emerges at the dawn of a new millennium. A new country with new horizons – and new divisions. There will be enormous new challenges, too, but the democratic structures are there to resolve them and grow through them. For as the graffito says, building a new nation, a great nation which this may yet become, is a continuous process. The construction never ends.

Confronting
the Ghosts

"**V**IVA VERWOERD!" Of all the ironies one encounters in the changing value system of the new South Africa, none is more startling than that chant of praise at an ANC rally for a name which more than any other is identified with apartheid. Hendrik Verwoerd, prime minister from 1958 until he was struck down by an assassin's hand in 1966, was both chief architect and the most ruthless implementer of the doctrine that turned South Africa into the world symbol of racial oppression. He was apartheid's Karl Marx and Stalin rolled into one.

Yet in mid-1993 his grandson, Wilhelm, joined the ANC together with his wife, Melanie, and at a rally in Cape Town soon afterwards that astonishing chant was raised in praise of them. Long live Verwoerd!

It is not an isolated case. As the transition process advanced, the Afrikaner community, which for nearly half a century had been one of the most solid political monoliths to be found anywhere, suddenly began breaking up like some polar ice cap after a long winter. Wilhelm Verwoerd was one of a dozen or more names from the Afrikaner establishment who defected to the ANC, while others, often members of the same high tribal families, moved in the opposite direction to join the parties of the far right. (Another example was poet Antjie Krog, who wrote a "Song of Praise" for President Mandela's inauguration, while her mother, author Dot Serfontein, joined the Conservative Party.) It was as though the old survival imperative that has always shaped the Afrikaner mind was now driving them to a critical choice – either to seek security by joining the dominant majority, or to move into a laager of resistance.

But for Wilhelm Verwoerd there was another and more personal motive – the expiation of guilt. "There is this personal cross I bear," he says, referring to his surname. "It is something I cannot escape. I have to confront the ghosts." F.W. de Klerk's insistence that South Africans should simply forget the past angers him. "There is no way we can do that," Verwoerd says. "Unless we confront the past and look at what happened, these ghosts will continue to haunt us. It must all come out so that the sunlight can heal the wounds."

Wilhelm Verwoerd was two years old when his grandfather was assassinated, and he grew up with an idealized image of the old ideologue. "I remember people responding to my surname and telling me what a great man my grandfather was, how things in South Africa would have been different if he had lived longer." But then the impressions began to change.

The young Verwoerd's early career tracked that of his ancestor to a remarkable degree: first studying theology at Stellenbosch University, then abroad for graduate studies, and home again to teach at Stellenbosch – the old man in applied psychology, the grandson in philosophy. But whereas Hendrik encountered the *Rassenkunde* of the National Socialist academics at Leipzig in the 1930s, young Wilhelm went to Utrecht in Holland where he was challenged by South African political exiles studying there. It was a tough experience. They wouldn't let him get away with his stock partyline rationalizations and gradually he began to acquire new perspectives. From there Wilhelm went to Oxford as a Rhodes scholar, where in addition to more contacts with exiles his readings in philosophy opened what in any event is a sharp mind. Then began the pilgrimage to confront the ghosts.

Wilhelm did not stand for Parliament on the ANC ticket in the April election because he wanted to continue his academic career. But his wife did – and she won. So now there is a Verwoerd on the ANC benches in that place where the Verwoerdian doctrine was enacted in all its evil thoroughness and where Hendrik banned the ANC in 1960. The irony is complete. It is the lesson of the trout hook.

PRYSLIED

In die sandkliphart
vandag
staan hy
kop en skraal skouers bo almal uit
houtskool en as is sy hare
die sandkleurige seun van Qunu
die man met die vlesige palmkussings
    van Nonqaphi Nosekeni
die stamdraer van Mgadla Mandela
'n klein swart ster op sy bo-lip
hy, heelmaker uit die Thembu-stam

ons prys hom
hy wat nie lag nie en nie huil nie
eerste ratelaar van Umkhonto we Sizwe
die swart pimpernel
hy wat nie lag nie en nie huil nie

Nelson Rolihlahla Mandela
jy maak die pante bymekaar
    van 'n verskeurde land
jy ryg die harte aan mekaar
    van swart en bruin en wit
jy draai ons na mekaar toe vir mekaar

Jy, opspoorder van harte
Jy, heelmaker van mense
So stig ons vrede
Vrede, die ma van groot nasies

SONG OF PRAISE

In this Sandstone heart
today
he stands
head and trim shoulders above all the rest
charcoal and ashes his hair
the sand-hued son of Qunu
the man with the fleshy palm cushions
    of Nonqaphi Nosekeni
the standard bearer of Mgadla Mandela
a small black star on his upper lip
he, healer of the Tembu

we praise him
he who neither laughs nor cries
first rattler of Umkhonto we Sizwe
the black pimpernel
he who neither laughs nor cries

Nelson Rolihlahla Mandela
you gather the panels
    of a torn land
you stitch up the hearts
    of black and brown and white
you turn us toward each other for one another

You, tracker of hearts
you, healer of people
So we shall establish peace
Peace, the mother of great nations

Nelson Rolihlahla Mandela
Wêna, Mfuni wezinhliziyo
Wêna, Msindisi wa Banthu
Ngalendlela, sizothola ukhuthula
Ukhuthula o mama we zizwe eziphakhemi

Poem by Antjie Krog. English translation by André P. Brink. Zulu
translation by Themba Nyathi. Read by actress Sandra Prinsloo
at the inauguration of President Mandela, May 10, 1994.

Addendum

FIRST EXECUTIVE BRANCH
OF THE NEW SOUTH AFRICA
MAY 1994

PRESIDENT: Nelson Rolihlahla Mandela (ANC)
FIRST DEPUTY PRESIDENT: Thabo Mvuyelwa Mbeki (ANC)
SECOND DEPUTY PRESIDENT: Frederik Willem de Klerk (NP)

CABINET MINISTERS
AGRICULTURE: Kraai van Niekerk (NP)
ARTS, CULTURE, SCIENCE AND TECHNOLOGY: Ben Ngubane (IFP)
CORRECTIONAL SERVICES: Sipho Mzimela (IFP)
DEFENCE: Joe Modise (ANC)
EDUCATION: Sibusiso Bengu (ANC)
ENVIRONMENT AFFAIRS: Dawid de Villiers (NP)
FINANCE: Derek Keys (NP)
FOREIGN AFFAIRS: Alfred Nzo (ANC)
HEALTH: Nkosazana Dlamini Zuma (ANC)
HOME AFFAIRS: Mangosuthu Buthelezi (IFP)
HOUSING: Joe Slovo (ANC)
JUSTICE: Dullah Omar (ANC)
LABOUR, MANPOWER: Tito Mboweni (ANC)
LAND AFFAIRS: Derek Hanekom (ANC)
MINERAL AND ENERGY AFFAIRS: Roelof Botha (NP)
POSTS, TELECOMMUNICATIONS AND BROADCASTING: Pallo Jordan (ANC)
PROVINCIAL AFFAIRS AND CONSTITUTIONAL DEVELOPMENT: Roelf Meyer (NP)
PUBLIC ENTERPRISES: Stella Sigcau (ANC)
PUBLIC SERVICE AND ADMINISTRATION: Zola Skweyiya (ANC)
PUBLIC WORKS: Jeff Radebe (ANC)
SAFETY AND SECURITY: Sidney Mufamadi (ANC)

SPORT AND RECREATION: Steve Tshwete (ANC)
TRADE, INDUSTRY AND TOURISM: Trevor Manuel (ANC)
TRANSPORT: Mac Maharaj (ANC)
WATER AFFAIRS AND FORESTRY: Kader Asmal (ANC)
WELFARE AND POPULATION DEVELOPMENT: Abe Williams (NP)
MINISTER WITHOUT PORTFOLIO: Jay Naidoo (ANC)

DEPUTY CABINET MINISTERS
AGRICULTURE: Thoko Msane (ANC)
ARTS, CULTURE, SCIENCE AND TECHNOLOGY: Winnie Mandela (ANC)
DEFENCE: Ronnie Kasrils (ANC)
EDUCATION: Renier Schoeman (NP)
ENVIRONMENT AFFAIRS: Bantu Holomisa (ANC)
FINANCE: Alec Erwin (ANC)
FOREIGN AFFAIRS: Aziz Pahad (ANC)
HOME AFFAIRS: Penuell Maduna (ANC)
JUSTICE: Chris Fismer (NP)
LAND AFFAIRS: Tobie Meyer (NP)
PROVINCIAL AFFAIRS AND CONSTITUTIONAL DEVELOP-MENT: Mohammed Valli Moosa (ANC)
SAFETY AND SECURITY: Joe Matthews (IFP)
WELFARE AND POPULATION DEVELOPMENT: Sankie Nkondo (ANC)

REGIONAL PREMIERS
EASTERN CAPE: Raymond Mhlaba (ANC)
EASTERN TRANSVAAL: Mathews Phosa (ANC)
KWAZULU/NATAL: Frank Mdlalose (IFP)
NORTHERN CAPE: Manne Amsley Dipico (ANC)
NORTHERN TRANSVAAL: Ngoako Ramatlhodi (ANC)
NORTHWEST: Popo Molefe (ANC)
ORANGE FREE STATE: Patrick Lekota (ANC)
PRETORIA/WITWATERSRAND/VEREENIGING (PWV): Tokyo Sexwale (ANC)
WESTERN CAPE: Hernus Kriel (NP)

Index